The Social Meanings of Language, Dialect and Accent

Language as SOCIAL ACTION

Howard Giles
General Editor

Vol. 16

The Language as Social Action series
is part of the Peter Lang Media and Communication list.
Every volume is peer reviewed and meets
the highest quality standards for content and production.

PETER LANG
New York • Washington, D.C./Baltimore • Bern
Frankfurt • Berlin • Brussels • Vienna • Oxford

The Social Meanings of Language, Dialect and Accent

International Perspectives on Speech Styles

EDITED BY **Howard Giles & Bernadette Watson**

PETER LANG
New York • Washington, D.C./Baltimore • Bern
Frankfurt • Berlin • Brussels • Vienna • Oxford

Library of Congress Cataloging-in-Publication Data

The Social Meanings of Language, Dialect and Accent: International
Perspectives on Speech Styles / Edited by Howard Giles, Bernadette Watson.
pages cm. — (Language as social action; Vol. 16)
Includes bibliographical references and index.
1. Speech and social status. 2. Linguistic demography.
3. Language spread. 4. Sociolinguistics.
I. Giles, Howard, editor of compilation.
II. Watson, Bernadette M., editor of compilation.
P40.5.S63S63   306.44—dc23   2012040727
ISBN 978-1-4331-1869-2 (hardcover)
ISBN 978-1-4331-1868-5 (paperback)
ISBN 978-1-4539-0981-2 (e-book)
ISSN 1529-2436

Bibliographic information published by **Die Deutsche Nationalbibliothek**.
Die Deutsche Nationalbibliothek lists this publication in the "Deutsche
Nationalbibliografie"; detailed bibliographic data is available
on the Internet at http://dnb.d-nb.de/.

The paper in this book meets the guidelines for permanence and durability
of the Committee on Production Guidelines for Book Longevity
of the Council of Library Resources.

© 2013 Peter Lang Publishing, Inc., New York
29 Broadway, 18th floor, New York, NY 10006
www.peterlang.com

All rights reserved.
Reprint or reproduction, even partially, in all forms such as microfilm,
xerography, microfiche, microcard, and offset strictly prohibited.

Printed in the United States of America

To Cindy Gallois

On the occasion of her "retirement" from the University of Queensland and in celebration of her enormous legacy in language attitudes research and theory, and for her MANY other areas of invaluable language and social psychological inquiry

Presented at ICLASP13, Leeuwarden, The Netherlands
June 20–23, 2012

Contents

1. Language Ideologies and Language Attitudes: A Foundational Framework   1
   Marko Dragojevic, Howard Giles, & Bernadette M. Watson

2. Language Attitudes in the Americas   26
   Agata Gluszek & Karolina Hansen

3. Language Attitudes in Western Europe   45
   Tamara Rakić & Melanie C. Steffens

4. Language Attitudes in the Nordic Countries   64
   Tore Kristiansen

5. Language Attitudes in the Maghreb Countries of North West Africa   84
   Eirlys E. Davies & Abdelali Bentahila

6. Language Attitudes in Southern Africa   105
   Desmond Painter & John Dixon

7. Language Attitudes in China Toward English   125
   Anping He & Sik Hung Ng

8. Language Attitudes in South Asia   141
   Itesh Sachdev & Tej Bhatia

9. Language Attitudes in Australia and New Zealand 157
   Ann Weatherall

Epilogue: Language Attitudes in Context 170
   Cindy Gallois

Contributors 181

Index 185

CHAPTER ONE

Language Ideologies and Language Attitudes:
A Foundational Framework

MARKO DRAGOJEVIC, HOWARD GILES, & BERNADETTE M. WATSON

Kava—1 DM
Kafa—don't have it
Kahva—bullet in the forehead

People readily form impressions of others during social interaction (Goffman, 1959). In addition to visual symbols of differences such as gender, age, and ethnicity, language plays a critical, and often a primary, role (Rakić, Steffens, & Mummendey, 2011) in how people perceive and evaluate their fellow interactants (e.g., Gallois & Callan, 1981; Gallois, Callan, & Johnstone, 1984; Giles & Marlow, 2011). Spoken language is inherently variable on all levels including pronunciation, grammar, and vocabulary. Although some of this variability reflects idiosyncratic differences across speakers, a significant portion of it is systematic and reflects regional, social, and contextual differences in language use (Lippi-Green, 1997). Because of these structured patterns of language use, linguistic forms can become indexical of (a pointer to) speakers' social identities (see Scherer & Giles, 1979; Silverstein, 2003). In this respect, the use of particular languages, accents (i.e., language varieties marked by a specific pronunciation) and dialects (i.e., language varieties marked by a specific grammar and vocabulary, in addition to pronunciation) can convey a significant amount of social information about speakers, such as their geographic background, ethnicity, and social class, as well as stereotypes attributed regarding their traits (Callan & Gallois, 1987; Giles & Billings, 2004; Fuertes et al., 2012a; Gluszek & Dovidio, 2010).

The tendency to socially stereotype speakers based on their use of language can have significant real world consequences, ranging from prejudice and discrimination (for a review, see Garrett, 2010) to matters of life and death. The "menu" presented in the opening lines of this chapter, which was prominently displayed in a café in Bosnia and Herzegovina during the height of the Yugoslav wars in the 1990s, provides a rather stark illustration of this point. The three items on the menu represent three different pronunciations for the word *coffee*, each indexing a particular social identity. For many locals in the region, *kava* indexes a Croatian, and by extension, Catholic identity; *kafa* indexes a Serbian and Orthodox Christian identity; and *kahva* indexes a Bosnian and Muslim identity (for a recent discussion of the inherent complexities involved in such distinctions, see Bugarski, 2012). As the "menu" makes rather clear, coffee at this particular (in this case Croatian[1]) café was readily served to Croatian patrons for the modest price of 1 DM (Deutsche Mark), for Serbs it was unavailable regardless of the depth of their pockets, and Muslims were better off ordering something else instead. Although such morbid repercussions of linguistic diversity may well be restricted to times of war, variability in language use *can* and *does* have very "real" communicative, social, and other consequences, which are often far from subtle even in peacetime. Indeed, a recent shooting at Oikos University in California, which left 7 people dead, was attributed by police to a former student who was "upset about being teased over [his] poor English skills" (Elias, 2012).

In this opening chapter, we draw on work in sociolinguistics, linguistic anthropology, and the social psychology of language to provide a general organizing framework for the present volume. We provide brief overviews of unique features of the chapters that follow this, and epilogue with a set of Principles that define the substance of findings emerging from language attitude research.

Linguistic indices such as lingua francas, accents and others do not go unnoticed across the world—although people clearly on occasion process such cues automatically and unconsciously (e.g., Gasiorek & Giles, 2012; Kristiansen, Garrett, & Coupland, 2005)—and people often construct and communicatively manage ideological schemas "that purport to explain the source and meaning of...linguistic differences" (Irvine & Gal, 2000, p. 37). Such schemas about language, or so-called "language ideologies," "enact" the links between language and speakers' social and personal identities, often imbuing them with moral and political connotations (Woolard & Schieffelin, 1994, p. 56), as well as shape intrapersonal attitudes and norms governing their expression. For example, Marlow and Giles (2010) investigated language criticism in Hawai'i and examined the contexts in which listeners criticized speakers and the subsequent responses of those criticized. They found criticism occurred across a variety of situations and the responses by speakers gave rise to reactions ranging from acquiescent apology to aggression. In what ensues, we explore parameters of language ideologies as foundational to, and informative of, the chapters that follow.

Language Ideologies

In the broadest sense, language ideologies reflect people's beliefs about what language is and how it should be used. Irvine (1989, p. 255) defines language ideologies as "the cultural (or subcultural) system of ideas about social and linguistic relationships, together with their loading of moral and political interests." People are socialized into and create language ideologies as a means of explaining the source and meaning of the links between linguistic and social phenomena. In this respect, language ideologies represent a set of interested positions about the role and use of language that attempt to justify and rationalize linguistic diversity. That is, they provide what Woolard and Schieffelin (1994, p. 62) call an "interpretive filter" through which people view, explain, and understand the relationship between language and society. At the face-to-face level of individual interactions, this filter provides the means by which strangers can form impressions of each other and enables them to reduce uncertainty about how to respond during this first (and maybe only) encounter (see Gudykunst & Ting-Toomey, 1990).

Irvine and Gal (2000) describe three semiotic processes through which people create ideological representations of linguistic variation: iconization, fractal recursivity, and erasure. *Iconization* refers to the process whereby people come to view linguistic features as iconic representations of speakers' inherent naturally ordained identities (Giles & Niedzielski, 1998). For example, these scholars describe how early European observers compared the click consonants of some Bantu languages to animal and bird sounds and, consequentially, came to view speakers of these languages as somehow subhuman (see Haslam, 2006). *Fractal recursivity* refers to "the projection of an opposition, salient at some level of relationship, onto some other level" (Irvine & Gal, 2000, p. 38). For example, Andronis (2004) shows how, in Ecuador, the ideological dichotomies *between* Spanish—the official language (which is seen as urban and modern)—and Quichua[2]—the language of the indigenous population (which is seen as rural and backward)—are recursively applied *within* the Quichua linguistic community. In this way, the standardized variety of Quichua is associated with modernity (like Spanish) whereas nonstandard varieties (e.g., Amazonian Quichua) are viewed as rural and backward. Finally, *erasure* refers to the process whereby "facts that are inconsistent with the ideological scheme either go unnoticed or get explained away" (Irvine & Gal, 2000, p. 38), such as when linguistic diversity is rendered invisible through the imposition of national languages. For example, Hassanpour (1992) describes how Turkey's desire for a linguistically homogenous state gave rise to oppressive language policies in the mid-twentieth century towards the country's Kurdish-speaking minority. Specifically, the Kurdish language was altogether banned in Turkey, the mere mention of the words "Kurd" and "Kurdistan" were outlawed, and those heard speaking Kurdish were fined or imprisoned (see also Blau, 2006; Kreyenbroek, 1992). These three semiotic processes demonstrate how language is a powerful medium that people use to differentiate and make social judgments about speakers of different linguistic forms.

The processes of *iconicity*, *fractal recursivity*, and *erasure* often operate in unison to create ideological representations that rationalize and justify linguistic diversity. Indeed, Painter and Dixon (chapter 6) describe how, upon their arrival in Southern Africa, early European settlers not only reduced the continuum of African languages into discrete categories of "missionary" languages—thus rendering invisible the diversity of the existing ethnolinguistic landscape (*erasure*)—but also animalized African speakers and their native languages, promising them salvation and "an alleviation of blackness" through the adoption of European languages (*iconicity*). This initial ideological dichotomy between African languages (which were seen as uncivilized), on the one hand, and European languages (which were seen as civilized), on the other, later became *recursively* applied to Afrikaans—a derivative of Dutch, spoken in South Africa. Specifically, whereas (standard) Afrikaans spoken by the white population came to be seen as civilized (like European languages), Afrikaans varieties spoken by the black population came to be seen as backward and uncivilized (like African languages).

Nationalist Ideology

Languages often come to be seen as emblematic of national identity and unity, as evident in popular discourse about the importance of learning the "mother tongue" and the romanticized association of *one* nation with *one* language (for the USA, see Barker et al., 2001). Indeed, such a nationalist ideology of language, which identifies a language with a people, is widely held across many parts of the world and has become a cultural truism (Gal & Irvine, 1995; Woolard & Schieffelin, 1994). The ideological linkage of *one* nation with *one* language is often dated to eighteenth-century German Romanticism and the writings of Johann Gottfried Herder and his contemporaries (see Bauman & Briggs, 2003; Woolard & Schieffelin, 1994). Herder believed that language captured the essence of a people and represented their national and cultural treasure. He considered the *Volk*, or common people, the guardians of the German language and culture through their folksongs, folktales, and myths. Herder valorized the power of a *pure*, uniform German language and literature, stripped of foreign (i.e., French) influences as the single most unifying force of the German people—to *be* German meant to *speak* the German language. Many, including the Brothers Grimm who helped establish an authentic German literature and thereby imbued the German language with literary and historical authenticity, embraced Herder's "nationalist project" (Bauman & Briggs, 2003, p. 197). Although in theory, the various rural and regional dialects embodied the true essence of the German language, in practice only one variety came to be regarded as the tongue of the fatherland. Emerging from the highlands in Southern Germany, this *Hochdeutsch*, or High German, became the standard language of the land (St Clair, 1982). Perhaps ironically, it was primarily in this very *Hochdeutsch*, rather than in rural and regional dialects of the *Volk*, that the Brothers Grimm wrote their famous "folk" texts (Robinson, 2010).

Nationalist sentiment surrounding language in eighteenth and nineteenth century Europe was hardly restricted to Germany. For example, Pederson (2009) describes how, around this same time, Denmark was transformed from being a multilingual state, once united by a common religion, to a unilingual state united by a common national language. Similarly, following the French Revolution, the Ile de France dialect came to represent one of the primary symbols of the French nation. Although standardization and purification policies had been taking place in France for centuries, such as the establishment of l'Académie Française in 1635, it was in the eighteenth and nineteenth centuries that systematic efforts by the government to *erase* regional and nonnative varieties and thus craft a unilingual French state took on a renewed fervor (Bourhis, 1982). Kristiansen (chapter 4) describes how a similar situation unfolded in nineteenth-century Finland, where western dialects came to be seen as "corrupted" by Swedish and features of the eastern regional dialects were systematically incorporated into the written standard as a way to "purify" it of foreign (i.e., Swedish) influence.

The nationalist ideology of language *naturalizes* the connection between language and nationality, by conceptualizing linguistic differences as universal truths or matters of biology (Gal & Irvine, 1995). To this end, Bernsand (2001) describes how the nationalist ideology has often been invoked in Ukraine to portray language as a natural extension of Ukrainian national identity, transmitted from mother to child as a collection of experiences of the nation. Indeed, languages often come to be seen as the property of nation states and "the absence of a distinct language can [be reason enough to] cast doubt on the legitimacy of claims to nationhood" (Woolard & Schieffelin, 1994, p. 60). Milroy (2001) points to the ideological nature of such claims and notes that Old English, considered by many to be the property of the English nation was, in 450AD, almost indistinguishable from related Germanic dialects in Europe and, thereby, cannot be considered solely the property of the English nation. Indeed, the long and uninterrupted history of a uniform English language on the British Isles may more accurately be described as cultural myth, created to historicize and legitimize the language, rather than be a "linguistic fact." In recent decades, the worldwide proliferation of English (e.g., International English) fundamentally challenges notions of language ownership and the legitimacy of any single nation's rights to prescriptivism of it. In this sense, English may be the property of the Indian nation, where it is a primary language, or the international English speaker, as much as it is the property of Britain or America.

Indeed, the very essence of what it means to be a native speaker and the links between language and nationhood are beginning to take on new meanings, given that, by some estimates, most of the world's population speaks more than one language with native proficiency (Grosjean, 2010). To this end, Maher and colleagues (2010) argue that multilingualism has now become the norm in many countries around the world, although it may not always be explicitly recognized or ordained as such by government bodies. In particular, Maher (2005) describes how multilingualism and multiculturalism have, in recent years, become "Cool" among younger generations in Japan, where the appropriation of nondominant (and previously stigmatized) languages and ethnicities has become commonplace. He argues that this reconstruction of ethnicity, which he calls "metroethnicity," fundamentally challenges traditional ideologies of monoethnic and monolingual nation states (Maher, 2010).

Similarly, Jørgensen (2012) notes that, despite prevailing monolingual norms in Denmark and Europe, Copenhagen youth frequently employ language features (e.g., vocabulary) associated with several different languages (e.g., Turkish, English, Danish) in the same conversation. He argues that such practices fundamentally challenge the ideological notion that languages are "separable" and "identifiable" collections of linguistic features that "naturally" belong together. Rather, he contends that the idea of separate languages is a socio-cultural construction—one that is often bound up in ideological rhetoric promoting the legitimacy of nation states—rather than a reflection of real-life linguistic practices, which tend to reflect "linguistic superdiversity" (p. 69).

In sum, Herder's vision, like that of his contemporary John Locke, was based on "linguistic and discursive standardization and regimes of purification" where "social and political cohesion demand one language, one meta-discursive order, one voice" (Bauman & Briggs, 2003, p. 195). In this way, his writings and the work of his contemporaries provided a model for national policies of language purification that are evident to this day (Bourhis, Sioufi, & Sachdev, 2012). The *erasure* of Slavic forms and the jailing of Slavic speakers in Greek Macedonia following World War I (for a discussion, see Irvine & Gal, 2000) and policies of linguistic purism in Croatia during the 1990s (Kordić, 2010) are but a few examples of systematic government efforts undertaken to create the illusion of monolingual states.

Nativeness as an Ideology

Working in tandem with a nationalist ideology of language, particularly in the perpetuation of foreign-accent discrimination, is what Shuck (2004, 2006) calls the "ideology of nativeness." Premised on a monolingual view of the world, the ideology of nativeness divides the social world into dichotomous, mutually exclusive, and (often) uncontested categories of *Us* and *Them* (Giles, 2012a; Giles, Reid, & Harwood, 2010a; Harwood & Giles, 2005). In the United States, this can be seen in the categorization of native English speakers as Americans and nonnative English speakers as foreign *Others* (Schmidt, 2002), even when their primary language may well be English (Shuck, 2004).

The ideology of nativeness exaggerates and rationalizes the distinction between native and nonnative speakers, primarily by classifying the latter as incomprehensible (Gallois & Callan, 1989; Gluszek, Newheiser, & Dovidio, 2011). Such beliefs are readily apparent at the discourse level, such as complaints about foreign accents being incomprehensible and moral indignation over immigrants who do not obtain native-like proficiency (Shuck, 2004). To this end, Weatherall (chapter 9) notes how complaints about telephone conversations with offshore call centers "somewhere up in India" are often rationalized based on non-native speakers' apparent "incomprehensibility." Moreover, Shuck (2006) notes that discourse about language is often "racialized," so that native speakers come to be conceptualized as, for example, American, White, and "accentless" or "accent-neutral" (see Gluszek & Hansen, chapter 2), whereas nonnative speakers come to be viewed as international, non-White, and accented. Indeed, Phillipson (1992) argues that language-based discrimination may represent a type of covert racism, providing "a more subtle way of hierarchizing social groups in the contemporary world" (p. 241). In parallel, Lippi-Green (1994) equates language-based discrimination in the workplace, particularly against foreign-accented speakers, to a contemporary form of institutionalized racism.

Shuck (2006) shows how the ideological distinction between *Us* and *Them* often remains intact to be *recursively* applied to other levels of opposition, even ones in which English speakers represent the *non*native category. For instance, she notes that American tourists often describe *native* Spanish speakers in Mexico as heavily accented. In other words, they recursively apply the Us/Them dichotomy, except now the socially desirable qualities associated with the *native* category, such as comprehensibility and fluency, are applied to *nonnative* Spanish speakers (i.e., the American tourists). In this way, even foreigners' communicative proficiency in their *own* language comes to be questioned (Shuck, 2006).

In sum, the ideology of nativeness draws on the nationalist ideology of language to enact and naturalize the links between nonnative speakers, foreignness, incomprehensibility, and race. People come to view the world in terms of dichotomous, mutually exclusive categories of *Us* and *Them*, on the one hand imbuing native speakers with socially desirable qualities and on the other denigrating and homogenizing nonnative speakers as foreign *Others*. The marginalization of nonnative speakers is often rationalized based on communicative inefficiency and incomprehensibility (Dovidio & Gluszek, 2012), qualities that remain intact to be *recursively* applied to other levels of opposition, such as race. In turn, language becomes a subtle tool of exclusion, which both laypersons and social institutions rely on to control access to social rewards.

Standard Language Ideology

Another common language ideology is that of a standard language (Milroy & Milroy, 1985; Silverstein, 1996). The standard language ideology extends the nationalist and nativeness ideologies by perpetuating not only a monolingual view of the world, but also the belief that there exists only one correct, or "best" *form* of a given language. Such a belief is widely accepted as a matter of common sense (Milroy, 2001). As Lippi-Green (1997, p. 64) notes, a standard language ideology represents "a bias toward an abstract, idealized, homogenous spoken language which is imposed and maintained by dominant bloc institutions and which names as its model the written language, but which is drawn primarily from the spoken language of the upper middle class."

Idealized in the form of a uniform pronunciation, grammar, and lexis, the standard functions as a model against which all other varieties of written and spoken language are judged. Although often thought of as the natural and correct way to speak, the standard glosses over the linguistic fact that language is naturally variable and that all varieties have the potential to be equally functional (Lippi-Green, 1997). Instead of being a naturally occurring form, the standard represents an abstraction that tries to impose an artificial uniformity on naturally occurring linguistic variability (Milroy, 2001). In other words, standardization attempts to create an artificially homogenous linguistic landscape by *erasing* inconsistencies and contradictions—it is the belief in what language *should* be, rather than what language *is* (Irvine & Gal, 2000; see Pederson (2009) and Edwards and Jacobson (1987) for a review of the complexities involved in ascribing status to such standard varieties). Indeed, many so-called "standard" forms, such as Classic Arabic, or *fusha* (Davies & Bentahila, chapter 5) and the "standard Portuguese" promoted by Brazilian TV networks (Gluszek & Hansen, chapter 2), have *no* native speakers, with the former being learned solely through formal education and the latter through media exposure.

As we noted, the notion that there are better and worse ways of speaking is often accepted as a matter of common sense for many people. Such an appeal, Milroy (2001, p. 536) notes, is so powerful that it "implies that any debate on the matter is superfluous." For instance, African American Vernacular English (AAVE), a "nonstandard" variety, is often dismissed by people as being incorrect due to a variety of features not present in Standard American English (SAE), such as multiple negation (e.g., I didn't go nowhere). Despite these lay notions of correctness, AAVE is just as "correct" and rule governed as other varieties of English (e.g., Labov, 1966) and forms that are stigmatized in AAVE, such as multiple negation are, in fact, "correct" in many languages of the world, such as Spanish (Milroy & Milroy, 1985). In other words, notions of correctness are ideological and not rooted in linguistic fact. The lack of standardization within Pacific languages reflects this point and as Milroy (2001) notes, Pacific languages "are fluid and highly variable: [and] it is not clear where one ends and another begins" (p. 542). Notions of correctness are therefore not relevant in some Pacific areas and the implications of this merit more investigation, and point the way to future work.

Chapters in this volume obviously provide examples of standard varieties and include SAE, Received Pronunciation (i.e., standard British English), Parisian French, and Castilian Spanish. Although these so-called "standard languages" represent no more than one of many dialects spoken in a nation, they tend to be the only ones officially recognized and legitimated by the government, reflecting the idealized forms of speech and writing present in dictionaries and grammar books (St. Clair, 1982), and are often associated with *status* (e.g., competence, intelligence) and prestige (Ball, Gallois, & Callan, 1989; Gallois et al., 2007; Giles & Marlow, 2011). However, despite lay notions of correctness and naturalness, Milroy (2001) argues that standard varieties do not inherently possess any value or prestige, but rather acquire it due to the prestige associated with their speakers (Giles & Niedzielski, 1998). In other words, prestige attributed to particular social groups comes to be *indexically* linked to standard varieties (see Stewart, 2012). For example, Bourhis (1982) describes how the Ile de France dialect spoken in the King's court came to be adopted as the standard language in France, with its purportedly superior status derived from the privileged position of the wealthy social class who originally spoke it. When a listener cannot discern the prestige value of an accent, a less prestigious accent may be highly rated. For example, this is true of both Australians and Americans who may favorably rate a strong Birmingham or Cockney accent as attractive. Many natives from England with such accents work hard to remove them because of the association with lower socioeconomic groups and low prestige amongst those native English who speak with more "respectable" accents (Coupland & Bishop, 2007; Giles & Powesland, 1975). Indeed, the tendency to equate the standard variety with high status appears to be rather undifferentiated across linguistic and social strata within a given society, with nonstandard speakers often consensually accepting the negative status evaluations assigned to them by others (Giles & Marlow, 2011).

Social institutions such as schools and the media promote and shape the standard language ideology by devaluing and marginalizing all varieties deemed nonstandard (Barker et al., 2001; Milroy & Milroy, 1985; Silverstein, 1996). For example, Telemundo—a Spanish-language television network in the U.S. with a majority Mexican-heritage viewership—coaches actors starring in their popular *telenovelas* to speak in a "neutral" (read Mexican) accent, rather than in their native regional and national (e.g., Colombian, Peruvian) varieties of Spanish (Ahrens, 2004). In other words, the network has attempted to *erase* linguistic variability from their *telenovelas* by rendering it virtually invisible, whilst simultaneously promoting a particular variety of the Spanish language (i.e., a Mexican accent), a move that has attracted criticism from some Latin American nations. Because social institutions tend to recognize only one language variety (e.g., the standard) as legitimately "correct," all other varieties come to be deemed "incorrect" or somehow lacking. In fact, nonstandard varieties are often not even thought of as *real* languages; instead, they are dialects, vernaculars, accents, or some other "marked" varieties (see He & Ng, chapter 7). Because standard language varieties tend to be associated with valued qualities within a culture, adherents of nonstandard forms are often labeled as social deviants (St. Clair, 1982). In turn, standard language varieties come to be indexically associated with symbolic and economic value, becoming a form of *linguistic capital* (Bourdieu, 1991) that government and social institutions instrumentally use to restrict social mobility (St. Clair, 1982).

The main rationalization of standardization is that a standard language is necessary for effective communication (Lippi-Green, 1994). The standard is believed to be associated with clarity of expression and lack of confusion—it is referentially *pure*. In the case of accent, phonological and intonational differences are thought to pose a barrier to clarity, understanding, and communicative efficiency. By assuming that the standard is something that can be naturally attained with proper training, hard work, and education, linguistic differences come to be equated with personal differences and those who so "insistently" choose not to adhere to the standard are often thought to be lacking in mental capacity or to suffer from some inherent flaw in character (for a discussion, see Silverstein, 1996). As a result, nonstandard varieties, and particularly foreign accents, come to be associated with incomprehensibility and speakers of such forms are often stigmatized (Gluszek & Dovidio, 2010). That said, Wotschke (1996) reviews the move to accept regional accents in post-war Britain. The reasons for this acceptance coincided with the increase in new universities for lower middle–class and working–class students. In addition, some students from these backgrounds were also gaining entry to Oxford and Cambridge. Thus, the new university educated graduates entered the workforce into varying positions of prestige and power and brought with them non-RP accents. As Wotschke notes the Oxbridge accent may still exist but is not as influential or important as it once was.

In light of the apparent value of the standard and institutional pressures to adopt it, it is noteworthy to observe that nonstandard varieties and minority languages continue to exist and have covert prestige in some quarters (see Trudgill, 1974; Ryan, 1979). For example, despite the institutional dominance of Standard English, nearly half of the population of Hawai'i continues to speak the relatively low status Pidgin, or Hawai'i Creole English (Kamana & Wilson, 1996). Indeed, Marlow and Giles (2010) found that although multiethnic locals in Hawai'i converged to Standard English in work and educational interactions, they nonetheless preferred to speak local Pidgin, even though its use evoked frequent criticism. Acknowledging that nonstandard language varieties fulfill important identity functions for their speakers by serving as symbols of ingroup solidarity, Woolard (1985) argues that the persistence of such forms is not simply due to a relaxation of pressures to adopt the standard in some (e.g., private) settings, but rather *competing* community pressures to produce "correct vernacular forms" in community contexts in which they are the speech norm. In this respect, nonstandard varieties come to possess "covert prestige," or value in their own right, and speakers who correctly employ such forms in community contexts tend to evoke favorable evaluations in terms of *solidarity* (e.g., friendly, trustworthy) from other members of their linguistic community, whereas those who transgress community norms by adopting the standard risk ridicule and social marginalization (Giles & Edwards, 2010).

Assessing What We Know in the 21st Century

Language ideologies provide the organizational schema through which linguistic diversity is viewed, interpreted, and evaluated. In this sense, language ideologies represent broad, socio-cultural schemas that shape the development of intrapersonal attitudes towards particular language varieties and their speakers. People come to view nonstandard language varieties as lacking in logic and correctness and *iconically* project these representations onto nonstandard speakers by downgrading them on a variety of traits such as intelligence and ambition. Facts inconsistent with ideological representations of nonstandard speakers, such as their actual education or competence, are often ignored and rendered invisible through processes of *erasure*. Finally, oppositions, such as the ideological portrayal of standard speakers as competent and nonstandard speakers as incompetent, come to be *recursively* projected onto other levels of social evaluation and functioning.

Moreover, prevailing language ideologies not only shape intrapersonal language attitudes, but also enable and constrain both the private and public expression of such attitudes, primarily by influencing norms of language use (cf. Jørgensen, 2012). Socio-cultural schemas of language use are deeply engrained in public consciousness, often to the point where language ideologies come to be accepted as matters of common sense or even as natural laws. In this way, claims such as "Only English should be spoken in the U.S." and "Some forms of English are better and more correct than others" become what Johnson (2012, p. 75) calls "stand-alone 'truths,'" requiring no substantiation or reasoning. Governmental policies, media representations, and educational practices are suffused by, and promote, such schemas. Such broad and pervasive institutional support, in turn, implicitly condones the private and public expression of attitudes consistent with prevailing language norms. Consequently, the derision and derogation of those who fail to linguistically conform (e.g., nonstandard/nonnative speech, code-switching) becomes both socially and morally acceptable (cf. St. Clair, 1982).In turn, the expression of such attitudes serves not only to reinforce, but also (re)produce existing ideological schemas and relationships of domination and subordination—in other words, language attitudes and ideologies often come to shape each other.

Nonetheless, despite the tendency of both standard and nonstandard speakers to associate the standard variety with high *status* (Giles& Marlow, 2011), nonstandard varieties and minority languages can possess covert prestige, with speakers of those forms sometimes evaluated more favorably in terms of *solidarity* by members of their own linguistic community. In this respect, whereas the association of the standard with high status tends to be rather uniform across social strata and linguistic groups, the ascription of solidarity value to a variety may be more differentiated across groups. To address this inherent complexity, Ryan, Giles, and Sebastian (1982) argued that, in addition to the level of standardization, another important factor that exerts an influence on language preference is a language's *vitality*, determined by (a) the *status* (e.g., economic, social, political power) and (b) *demographics* (e.g., number and distribution) of its speakers, as well as (c) its *institutional support*. These scholars argued that whereas the status value ascribed to a given variety tends to be closely associated with its degree of standardization, its solidarity value tends to be more closely linked to its vitality—as such, we might expect to find varieties *increasing* in vitality to enjoy more covert prestige in the speech community in which they are the speech norm than varieties decreasing in vitality. To this end, Rakić and Steffens (chapter 3) note that although standard German (i.e., Hochdeutsch) is an official language in Switzerland, Swiss German—the nonstandard variety—tends to maintain a high degree of vitality among the local population and is spoken in a wider range of settings than the standard. As such, Swiss German speakers tend to be evaluated more favorably in terms of solidarity than standard German speakers in Switzerland. The opposite pattern tends to emerge for nonstandard varieties *decreasing* in vitality. For example, Sachdev and Bhatia (chapter 8) note how some linguistic minorities in India actually take "pride" in confessing a *lack* of proficiency in their mother tongue to other members of their linguistic community. Although standardization and vitality are closely related constructs that often exert a mutual influence on one another—that is, standardization is likely to enhance the vitality of a language and languages with increasing vitality are more likely to achieve standardization—they are distinct, in that standard languages may possess relatively low vitality (e.g., Latin) and languages with increasing vitality may be relatively unstandardized (e.g., African American Vernacular English).

Both standardization and vitality are subject to the ideological forces that operate within a given society. As we have shown throughout, the nationalist, nativeness, and standard language ideologies often operate in unison to undermine the legitimacy, status, and survival of nonstandard varieties and minority languages. As such, to the extent that these ideologies are engrained in the public and national consciousness, they are likely to exert a negative force on nonstandard/minority languages' vitality and undermine their linguistic "wellness," such as through "assimilationist" and "ethnist" government policies which require minorities to relinquish their own languages in favor of the national standard (for a discussion, see Bourhis et al., 2012); in turn, decreased vitality is likely to undermine a language's potential for standardization. Serving as a heuristic, the two-dimensional model in Figure 1.1 locates along these two dimensions some of the many language varieties

Figure 1.1: The two primary sociocultural constructs affecting language attitudes: standardization and vitality.

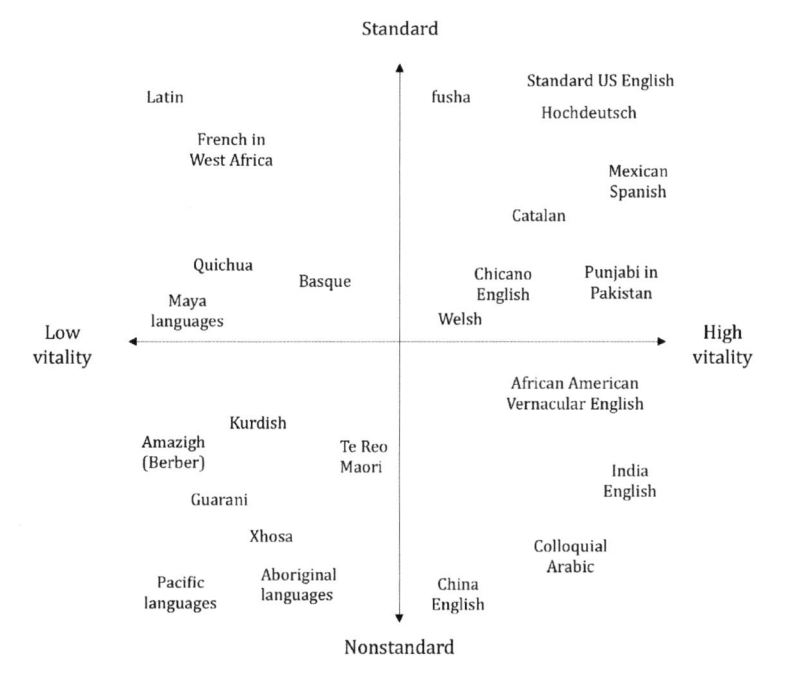

covered in the chapters that follow, although we concede that language attitudes situations can be fruitfully located in other intergroup dimensions (see Giles, Reid, & Harwood, 2010b). The extent to which this model will reconfigure over the next decade or so will be a fascinating study in language dynamics.

Overview of the Volume

This volume is all about how languages, dialects and accents induce people to form a variety of social judgments about users of these forms. It is timely to dedicate it to and acknowledge Cindy Gallois' past contributions to language attitudes in the second decade of the 21st century for at least two major reasons. First, issues such as these, apart from monographs built on specific research programs (e.g., Garrett, Coupland, & Williams, 2003) and/or traditional reviews that tend to be largely ahistorical glossing over broader sociocultural issues (e.g., Garrett, 2010), have not been comprehensively overviewed since the early 1980s (Ryan & Giles, 1982); that is more than a quarter of a century ago. Work in the so-called language attitudes tradition flourished in the 1960s through the 1980s due to the seminal work of Labov (1966) and Lambert (1967; see Giles & Coupland, 1991), yet was rendered relatively silent in the 1990s through the early 2000s. Second and gratifyingly, such work is commanding renewed cross-disciplinary attention and is back in vogue (e.g., Grondelaeers, van Hout, & Steggs, 2010; Heaton & Nygaard, 2011; Kinzler, Corriveau, & Harris, 2011; Rakić et al., 2011; Reid et al., 2012) and being afforded theoretical bite (e.g., Dovidio & Gluszek, 2012; Giles, 2011; Giles & Rakić, in press; Giles & Marlow, 2011). Hence, this volume fills a void and is unique to the extent that it reviews work on evaluations to speech styles across nations and acknowledges the unique socio-cultural and historical forces that shape those evaluations; no previous volume has embraced this comparative perspective globally. That said, not all international sites are afforded prominence. The chapters on regions selected here (some small and others continental) are devoted to locations where many investigations have been conducted. The contents of this volume include scholars who are recognized for their contributions to this field of inquiry. In addition, the chapters here address some of the limitations of language attitude research highlighted by Gallois, Watson, and Brabant (2007). They noted that all too often research into language attitudes assumes a link between individuals' attitudes to an entity and their subsequent communication behavior. This assumption, they argue, is flawed. Communication behavior is governed by a number of components, each playing its part in different ways across situations. These include interpersonal and contextual information, intergroup salience and relations. Furthermore, each of these is dynamic and changing (Dragojevic & Giles, in press), which is the exciting challenge for social psychologists of language as they invoke theoretical frameworks to unpack these complexities. In what follows, we overview the chapters in this book by highlighting the unique features associated with their socio-geographical locations.

Gluszek and Hansen (chapter 2) spread their review net widely up and down the continents of North and South America, examining the attitudes towards many languages, dialects, and accents, including Spanish, English, Portuguese, AAVE, and indigenous languages such as Quichua, Guarani, or Aymara. They examine the social perceptions and attributed comprehensibility of these varieties in workplace and education broadly, and bilingual programs specifically, as well as in the media. As elsewhere in this volume, they discuss the apparent growing tolerance towards (sometimes endangered) indigenous languages and the language policies implemented to protect them. Gluszek and Hansen also discuss, in ways not always manifest in the literature, the relationship between language attitudes and the media. In particular, they look to how different accents can be strategically adopted in the movies, on TV and radio in order to evoke particular social images (e.g., of a villain) and how the media has created a standard Portuguese accent in Brazil and "accent-neutral Spanish." Throughout, Gluszek and Hansen adopt a socio-historical perspective on how language attitudes develop as well as explore the ways in which intergroup competition is linked to language choices.

The chapter on Western Europe by Rakić and Steffens (chapter 3) also grapples with a rich panoply of language attitude situations on their radar screen, some monolingual (e.g., Greece and Portugal) and others plurilingual (e.g., Malta and Luxembourg). They examine perceptions and attributions of languages that transcend national borders, as in the case of French and German in Belgium and Switzerland, respectively. Rakić and Steffens also look at lingua francas such as English, the language attitude situations of The Netherlands, Italy, Luxembourg, and Malta, immigrant and minority languages (e.g., Turkish in Germany and Welsh in Britain), as well as a range of different accents of these varieties (e.g., Irish English, Breton and Parisian French, and Bavarian German). Rakić and Steffens, who take an intergroup perspective throughout, point out that what is a standard variety in one country can be nonstandard in another, with accent sometimes being a stronger marker of group identity than a language itself. Common with other chapters, they take a valued historical, dynamic perspective as in the case of attitudes towards and use of Catalan and Basque in pre- and post-Franco eras.

Staying in Europe but moving to Scandinavia where language attitude studies have their own vitality, Kristiansen (chapter 4) examines how a complex array of historical, political, and ideological forces—stretching back to the Viking Age—came to shape the linguistic landscapes in the Nordic countries of Denmark, Norway, Sweden, Iceland, and Finland. The current diversity, he argues, is in part due to a long history and patterns of Danish and Swedish domination in the region. For instance, the latter had a marked influence on the development of written norms in Norway and Finland. Recognizing that varieties spoken in their capital cities had become "corrupted" by Danish and Swedish respectively, both countries incorporated features of their "purer" regional dialects into their standard varieties. Turning to recent times, Kristiansen provides compelling evidence to show that direct and indirect elicitation methods often yield seemingly contradictory results; whereas Danish "local patriotism" appears to trump the "standard" with the former technique, the opposite emerges with the latter. In addition, Nordic countries' attitudes towards the influence of English on their national languages are explored, showing that countries appearing the most positive towards it "overtly" are least positive about it "covertly."

Davies and Bentahila (chapter 5) paint a rare picture of contemporary language attitudes in the Maghreb countries of North West Africa (i.e., Algeria, Morocco, and Tunisia). They reveal a rich mosaic of attitudes—oftentimes ambivalent - comparatively associated with written (and spoken) fushas, colloquial Arabic, Berber, various accented varieties of French, and code-switches between some of these. As with others in the volume where connections are made with national, ethnic and youth identities and cultures, this chapter provides ample illustrations of some of the themes we have outlined thus far. Davies and Bentahila also point out that even language varieties imbued with notions of purity, which are supported by formalized language academies, can sometimes be considered unsuccessful. Furthermore, government language planning might boomerang to the extent that it can ultimately revitalize French usage—the colonizers' language—in the quest for making people more marketable in the global economy. In the latter regard, this chapter—which also argues convincingly how methods employed can dictate different attitude profiles—indicates how new communication technologies can make language use and attitudes a child of their time and that the pace of change in this regard can be somewhat dramatic affecting as it can the linguistic landscape and evolving literature.

Moving to the southern region of the African continent, Painter and Dixon (chapter 6) also expend effort after delineating the *historical* development (and hegemony) of colonial languages—in this case, English and Afrikaans—vis-à-vis indigenous languages but, this time, in the context of racialization and de-racialization processes in the pre- and post-Apartheid eras. The argument that African languages were provided with institutional support to further subjugate their speakers' social positions, opportunities, and self-esteem is a compelling position to take, and their more recent de-stigmatization is an intriguing development. Painter and Dixon overview research, sometimes using the matched-guise technique[3], which assesses, again comparatively, various combinations of English (including Indian and Black South African varieties) in contrast with varieties (e.g., Cape) of Afrikaans, Zulu, and Xhosa. Important features of this chapter are the discussion of the ways in which language communities can practice appropriation of, and *own*, other groups' language varieties to meet their own collective means, and do so in ways that are discursively constructed.

Turning to the Asian context, He and Ng (chapter 7) explore the social meanings attached to English in China—which has an incredible number of urban learners of this language—and the position of government, teachers, and others in influencing proficiency and communicative competence in varieties and mixes of varieties of it (e.g., British, American, and China Englishes). Not only is English imbued, as elsewhere, with utilitarian values in a modernizing society, but it has what He and Ng call "humanistic" values in terms of broadening cultural awareness, enhancing civic and social responsibilities, and even in modifying conceptions of the self; and all this in the context of China harboring well over a 100 mother tongues. The impact of attitudes in fostering different social motivations for learning English (see also, Gardner, 2011) as well as so-called "productive bi- and trilingualism" are discussed. Intriguingly, international events such as the Beijing Olympics and the Shanghai World Exhibition—along with the one million volunteers supporting the former in their speaking and accommodating foreign English (amongst other) tourists—are regarded as important in broadening cultural awareness amongst the Chinese people. This cultural function of English goes hand in hand with China's quest of modernity on the one hand, and on the other hand, with vigorous debate among Chinese educators on the feasibility of developing a China English in association with China's peaceful rise in the international community of nations (Ng, Ye, & Lee, 2011).

Sachdev and Bhatia (chapter 8) examine the diverse linguistic landscape of South Asia, exploring some of the historical forces that have shaped it over the centuries—such as the "Persianization" of Kashmir and the "Englishization" of India—as well as contemporary government policies and ideologies that continue to exert a significant influence. Despite restrictive language policies in many South Asian countries—for example, Bangladesh and the Maldives both have only one official language and Punjabi continues to have unofficial status in Pakistan, despite being spoken by the majority of the population—Sachdev and Bhatia note that multilingualism, language-mixing, and code-switching are the norm, rather than the exception. This is particularly true in India, where educational policies have predominantly been favorable towards mother-tongue instruction and where popular media (e.g., Bollywood) has played a significant role in promoting mutual intelligibility between urban and rural varieties of Hindi, for example. India's relatively liberal language policies have also contributed significantly to the revitalization of Punjabi, in part due to its recognition as an official language in the northern Indian state of Punjab. Nonetheless, many minority languages in South Asia continue to suffer from low vitality and be overshadowed by prestige varieties associated with economic and social status, such as Hindi and English.

Moving to the Antipodes, Weatherall (chapter 9) examines how colonialism, racism, and linguistic imperialism of English undermined the value of indigenous languages in Australia and New Zealand, rendering a once rich and diverse linguistic landscape desolate, with the majority of indigenous languages now either endangered or extinct. Weatherall gives due attention to a number of distinctive varieties—including English, New Zealand Sign, Samoan, Te Reo Maori (the indigenous language of New Zealand), and Aboriginal languages in Australia—examining contemporary language attitudes, as well as the effectiveness of recent government efforts at improving the subjective well-being of minority language communities (see also Bourhis et al., 2012). Although such efforts appear to have had a positive impact on the deaf community of New Zealand, increased institutional support of Te Reo Maori—in the form of media presence and a Te Reo Maori version of the national anthem—has done little to revitalize it, with the majority of Maori unable to speak their native language. Yet despite the apparent low vitality of indigenous varieties, Weatherall notes that contemporary "hybrid" varieties of nonstandard English, such as Maori English, Aboriginal English, and Pacifika English, appear to be on the rise as youth seek to establish their unique ethnolinguistic identities. The future of aboriginal languages in Australia remains uncertain and for linguists and language attitude scholars this raises many questions as to their sustainability and vitality.

Finally, the volume closes with an Epilogue from Cindy Gallois wherein she overviews the preceding chapters with respect to exploring their dissimilarities, pointing expansively to refreshing vistas in which this research domain may blossom in the years to come. Amongst other pertinent issues, she encourages research that actively recognizes that a speech community's perceptions of its social history are an integral element shaping their language attitudes as well as encourages us to expend more effort after analyzing language attitudes-in-action by observing how perceptions are enacted in communicative behavior.

Conclusion

Language attitudes do not exist in a social vacuum, nor are they stable and immutable frames of reference. Rather, they are a product of diverse, and sometimes competing, cultural, historical, and ideological forces, and can quickly shift in response to the radically changing political and technological landscape that constitutes the modern (globalized) world (see Coluzzi, 2012). Our opening analysis of language ideologies and the chapters in this volume have led to the crafting of Propositions about the dynamics of language attitudes. Inevitably, these will be refined by us—and perhaps blended with or amended in light of recent principles of intergroup communication (Giles, 2012b; Hogg & Giles, 2012)—and added to by others over the coming years. Yet despite their embryonic character, they function as a viable organizing heuristic for capturing not only the essence of the above ideological frames and the field of language attitudes in general (see Giles & Rakić, in press) but, also, for illustrating many (but obviously hardly all) of the important features inherent in the chapters that follow.

I: When language varieties are expressed in interaction and in the media, they can be socially diagnostic of other speakers' attributes. Such language attitude schemas can be learned and invoked very early in the lifespan and sometimes can be more potent in forging social judgments than other prevailing physical cues as well as influence decision-making in applied contexts, such as the workplace, medical, and counseling clinics.

II: Language varieties can be distinguished between those imbued with attributions of natural, cultured sophistication on one hand or innate inferiority on the other, with speakers of them, in turn, being socially dichotomized (and imperialized) into the comprehensible elite and the cognitively and communicatively inadequate, respectively.

III: Accordingly, socioeconomically privileged interest groups can spread ideologies, established and sustained by means of (sometimes racialized and dehumanizing) institutional structures and normative pressures they control, and implement policies to subvert the sociopolitical influence of those with competing linguistic interests and language varieties.

IV: However, stigmatized language varieties when internalized by the speech community implicated can lead to reductions in collective wellbeing and increased psychological stress. That said, they can also fulfill important social identity-enhancing, community-promoting, and bonding/solidarity functions for their speakers. Hence, these varieties can assume significant social capital in certain localized contexts, and especially when embraced by different layers of the social strata. Furthermore, such speakers can be attributed by outsiders with traits of social attractiveness, such as trustworthiness and kindness.

V: Nonetheless, language attitudes are not immutable frames of reference. Intergroup dynamics (be it, for example, changes in youth cultures, the fluctuating power relations between ethnic and national groups, and consequent shifts in group vitality such as institutional support mechanisms), globalization and international events, and new technologies (e.g., satellite TV, computer-mediated communication, and social media) can reconstitute previous judgmental fashions. In this way, existing ideological schemas can be reshaped and accepted, sometimes by means of governmental planning, and in ways that can maintain, preserve, and revitalize certain language varieties.

VI: Language attitudes attending spoken, signed, and written varieties can be value-laden (i.e., linked to modernity, rurality, social mobility, and/or religiosity, etc.) as well as associated with clear-cut affective meanings (anger, contempt, openness, and/or pride, etc.) and linguistic rights. Yet they can also be ambivalent (and sometimes seemingly contradictory) depending on the social groups targeted, methods employed, and the plethora of private, electronic, public and literary contexts in which they are evoked.

VII: Language attitudes are not merely cognitive and affective representations that can facilitate or impede motivations for learning and becoming communicatively competent in specific language varieties. Rather, they can also be rhetorical cogs in larger-scale argumentative narrative performances, designed (at least in part) to justify some ideological position(s).

As chapters in this volume attest, language attitudes are not only a product of the present times, but also a reflection of complex histories of domination and subordination that, in some cases, can be traced back hundreds of years. As such, language attitudes represent a glimpse into the past as much as into the present, and in order to fully grasp the complex and intricate nature of languages' social meanings, we must first understand the histories, relationships, and ideologies of the people who speak them.

Notes

1. It is not our intention to single out Croatia—similar anecdotes are available from other former Yugoslav Republics (i.e., with different belligerents) and we suspect that they are prevalent worldwide, particularly in times of war.
2. Quichua belongs to the Quechua language family.
3. Lambert's (e.g., 1967) matched-guise technique has invited debate and criticism over the decades (e.g., Garrett, 2010; Giles & Bourhis, 1976; Grondelaers et al., 2010) and was devised to tap, under controlled experimental conditions, private attitudes towards language varieties. It involves bidialectal and bilingual speakers, ideally authentically, producing the same so-called neutral passages of prose (see Giles & Coupland, 1991) in different linguistic forms, but controlling for extraneous stereotypical representations and/or paralinguistic and intonational features, such as speech rate and pitch. For an overview of extant methods across the language attitudes terrain, see Ryan, Giles, and Hewstone (1988), and for new ways of eliciting more implicit language attitudes, see Pantos and Perkins (in press) and Campbell-Kibler (in press). For a distinction between attitudes towards *linguistic forms* and attitudes towards *speakers* of those forms, as well as methods of assessing the former, see Schoel, Roessel, Eck, Janssen, and Petrovic (in press).

References

Ahrens, F. (2004, August 2). Accent on higher TV ratings. *The Washington Post.* Retrieved from http://www.washingtonpost.com
Andronis, M. A. (2004). Iconization, fractal recursivity, and erasure: Linguistic ideologies and standardization in Quichua-speaking Ecuador. *Texas Linguistic Forum, 47,* 263–269.
Ball, P., Gallois, C., & Callan, V. J. (1989).Language attitudes: A perspective from social psychology. In P. Collins and D. Blair (Eds.), *Australian English: The language of a new society* (pp. 89-102). Queensland, Australia: University of Queensland Press.
Barker, V., Giles, H., Noels, K., Duck, J., Hecht, M., & Clément, R. (2001).The English-only movement: A communication perspective. *Journal of Communication, 51,* 3–37.
Bauman, B., & Briggs, C. L. (2003).*Voices of modernity: Language ideologies and the politics of inequality.* Cambridge, MA: Cambridge University Press.
Bernsand, N. (2001). Surzhyk and national identity in Ukrainian nationalist language ideology. *Berliner Osteuropa Info, 17,* 38–47.
Blau, J. (2006). Refinement and oppression of Kurdish language. In F. A. Jabar & H. Dawod (Eds.), *The Kurds: Nationalism and politics* (pp. 103–112).Beirut, Lebanon: SAQI.
Bourdieu, P. (1991). *Language and symbolic power.* Cambridge, MA: Harvard University Press.
Bourhis, R. Y. (1982). Language policies and language attitudes: Le monde de la Francophonie. In E. B. Ryan & H. Giles (Eds.), *Attitudes towards language variation: Social and applied contexts* (pp. 34–62). London: Edward Arnold.
Bourhis, R. Y., Sioufi, R., & Sachdev, I. (2012).Ethnolinguistic interaction and multilingual communication. In H. Giles (Ed.), *Handbook of intergroup communication* (pp. 100–115). New York: Routledge.
Bugarski, R. (2012). Language, identity and borders in the former Serbo-Croatian area. *Journal of Multilingual and Multicultural Development, 33,* 219–235.
Callan, V. J., & Gallois, C. (1987). Anglo-Australians' and immigrants' attitudes toward language and accent: A review of experimental and survey research. *International Migration Review, 21,* 48–69.
Campbell-Kibler, K. (in press).The implicit association test and sociolinguistic meaning. *Lingua.*
Coluzzi, P. (2012). Modernity and globalization: Is the presence of English and of cultural products in English a sign of linguistic and cultural imperialism? Results of a study conducted in Brunei Darussalam and Malaysia. *Journal of Multilingual and Multicultural Development, 33,* 117–131.
Coupland, N., & Bishop, H. (2007). Ideologized values for British accents. *Journal of Sociolinguistics, 11,* 74–93.
Dovidio,J. F., & Gluszek, A. (2012). Accents, nonverbal behavior, and intergroup bias. In H. Giles (Ed.), *The handbook of intergroup communication* (pp. 87–99). New York: Routledge.
Dragojevic, M., & Giles, H. (in press). Language and interpersonal communication: Their intergroup dynamics. In C.R. Berger (Ed.), *Handbook of interpersonal communication.* Berlin: De Gruyter Mouton.
Edwards, J. R., & Jacobsen, M.(1987).Standard and regional standard speech: Distinctions and similarities. *Language in Society, 16,*369–80.
Elias, P. (2012, April 3). Oikos University shooting: Suspect in deadly attack was upset about being teased over poor English skills, police say. *Huffington Post.* Retrieved from http://www.huffingtonpost.com

Fuertes, J. N., Gottdiener, W., Martin, H., Gilbert, T. C., & Giles, H. (2012). A meta-analysis of the effects of speakers' accents on interpersonal evaluations. *European Journal of Social Psychology, 42*, 120–133.
Gal, S., & Irvine, J. (1995). The boundaries of languages and disciplines: How ideologies construct difference. *Social Research, 62*, 967–1001.
Gallois, C., & Callan, V. J. (1981). Personality judgments elicited by accented English speech. *Journal of Cross-Cultural Psychology, 12*, 347–359.
Gallois, C., & Callan, V. J. (1989). Attitudes to spoken Australian English: Judgments of ingroup and ethnic outgroup speakers. In D. Bradley, R. D. Sussex, & G. K. Scott (Eds.), *Studies in Australian English* (pp. 149–160). Bundoora, Australia: Department of Linguistics, La Trobe University for the Australian Linguistic Society.
Gallois, C., Callan, V. J., & Johnstone, M. (1984). Personality judgments of Australian and Aborigine and White speakers: Ethnicity, sex, and context. *Journal of Language and Social Psychology, 3*, 39–57.
Gallois, C., Watson, B., & Brabant, M. (2007). Attitudes to language and communication. In M. Hellinger & A. Pauwels (Eds.), *Handbook of language and communication: Diversity and change* (pp. 597–620). Berlin, Germany: Mouton de Gruyter.
Garrett, P. (2010). *Attitudes to language*. Cambridge, UK: Cambridge University Press.
Garrett, P., Coupland, N., & Williams, A. (2003). *Investigating language attitudes: Social meanings of dialect, ethnicity and performance*. Cardiff, UK: University of Wales Press.
Gasiorek, J., & Giles, H. (2012). Effects of inferred motive on evaluations of nonaccommodative communication. *Human Communication Research, 38*, 309–332.
Giles, H. (2011). Language attitudes: The role of motivated information management. *Canadian Issues, Fall*, 28–34.
Giles, H. (Ed.). (2012a). *The handbook of intergroup communication*. New York: Routledge.
Giles, H. (2012b). Principles of intergroup communication. In H. Giles (Ed.), *The handbook of intergroup communication* (pp. 3–16). New York: Routledge.
Giles, H., & Billings, A. (2004). Language attitudes. In A. Davies & E. Elder (Eds.), *Handbook of applied linguistics* (pp. 187–209). Oxford, UK: Blackwell.
Giles, H., & Coupland, N. (1991). Language attitudes: Discursive, contextual and gerontological considerations. In A.G. Reynolds (Ed.), *Bilingualism, multiculturalism, and second language learning: The McGill Conference in honor of Wallace E. Lambert* (pp. 21–42). Hillsdale, NJ: Erlbaum.
Giles, H., & Edwards, J. R. (2010). Attitudes to language: Past, present and future. In K. Malmkjaer (Ed.), *The Routledge linguistics encyclopedia* (3rd ed., pp. 35–40). London, UK: Routledge.
Giles, H., & Marlow, M. (2011). Theorizing language attitudes: Past frameworks, an integrative model, and new directions. In C. Salmon (Ed.), *Communication yearbook 35* (pp. 161–197). Thousand Oaks, CA: Sage.
Giles, H., & Niedzielski, N. (1998). Italian is beautiful, German is ugly. In L. Bauer & P. Trudgill (Eds.), *Language myths* (pp. 85–93). London: Penguin.
Giles, H., & Powesland, P. F. (1975). *Speech style and social evaluation*. London: Academic Press.
Giles, H., & Rakić, T. (in press). Language attitudes: The social determinants and consequences of language variation. In T. Holtgraves (Ed.), *The Oxford handbook of language and social psychology*. New York: Oxford University Press.

Giles, H., Reid, S. A., & Harwood, J. (Eds.). (2010a). *The dynamics of intergroup communication.* New York: Peter Lang.

Giles, H., Reid, S. A., & Harwood, J. (Eds.). (2010b). Introducing the dynamics of intergroup communication. In H. Giles (Ed.), *The dynamics of intergroup communication* (pp. 1–16). New York: Peter Lang.

Goffman, E. (1959). *The presentation of self in everyday life.* New York: Anchor Books.

Gluszek, A., & Dovidio, J. F. (2010). A social psychological perspective on the stigma of non-native accents in communication. *Personality and Social Psychology Review, 14,* 214–237.

Gluszek, A., Newheiser, A.-K., & Dovidio, J. F. (2011). Social psychological orientations and accent strength. *Journal of Language and Social Psychology, 30,* 28–45.

Grondelaers, S., van Hout, R., & Steegs, M. (2010). Evaluating regional accent variation in Standard Dutch. *Journal of Language and Social Psychology, 29,* 101–116.

Grosjean, F. (2010). *Bilingual: Life and reality.* Cambridge, MA: Harvard University Press.

Gudkykunst, W. B., & Ting-Toomey, S. (1990).Ethnic identity, language, and communication breakdowns. In W. P. Robinson & H. Giles (Eds.), *The new handbook of language and social psychology* (pp. 309–328). Chichester, UK: Wiley.

Harwood, J., & Giles, H. (Eds.). (2005). *Intergroup communication: Multiple perspectives.* New York: Peter Lang.

Haslam, N. (2006). Dehumanization: An integrative review. *Personality and Social Psychology Review, 10,* 252–264.

Hassanpour, A. (1992). *Nationalism and language in Kurdistan, 1918–1985.* San Francisco: Mellen Research University Press.

Heaton, H., & Nygaard, L. C.(2011). Charm or harm: Effect of passage content on listener attitudes toward American English accents. *Journal of Language and Social Psychology, 30,* 202–211.

Hogg, M. A., & Giles, H. (2012). Norm talk and identity in intergroup communication. In H. Giles (Ed.), *The handbook of intergroup communication* (pp. 373–387). New York: Routledge.

Irvine, J. T. (1989). When talk isn't cheap: Language and political economy. *American Ethnologist, 16,* 248–267.

Irvine, J. T., & Gal, S. (2000). Language ideology and linguistic differentiation. In P. V. Kroskrity (Ed.), *Regimes of language: Ideologies, polities, and identities* (pp. 35–84). Santa Fe, NM: School of American Research Press.

Johnson, F. L. (2012). Rhetorical positioning of US policy statements about multilingual education—with reference to the EU. *Language, Culture and Curriculum, 25,* 73–88.

Jørgensen, J. N. (2012). Ideologies and norms in language and education policies in Europe and their relationship with everyday language behaviors. *Language, Culture and Curriculum, 25,* 57–72.

Kamana, K., & Wilson, W. H. (1996).Hawaiian language programs. In G. Cantoni (Ed.), *Stabilizing indigenous languages* (pp. 153–156). Flagstaff, AZ: Northern Arizona University.

Kinzler, K. D., Corriveau, K. H., & Harris, P. L. (2011). Children's selective trust in native accent speakers. *Developmental Science, 14,* 106–111.

Kordić, S. (2010). *Jezikinacionalizam* [Language and nationalism].Zagreb, Croatia: Durieux.

Kreyenbroek, P. G. (1992). On the Kurdish language. In P. G. Kreyenbroek & S. Sperl (Eds.), *The Kurds: A contemporary overview* (pp. 68–83). London, UK: Routledge.

Kristiansen, T., Garrett, P., & Coupland, N. (Eds.). (2005). Subjective processes in language variation and change. *Acta Linguistica Hafniensia, 37,* 1–250.

Labov, W. (1966). *The social stratification of English in New York City*. Washington, DC: Center for Applied Linguistics.
Lambert, W. E. (1967). A social psychology of bilingualism. *Journal of Social Issues, 23*, 91–109.
Lippi-Green, R. (1994). Accent, standard language ideology, and discriminatory pretext in the courts. *Language in Society, 23*, 163–198.
Lippi-Green, R. (1997). *English with an accent*. London: Routledge.
Maher, J. C. (2005). Metroethnicity, language and the principle of cool. *International Journal of the Sociology of Language, 175/176*, 83–102.
Maher, J. C. (2010). Metroethnicies and metrolanguages. In N. Coupland (Ed.), *The handbook of language and globalization* (pp. 575–591). Oxford, UK: Blackwell.
Maher, C. J., Millar, M., Sayanagi, N., Rackham, D., Nishozono-Maher, A., Usui, N., & Buckley, L. (2010). Multilingual awareness in Japan: A national survey of young people's attitudes. *The Japan Journal of Multilingualism and Multiculturalism, 16*, 37–49.
Marlow, M., & Giles, H. (2008). "Who you tinkYou, talkinpropah?" Hawaiian Pidgin demarginalized. *Journal of Multicultural Discourses, 2*, 53–69.
Marlow, M. L., & Giles, H. (2010). 'We won't get ahead speaking like that!': Expressing managing language criticism in Hawai'i. *Journal of Multilingual and Multicultural Development, 31*, 237–251.
Milroy, J. (2001). Language ideologies and consequences of standardization. *Journal of Sociolinguistics, 5*, 530–555.
Milroy, J., & Milroy, L. (1985). *Authority in language: Investigating language prescription and standardization*. London: Routledge & Kegan Paul.
Ng, S.H., Ye, J., & Lee, C.C. (2011). Media discourse on globalization in China: A social-psychological analysis. *Journal of Language and Social Psychology, 30*, 138–157.
Pantos, A. J., & Perkins, A. W. (in press). Measuring implicit and explicit attitudes toward foreign accented speech. *Journal of Language and Social Psychology, 32* (1).
Pedersen, I. L. (2009).The social embedding of standard ideology through four hundred years of standardization. In M. Maegaard, Gregersen, F., Quist, P., & Jørgensen, J. N. (Eds.), *Language attitudes, standardization and language change* (pp. 51–68).Oslo, Norway: Novus Forlag.
Phillipson, R. (1992). *Linguistic imperialism*. Oxford, UK: Oxford University Press.
Rakić, T., Steffens, M. C., & Mummendey, A. (2011). Blinded by the accent! The minor role of looks in ethnic categorization. *Journal of Personality and Social Psychology, 100*, 16–29.
Reid, S. A., Zhang, J., Anderson, G. L., Gasiorek, J., Bonilla, D., & Peinado, S. (2012). Parasite primes make foreign accented English sound distant to people who are disgusted by pathogenes (but not by sex or morality). *Evolution and Human Behavior, 33*, 471–478.
Robinson, O. W. (2010). *Grimm language: Grammar, gender and genuineness in the fairy tales*. Philadelphia, PA: John Benjamins.
Ryan, E. B. (1979).Why do nonstandard varieties persist? In H. Giles & R. N. St. Clair (Eds.), *Language and social psychology* (pp. 145–157). Oxford, UK: Blackwell.
Ryan, E. B., Giles, H., & Hewstone, M. (1988). The measurement of language attitudes. In U. Ammon, N. Dittmar, & K. J. Mattheier (Eds.), *Sociolinguistics: An international handbook of the science of language* (Vol. II, pp. 1068–1081). Berlin, Germany: Mouton de Gruyter.
Ryan, E. B., Giles, H., & Sebastian, R. J. (1982). An integrative perspective for the study of attitudes toward language variation. In E. B. Ryan & H. Giles (Eds.), *Attitudes towards language variation: Social and applied contexts* (pp. 1–19). London: Edward Arnold.

Scherer, K. R., & Giles, H. (Eds.).(1979). *Social markers in speech*. Cambridge, UK: Cambridge University Press.
Schmidt, R. (2002). Racialization and language policy: The case of the U.S.A. *Multilingua, 21*, 141–161.
Schoel, C., Roessel, J., Eck, J., Janssen, J., & Petrovic, B. (in press). 'Attitudes Toward Languages' (AToL) scale: A global instrument. *Journal of Language and Social Psychology*.
Shuck, G. (2004).Conversational performance and the poetic construction of ideology. *Language in Society, 33*, 195–222.
Shuck, G. (2006). Racializing the nonnative English speaker. *Journal of Language, Identity, and Education, 5*, 259–276.
Silverstein, M. (1996). Monoglot "standard" in America: Standardization and metaphors of linguistic homogeneity. In D. Brenneis & R. H. S. Maucaulay (Eds.), *The matrix of language: Contemporary linguistic anthropology* (pp. 284–306). Boulder, CO: Westview Press.
Silverstein, M. (2003). Indexical order and the dialectics of sociolinguistic life. *Language & Communication, 23*, 193–229.
St. Clair, R. N. (1982). From social history to language attitudes. In E. B. Ryan & H. Giles (Eds.), *Attitudes towards language variation: Social and applied contexts* (pp. 164–174). London: Edward Arnold.
Stewart. C. M. (2012). Mapping language ideologies in multi-ethnic urban Europe: The case of Parisian French. *Journal of Multilingual and Multicultural Development, 33*, 187–202.
Trudgill, P. (1974). *Sociolinguistics: An introduction*. Harmondsworth, UK: Penguin.
Woolard, K. A. (1985). Language variation and cultural hegemony: Toward an integration of sociolinguistic and social theory. *American Ethnologist, 12*, 738–748.
Woolard, K. A., & Schieffelin, B. B. (1994). Language ideology. *Annual Review of Anthropology, 23*, 55–82.
Wotschke, I., (1996).Socio-regional speech versus "Oxford accent" trends and fashions in the pronunciation of English English. *Hermes, Journal of Linguistics, 17*,213–237.

CHAPTER TWO

Language Attitudes in the Americas

AGATA GLUSZEK & KAROLINA HANSEN

Two languages dominate the American continents: Spanish (with approximately 300 million native speakers)[1] and English (with about 235 million native speakers); Portuguese (roughly 163 million native speakers; Lewis, 2009) follows them. The remainder of the population of the two continents (over 50 million) speaks a variety of other native languages (including Quechua with over 10 million, French with approximately 8.3 million, and Haitian Creole with about 7.7 million native speakers; Lewis, 2009). Within each language, different dialects and accents abound. Geographically, languages both co-exist and are spread out. For instance, in the Canadian provinces of Quebec and New Brunswick, English and French co-exist. Quechua is spoken in parts of Ecuador, Peru, Bolivia, Chile, and Argentina. In fact, the movement and interactions of speakers of different linguistic backgrounds—whether in terms of a native language, a dialect, or an accent—are constant elements of the two continents.

In general, language, dialect, and accent constitute a significant social force (for recent reviews, see Giles & Marlow, 2011; Gluszek & Dovidio, 2010a). Throughout the world and history, one's linguistic background has often been a cause for prejudice and discrimination, sometimes ending tragically (see Dragojevic, Giles, & Watson, chapter 1). It has also been a source of pride, serving as a unifying force for ethnolinguistic groups and a way to positively distinguish one's ingroup from the (often oppressing) outgroup (Gallois, Ogay, & Giles, 2005). Recent research and evolutionary theory suggest that the way one speaks—as exemplified by one's *manner of pronunciation* (Giles, 1970)—has been an important cue in identifying a person as an outgroup member. When lacking visible cues to distinguish ingroup from outgroup members, we use language and accent to detect the distinction (Kinzler, Shutts, De-Jesus, & Spelke, 2009). Even when visible cues are present, we nevertheless turn to language—not appearance—to categorize a person as either belonging to our group or not (Hansen, Rakić, & Steffens, 2012; Rakić, Steffens, & Mummendey, 2011). These tendencies may stem from the fact that throughout history people lived in close proximity to those who physically looked very similar to them but often differed in auditory cues, whether speaking a different language, dialect or with a different accent (Kinzler et al., 2009). Thus, the only way to distinguish a friend from a potential foe was to listen closely. Research shows that in fact we are extremely sensitive to cues of foreignness, detecting non-native speech in milliseconds (Flege, 1984) and in speech played backwards (Munro, Derwing, & Burgess, 2003).

The sensitivity to others' linguistic backgrounds has real consequences for speakers and listeners alike. People's attitudes to those who speak differently tend to be negative (Gluszek & Dovidio, 2010a) and result in stereotyping, prejudice, and discrimination in all aspects of everyday life, including education, employment, and the media (Lippi-Green, 2012). Attitudes influence language policies, which, in turn, can dampen or exacerbate the negative consequences of speaking in a non-standard way (Padilla et al., 1991). In the present chapter, we discuss how the social meaning of languages, dialects, and accents shapes the social landscape of the American continents. We focus on education, employment, the role of the media, and language policies. After reviewing current literature, we propose a framework for understanding the relationships between major languages spoken on the American continents and how they may evolve in the future given demographic changes and the increased mobility of the speakers of the various languages. Because the majority of research on language attitudes has been conducted in the US and Canada, in our discussion we focus on these findings, and whenever possible demonstrate how the same processes apply or may apply in other countries of the Americas.

Languages, Dialects, and Accents

The Spanish language is spoken by a significant portion of the population in South and Central America and the Caribbean, with Mexico having the largest population of Spanish speakers (Lewis, 2009). The English language dominates Northern America (the United States and Canada), Belize, and some parts of the Caribbean[2] (Lewis, 2009). English is also the most commonly studied second language in the world, including in South and Central America (Graddol, 2006). The third most prevalent language is Portuguese, spoken mostly in Brazil and parts of Uruguay and Paraguay (Lewis, 2009). In addition, the American continents are a home to an estimated 993 living languages (Lewis, 2009). Each language includes numerous cultural and regional dialects, or linguistic varieties that differ from each other in vocabulary, grammar, and pronunciation (Lippi-Green, 2012). For example, African-American Vernacular English (AAVE) is a cultural dialect of American English, and Argentinean Spanish is a geographical dialect of Spanish. Frequently, dialects have different pronunciation, referred to as a regional or ethnic accent. However, accents are also a common characteristic of non-native speakers of any language, to which we refer as non-native accents. Collectively, we refer to regional, ethnic, and non-native accents as non-standard accents.

Speaking a different language or with a non-standard accent is often associated with a range of negative stereotypic perceptions (Gluszek & Dovidio, 2010a; Lippi-Green, 2012). Individuals who have non-native or regional accents are viewed as less intelligent and competent than people with standard accents, and as speaking the language poorly (for a review, see Gluszek & Dovidio, 2010a). Research has identified three dimensions on which the ratings tend to converge: social status (competence), solidarity (social attractiveness), and dynamism (level of activity; Fuertes et al., 2012). Speakers with non-standard accents tend to be rated low in status, especially when their accents are perceived as difficult to comprehend (Bresnahan et al., 2002). Although such speakers are sometimes perceived higher on the solidarity dimension, a recent meta-analysis found that in general non-standard-accented speakers are rated lower than standard-accented speakers on all three dimensions of status, solidarity, and dynamism (see Fuertes et al., 2012).

Negative attitudes toward linguistic varieties may result in overt behaviors directed at the group, or discrimination (Gluszek & Dovidio, 2010a). Language and accent discrimination differ from other forms of discrimination in that they are still widely accepted in society (Lippi-Green, 2012). Research findings suggest that subtle and blatant discrimination is common across languages and countries of the Americas. In the next three sections, we discuss three areas—education, employment, and the media—where speaking a different language or with a non-standard accent matters.

Education

Language ideology and the myth of the standard language/accent (see Dragojevic et al., this volume, and Lippi-Green, 2012) are deeply embedded in educational systems of most countries in the Americas (Hornberger, 2000; Lippi-Green, 2012). From an early age, children learn not only to read and write, but also to discern the *right* way to read, write, and *speak*. Usually only one form of a written and spoken language—the one that is already deemed as the standard for the given language—is imposed as the appropriate one for children to perfect. Other varieties of the language (e.g., African American Vernacular English) or languages (e.g., Spanish in the US) are often portrayed as inappropriate in the school context and beyond (Lippi-Green, 2012). Such politics stand in contrast to linguists' views (Milroy, 2001) but rarely do teachers call for valuing local accents and dialects at school (Santos Mota, 2002). Even in the countries that openly support bilingual and multilingual education such as Canada (e.g., Bourhis, Montaruli, & Amiot, 2007) and many Latin American countries (Mexico, Guatemala, Peru, or Bolivia; Mar-Molinero, 1995), one language is often afforded more social prestige.

In the United States, the National Council of Teachers of English (NCTE) and the International Reading Association (IRA) suggest what children should learn. Their latest publication is from 1996, but it still reflects current practices in schools across the country. Initially, it may appear that the Council and Association's approach to language varieties is highly accepting:

> We know, of course, that our students come from many different language communities. [...] that no single "standard" of English exists around the world, or even within a single country. All of us who speak English speak different varieties of English depending on whom we are communicating with, the circumstances involved, the purpose of the exchange, and other factors. (IRA & NCTE, 1996, p. 16)

However, after this initial open acknowledgement, the tone changes somewhat:

> Nonetheless, some varieties of English are more useful than others for higher education, for employment, and for participation in what the Conference on College Composition and Communication (1993) in a language policy statement calls "the language of wider communication." Therefore, although we respect the diversity in spoken and written English, we believe that all students should learn this language of wider communication. (IRA & NCTE, 1996, p. 16)

This seeming acceptance and respect for other language varieties quickly gives in to the recommendation that *all* students *should* learn "the language of wider communication." Thus, students speaking African American Vernacular English—a dialect of English with its own grammar rules and vocabulary spoken mostly by African Americans in the US—speak "a less useful" form of the English language, as do students of Mexican ethnic origin in California and the Southwest who speak Chicano English. However, native English speakers of upper classes across the country speak the "appropriate" form of the English language (Lippi-Green, 2012). Furthermore, many states have laws that require students to be taught in English, in stark disregard for research suggesting that students benefit from being taught in their own language before gradually being introduced to the mainstream language (The Linguistic Society of America, 2010).

Latin American countries developed similar policies in the era of colonization and Spanish and Portuguese "linguistic imperialism" (Rajagopalan, 2005). However, in the last few decades Latin American countries have started acknowledging the importance of cultural diversity and valuing local, mainly indigenous, languages (Chareille, 2003). In a search for a new national identity different from the postcolonial one, some countries started recognizing bilingualism and multi-ethnicity as important parts of their identity politics (Hornberger, 2000; Plaza Martínez & Albó, 1989). They initiated programs of bilingual indigenous-Spanish education at schools, for example, in Maya languages in Guatemala or in Quechua and Aymarain in Peru, Ecuador, and Bolivia (Cummings & Tamayo, 1994; Hornberger, 2000). Among other goals, the aim of bilingual education was to save indigenous languages from extinction and help indigenous populations become more fluent in Spanish. Nevertheless, skeptics argue that these goals are not being fulfilled and indigenous languages still have lower status than Spanish and Portuguese (Niño-Murcia, 2003). In addition, criticisms have been raised that "it is the white man [sic] that decides what is good for indigenous populations" (Rajagopalan, 2005, p. 88). Thus, it is unsurprising that attitudes to bilingual teaching programs are sometimes negative as parents are aware of the higher status afforded to the standard Spanish in the job market and expect schools to teach only Spanish to their children (Cummings & Tamayo, 1994).

Standard language ideology dictates not only what children should learn, but also who should—and more importantly who should *not*—do the teaching (Lippi-Green, 2012). For example, in 2010 the Arizona Department of Education and State Board of Education instructed Arizona schools to remove teachers who speak English with "heavy accents" from English Language Learner (ELL) classrooms, which prompted an outcry among teachers and various associations. The Linguistic Society of America (2010) issued a resolution condemning such a move stating that it "is based on uninformed linguistic and educational assumptions about accents and the role of accents in language teaching and learning."

The concerns over language and accent of those who are teaching are not limited to primary education. Colleges and universities also serve as a battleground for language and accent ideologies. In the United States, the issue of non-natively speaking instructors who teach undergraduate classes is highly debated (Alberts, 2008; Rubin, 1992). In Latin America, students also complain about classes taught by non-natively speaking graduate students and faculty (Shoemaker, 2011). Yet, on average, undergraduates do not perform worse in such classes (Fleisher, Hashimoto, & Weinberg, 2002). In fact, experimental studies demonstrated that often it is the perception of an accent, not the accent per se, that leads to negative evaluations of non-native teachers (Rubin, 1992). Moreover, listener expectations and biases are often responsible for issues with comprehensibility (Lindemann, 2011; Rubin, 1992).

One of the main reasons why non-standard language and pronunciation varieties are discouraged in educational systems across the Americas is that children who grow up speaking differently face a number of disadvantages when they enter young adulthood, from prejudices in the higher education system to discrimination in the workplace. As we discuss below, such concerns are not baseless. However, subscription to the standard language ideology, or the "language of wider communication," in education is partially responsible for creating societies in which language varieties are not accepted (Lippi-Green, 2012).

Employment

Negative attitudes toward non-standard speech extend beyond the walls of educational institutions and affect speakers as they enter employment and progress through their careers. Discrimination in employment based on one's language or accent is prevalent in countries across both American continents. In the United States, research has found that individuals who speak with regional or non-native accents are perceived as less hirable (e.g., Segrest Purkiss et al., 2006) and are more likely to be assigned to lower status positions than are those with standard accents (de la Zerda & Hopper, 1979). Similar results were found in Costa Rica; participants assigned lower status occupations to the speakers who used a stigmatized form of pronunciation (Berk-Seligson, 1984).

Researchers have demonstrated that the language (or languages) a person speaks has consequences on employment and income. In the US, Mexican American employees speaking with a Mexican accent earn less than Mexican American employees with an American accent, independent of language proficiency (Davila, Bohara, & Saenz, 1993). In Canada, similar results have been reported (Creese & Kambere, 2003; Hakak, Holzinger, & Zikic, 2010). In Paraguay, the vast majority of the population speaks Guarani, an indigenous language. However, the Spanish language is afforded a higher prestige and monolingual Spanish speakers on average earn more than either bilingual Spanish-Guarani or monolingual Guarani speakers (Patrinos, Velez, & Psacharopoulos, 1994). Similar findings have been reported for speakers of indigenous languages and for immigrant guest workers in other Latin American countries, such as Argentina (Preston, 2002), Bolivia (Chiswick,

Patrinos, & Hurst, 2000), Costa Rica (Funkhouser, Pérez Sáinz, & Sojo, 2002; Garcia, 2004), Peru (MacIsaac & Patrinos, 1995), and Guatemala (Beckett & Pebley, 2003; Patrinos, 1997).

It is important to note that most countries of the Americas prohibit discrimination based on language and accent and many of Latin American countries guarantee bilingual education for Indigenous people (UNESCO, 2003). However, even in countries with strong anti-discrimination laws, such as the US, the law allows for exceptions. For example, employers can refuse to hire or can fire a person if they believe that his or her "accent seriously interferes with the employee's job performance" (US Equal Employment Opportunity Commission, 2012). However, objective criteria for assessing accent effects on one's performance are non-existent, and courts often rely on employers' or their own subjective opinions to determine whether a person's accent is problematic (Lippi-Green, 1994). Furthermore, employers in the United States readily admit that they discriminate based on a person's foreign appearance or accent (Lippi-Green, 1994). Since prejudices can affect behavior and decisions in unconscious ways (Dovidio, 2001), courts' and employers' potential biases affect non-standard speakers' lives with few safeguards (Lippi-Green, 2012; Matsuda, 1991). Moreover, those who perceive accent as a barrier in social and professional interactions may experience negative psychological health outcomes. For instance, Wated and Sanchez (2006) found that possessing a non-native accent served as a significant predictor of stress experienced at work for Hispanic workers in the US.

On one hand, employees in the Americas are often discriminated based on their language or accent; on the other hand, however, language can be an asset when applying for specific kinds of jobs, such as in call centers. A growing need for low-cost customer service can be solved thanks to technological advances by employing operators who do not need to be in the same country as their clients. However, impressions transmitted by the voice are important. Therefore, companies seek places where people already speak the language with an accent perceived as weak and understandable, or even pleasant. Brazilians, for example, claim that their Portuguese accent in English is weaker and more pleasant than a Spanish accent (Coutinho de Arrida, Notarnicola Filho, & Vernes Almeida, 2011). Companies serving Spanish-speaking clients do not want their employees to be associated with negative stereotypes of specific national or ethnic groups and are looking for Spanish speakers with an unidentifiable "neutral" accent. Therefore, various Latin American countries advertise their accent as the most "neutral" and suitable for transnational call centers (Rivas, 2007).

In sum, a non-standard language, dialect, or accent in general has negative consequences for the speaker concerning employment opportunities. Most research, however, has been conducted in the US and Canada and more research is needed to better understand the effects of languages, dialects, and accents on employment and how these effects have changed in the past two decades.

The Media

The myth of a standard language or accent and stereotypical conceptions associated with non-standard forms are perpetuated by the media across the Americas. The exposure to such stereotypical portrayals begins early in life through cartoons and Disney movies (Lippi-Green, 2012). For example, in the original English language version of *Aladdin*, the main characters speak with an American accent, but the bad characters have a distinctive Arabic accent (Lippi-Green, 2012). Furthermore, in the United States, a content analysis of a random sample of cable cartoons for children revealed that villains spoke with stereotypically negative accents (German, Russian, and other Eastern European) whereas heroes spoke with American and British English accents (Dobrow & Gidney, 1998). Similar patterns of stereotyping appear in movies and TV shows directed at adults (Lippi-Green, 2012). For example, on prime time television, Hispanic/Latino characters are more likely to have an accent and be less articulate than members of other groups (Mastro & Behm-Morawitz, 2005).

While movies often use accents as "mental shortcuts" to easily categorize and stereotypically depict characters, at the same time they require actors to be "accent-flexible." If, for any reason, actors are unable to shed their native or regional accents, they risk not being hired or being typecast. For example, Bela Lugosi, a Hungarian actor typecast as Dracula, pointedly noted, "If my accent betrayed my foreign birth, it also stamped me as an enemy, in the imagination of the producers" (IMDB, 2012). Thus, film and theatre college departments offer an array of accent training classes to teach students both how to acquire the ability to speak with other accents and how to neutralize their own. This phenomenon is not limited to the English language. In the Spanish language media, a "neutralized" Spanish is gaining popularity (Ahrens, 2004). The largest Mexican TV channel employs numerous coaches to teach its actors coming from various Latin American countries to speak a neutral way. Even in a soap opera about Roma people in Mexico, which features actors from Colombia, Argentina, Peru, Spain, and Mexico, all actors speak in such a neutralized Mexican Spanish. As Ahrens (2004) notes, it seems that "accent-neutral Spanish is the sound of a coming media culture."

The media not only promote the standard variety, but also shape what is regarded as standard. For example, the largest Brazilian TV channel promotes a "standard Portuguese" that is in fact an otherwise non-existent language variety (Massini-Cagliari, 2004). Strong influence of the media was shown in a study of attitudes towards different dialects of Portuguese spoken in five large Brazilian cities: None of the dialects was perceived as appropriate to become the standard for the entire country (Ramos, 1997). Furthermore, speakers of the dialects deemed most fitting to become a standard, perceived themselves as speaking most similarly to the language used in the media, demonstrating that the media play a strong role in setting the standards of pronunciation in Brazil (Medeiros, 2006; Ramos, 1997). However, the larger the perceived difference between people's own dialect and the pronunciation used in the media, the prouder they felt about their own dialect (Ramos, 1997).

While large TV and radio stations are promoting and creating a standard pronunciation, smaller stations seek to promote underrepresented languages and political and social communities (Beltrán & Reyes, 1993; Lipski, 1991). For example, Bolivia and Ecuador have developed a wide and sophisticated system of local radio stations, run by farmers, physical workers, and indigenous people (Beltrán & Reyes, 1993). The radio stations are perceived as giving a voice to the groups who are not adequately represented in the media and the speakers often use non-standard varieties of Spanish or speak in indigenous languages. Similarly, underground radio stations in Central America and the Caribbean have been serving as an important voice of social and political movements. Their ideological beliefs are also reflected in the use of local accents and in the choice of words, for example, in Cuba by using "you" instead of "comrade" (Lipski, 1991).

Natural non-standard accents appear in the small-scale media, but the large-scale media are more likely to portray actors imitating various accents (to varying degrees of success). This phenomenon may serve as a basis for an erroneous belief among speakers with non-standard pronunciation that accents can be easily altered or even eliminated (Lippi-Green, 2012; Scovel, 2000). Although accent strength diminishes the longer one resides in a given country and the more one uses the non-native language, researchers generally tend to agree that individuals who learn a language later in life are highly unlikely to acquire a native-like pronunciation (e.g., Flege, 1988; Piske, MacKay, & Flege, 2001; Scovel, 2000). Even actors who are successful at imitating other accents put a considerable effort in having to speak in a way that is unnatural to them and revert to their usual way of speaking when cameras are turned off (Lippi-Green, 2012).

The ways in which the media portray accents and languages can significantly affect how children and adults respond to people who speak in a non-standard way. Specifically, people spend a significant portion of their waking life watching TV. For example, on average Americans watch 36 hours of television per week (Nielsen, 2011), Argentineans 31, Brazilians 29.5, and Mexicans 26.5 (TGI, 2009). Television affects people's visions of the reality and their behaviors (Bryant & Oliver, 2009), including their perceptions on speech, favoring the use of standard grammatical variants (PEUL, 1991). With the wider access to TV also in more remote communities, the media are making people more aware of the standard pronunciation and may be even causing convergence to the standard. For instance, in towns on the Brazilian-Uruguayan border only older people continue to speak a mixture of Portuguese and Spanish. Younger generations realize the higher status of standard Brazilian Portuguese and have access to TV to learn to speak the TV-like-Portuguese (Carvalho, 2004). Furthermore, as people engage in more media-related entrainment (e.g., video games), which follow similar patterns as TV (e.g., accents in video games), the media's importance in shaping people's responses to languages and accents should not be underestimated.

Framework and Future

Languages and accents matter on both interpersonal and intergroup levels because, in the words of Milroy (2001), "language in use is necessarily a social phenomenon" (p. 545). Interpersonal interactions between people from different language backgrounds are often characterized by anxiety (Stephan & Stephan, 2000), suspicion, and distrust (Lev-Ari &Keysar, 2010). Moreover, people often experience a general negative affect in response to non-standard accents (Bresnahan et al., 2002). They may become irritated when unable to understand an accent or when they have to expend additional cognitive resources to listen to an accented speech (Spencer-Rodgers & McGovern, 2002). Individuals with non-standard speech may not only feel stigmatized and discriminated against but also experience enduring communication challenges (Gluszek & Dovidio, 2010b). Thus, it is important to examine the present and future effects of languages, dialects, and accents on individuals and societies at large.

In regards to present research on languages, accents, and dialects, we have very broadly summarized some areas of findings thus far. It is an extensive and complex topic and much research is still needed, especially in the area of how larger demographic and societal changes affect languages and accents. Furthermore, as much as some would like to keep "standards" fossilized and unchanging, languages, dialects, and accents are constantly changing (Milroy, 2001). Factors that affect how people speak vary as well (see Bourhis et al., 2005). For example, language policies in many Latin American countries concerning indigenous languages have shifted significantly in the past half-century (Rajagopalan, 2005).

Several factors influence language and accent use and change. In Figure 1, we propose five main factors that we find especially important in the Americas. One of them is the movement of people and competition among them, both within and between countries (Graddol, 2006). In the Americas, over 57 million people are international migrants and over 5 million are internally displaced persons (International Organization for Migration, 2010). These numbers does not include voluntary internal migration between various regions and urban migration. Such movements may lead to intergroup competition, perceived or actual, for what is seen as limited resources within a country (Esses, Jackson, & Armstrong, 1998). In times of economic recessions, anxieties over diminishing resources are heightened. People may believe that there is not enough for everyone, which may lead to perceived competition for limited resources. However, some groups are perceived as being more threatening than others, especially when they are particularly salient and distinctive due to their characteristics (Esses et al., 1998). One such distinctive trait is the way a person speaks. As a result, linguistic minority groups may be particularly willing to give up their languages or dialects and attempt to sound more like the majority group members. However, such groups may also resist negative stereotyping and seek to establish positive ingroup identity by emphasizing their different way of speaking (Giles & Johnson, 1981, 1987). In either case, intergroup competition may influence language, dialect, and accent use and change.

Various language policies and proposals, such as the English-only movement in the US (Lippi-Green, 2012; Padilla et al., 1991), are often motivated by perceived competition with immigrants. Restrictive policies may serve as the means of excluding those who speak in a non-standard way, such as Arizona's efforts to remove teachers who speak accented English mentioned above. Policies can also serve as a way to forcefully assimilate others into the mainstream way of speaking, even though they would be highly unlikely to succeed because it is extremely difficult to change one's accent (Scovel, 2000). Language policies and native-language movements may affect non-native speakers of that language negatively on both psychological and social levels (Padilla et al., 1991). In addition, institutionalized support for a standard pronunciation of a language in education and in the media discriminates against speakers with non-standard accents (Lippi-Green, 2012).

Language policies can also increase the prestige of declining languages, encourage the preservation of minority languages, and foster bi- and multi-lingualism (Moseley, 2010). In countries or regions where two languages are spoken, language policies may increase the prestige of the target language. For example, in the Canadian province of Quebec, the successive Charters of the French Language increased the status of the then waning French language (Bourhis et al., 2007). Similarly, in the last decades many Latin American governments granted official national language status to the most widely spoken indigenous languages (e.g., Quechua in Peru or Quechua and Aymara in Bolivia, Rajagopalan, 2005). In addition to legitimizing indigenous languages and valuing multiculturalism, it is also an attempt to prevent language loss. It is yet difficult to judge the results of these policies.

Another factor that influences language use and change is a general perception of the linguistic landscape, such as the degree to which a language is supported institutionally (e.g., signs) or is present in the media (Dailey, Giles, & Jansma, 2005). For instance, one study found that Hispanic raters perceived American-accented speakers less favorably in a more Spanish-oriented linguistic climate and more favorably in an English-oriented linguistic landscape, but that linguistic landscape had no effect on American-accented speakers' ratings (Dailey et al., 2005). In a different study, however, when European Americans perceived the media as more Spanish-oriented they tended to support immigrants and immigration more (Barker & Giles, 2004). Future research may determine the causes of these different patterns. It is likely that the effects of the linguistic landscape on people's attitudes and language use depend on the degree to which they perceive the language is supported. For example, a few signs in a foreign language on private buildings are likely to have different effects than similar signs in all public buildings, documents and forms, and on a local TV and radio stations.

In addition to the external factors affecting language and accent use and change, the linguistic groups' attitudes toward their own language variety are important internal factors (Giles & Johnson, 1987). For example, if speakers of endangered indigenous languages do not perceive their language as an important part of self-identity, or in fact, see it as a barrier for the younger generation entering the mainstream culture and gaining economic power, there is very little external factors (e.g., language policies) can do to stop the language from dying. If, however, speakers of a minority language or with a non-standard accent perceive their linguistic background in a positive way and as an important part of their identity, they are more likely to maintain their unique way of speaking as a way to distinguish themselves from other groups (Giles & Johnson, 1987). Thus, linguistic groups' attitudes toward their own way of speaking are an important factor in language and accent use and change.

These main elements, including the media discussed in the previous section, exert incessant pressures on linguistic varieties yet are also constantly changing themselves. Their influence increases and decreases depending on yet a variety of other factors. Therefore, the future variations in languages, dialects, and accents can only be speculated. However, given that language is a meaningful cue in distinguishing ingroup from outgroup members, both in the presence and absence of any visual cues (Hansen et al., 2012; Rakić et al., 2011) and that stigmatized varieties of a language persist as a way for groups to positively distinguish themselves from others (Giles & Johnson, 1987), various ways of speaking on the American continents are unlikely to disappear. In fact, as countries continue to experience international and national migration, the way one looks may become less significant and the way one speaks even more critical. In Figure 2.1, we suggest how the relationship between languages and accents might change within the current century.

Figure 2.1: Languages of the Americas: The current landscape (left) and potential changes this century (right).

| Competition | Language Policies | Linguistic Landscape | Media | Ethnolinguistic Identity | Competition | Language Policies | Linguistic Landscape | Media | Ethnolinguistic Identity |

Haitian — English — French
Immigrant Languages
Spanish
Portuguese
Indigenous Languages
Quechua

Haitian — English — French
Immigrant Lang.
Spanish
Portuguese
Indigenous Lang.
Quechua

We believe that drastic changes are unlikely to occur. Although indigenous languages will probably keep disappearing from the linguistic map of both Americas (Hawkins, 2005; Moseley, 2010), it is highly unlikely that the continents will become dominated by the English language alone as many often foretell (Graddol, 2006). A detailed report on the current and predicted trends in the English language suggests that the dominance of this language is waning while the importance of Spanish, Chinese, and Arabic is growing (Graddol, 2006). Increasingly, the model of a native English speaker as the ideal target for non-native speakers is also becoming obsolete. At the same time, we think that the awareness of the importance of bilingualism, acceptance of various forms of pronunciation, and an understanding of language learning and language processes will continue to rise.

One way to facilitate increased language, accent, and dialect tolerance is through language-related policies (Graddol, 2006). However, as we discussed above, policies by themselves may not be enough to change general negative attitudes toward linguistic varieties (e.g., Rajagopalan, 2005). This could be due to deeply ingrained human sensitivity to variations in how others speak and weak social norms against language and accent discrimination, partially fueled by standard language ideologies (Lippi-Green, 2012).

As we have seen in the past half century, norms against discrimination based on certain characteristics, such as race and ethnicity, can be embraced by societies. Achieving a similar degree of success with languages and accents may prove more difficult. First, speakers who use non-standard languages or pronunciation are not united in groups of non-native or non-standard speakers. They may differ not only in their ways of speaking, but also in mainstream language proficiency, cultural backgrounds, or religion. Second, race and ethnicity are visible cues and one can learn quickly and consciously that it is not socially appropriate to discriminate based on such cues. However, auditory cues are often present only after seeing someone and can be surprising (Hansen et al., 2012). For example, we may expect a Middle Eastern–looking person to speak with a foreign accent and if she or he does not, we may be bemused but evaluate such person positively. However, when a seemingly native speaker speaks with a foreign accent, we would evaluate this person negatively (Hansen et al., 2012). In any case, we would be surprised and such situations may require additional cognitive processing, which may interfere with learning not to discriminate. Finally, the standard language ideology is deeply ingrained in the society and its institutions, the media, and the public discourse (see Chapter 1, this volume, also Lippi-Green, 2012; Milroy 2001). Thus, changing language policies only on the institutional level may be not enough to change also the social meaning of languages, dialects, and accents.

Conclusion

In our brief discussion of languages, dialects, and accents in the Americas, we focused on education, employment, and the media—the three areas of waking life to which people devote most time. The general patterns of social meanings of the linguistic varieties are similar, even if details differ between countries. For example, although the history, attitudes, and policies surrounding indigenous languages in Bolivia are quite different from immigrant languages in the United States, the general patterns of stereotyping and discrimination are analogous. During the past few decades, many countries started valuing their cultural and linguistic diversity and introduced policies to preserve and support this diversity. However, policies are not enough to increase the status of non-standard ways of speaking. Market and media globalization support standard English, create "standard" Portuguese, or even try to unify all varieties of Spanish by erasing national markers and creating a "neutralized Spanish." As mentioned in the opening chapter of this book, "the standard represents an abstraction that tries to impose an artificial uniformity on naturally occurring linguistic variability" (Dragojevic et al., this volume, p. 8; Milroy, 2001). This struggle between the artificial ideals and the inescapable linguistic variability of the real world is likely to continue, affecting both the linguistic map and social landscape of the Americas.

Notes

1. All numbers are approximate and based on the data from various years. Current estimates are likely to be higher.

2. Specifically, English is considered a native language of the following Caribbean countries and territories: Anguilla, Antigua and Barbuda, Bahamas, Barbados, Cayman Islands, Dominica, Grenada, Guyana, Jamaica, Saint Kitts and Nevis, Saint Lucia, Trinidad and Tobago, U.S. Virgin Islands, and British Virgin Islands.

References

Ahrens, F. (2004). Accent on higher TV ratings: Spanish-language network Telemundo coaches actors to use Mexican dialect. *Washington Post*, 2 August, page A1.

Alberts, H. C. (2008). The challenges and opportunities of foreign-born instructors in the classroom. *Journal of Geography in Higher Education, 32*, 189–203.

Barker, V., & Giles, H. (2004). English-only policies: Perceived support and social limitation. *Language and Communication, 24*, 77–95.

Beckett, M., & Pebley, A. R. (2003). Ethnicity, language, and economic well-being in rural Guatemala. *Rural Sociology, 68*(3), 434–458.

Beltrán, L. R., & Reyes, J. (1993). Radio popular en Bolivia: La lucha de los obreros y campesinos para democratizar la comunicación [Popular radio in Bolivia: The struggle of the workers and farmers to democratize the communication]. *Diálogos de la Comunicación, 35*, 14–32.

Berk-Seligson, S. (1984). Subjective reactions to phonological variation in Costa Rican Spanish. *The Journal of Psycholinguistic Research, 13*, 415–442.

Bourhis, R. Y., Montaruli, E., & Amiot, C. E. (2007). Language planning and French-English bilingual communication: Montreal field studies from 1977 to 1997. *International Journal of the Sociology of Language, 185*, 187–224.

Bresnahan, M. J., Ohashi, R., Nebashi, R., Liu, W. Y., & Shearman, S. M. (2002). Attitudinal and affective response toward accented English. *Language and Communication, 22*, 171–185.

Bryant, J., & Oliver, M. B. (Eds.). (2009). *Media effects: Advances in theory and research* (3rd ed.). New York: Routledge.

Carvalho, A. M. (2004). I speak like the guys on TV: Palatalization and the urbanization of Uruguayan Portuguese. *Language, Variation and Change, 16*, 127–151.

Chareille, S. (2003). Planificación lingüística y constitución de un bloque regional: El caso del Mercosur (Argentina, Brasil, Paraguay y Uruguay) y de Chile [Language planning and the constitution of a regional bloc: The case of Mercosur (Argentina, Brazil, Paraguay, and Uruguay) and Chile]. *Language Problems and Language Planning, 27*, 63–71.

Chiswick, B. R., Patrinos, H. A., & Hurst, M. E. (2000). Indigenous language skills and the labor market in a developing economy: Bolivia. *Economic Development and Cultural Change, 48*, 349–367.

Coutinho de Arrida, M. C., Notarnicola Filho, O., & Vernes Almeida, N. (2011). *Revista Brasileria de Casos de Ensino em Administração, 1*(1). Retrieved from http://bibliotecadigital.fgv.br/ojs/index.php/gvcasos/article/view/3067/2167.

Creese, G., & Kambere, E. N. (2003). What colour is your English? *Canadian Review of Sociology and Anthropology, 40*, 565–573.

Cummings, S. M., & Tamayo, S. (1994). Language and education in Latin America: An overview. *Human Resources Development and Operations Policy Working Papers, 30*, paper Nr. 13068. Retrieved from http://go.worldbank.org/WTZKH4FN60

Dailey, R. M., Giles, H., & Jansma, L. L. (2005). Language attitudes in an Anglo-Hispanic context: The role of the linguistic landscape. *Language and Communication, 25*, 27–38.

Davila, A., Bohara, A. K., & Saenz, R. (1993).Accent penalties and the earnings of Mexican Americans. *Social Science Quarterly, 74*, 902–916.

de la Zerda, N., & Hopper, R. (1979). Employment interviewers' reactions to Mexican American speech. *Communication Monographs, 46*, 126–134.

Dobrow, J. R., & Gidney, C. L. (1998). The good, the bad, and the foreign: The use of dialect in children's animated television. *The Annals of the American Academy of Political and Social Science, 557*, 105–119.

Dovidio, J. F. (2001). On the nature of contemporary prejudice: The third wave. *Journal of Social Issues, 57*, 829–849.

Esses, V. M., Jackson, L. M., & Armstrong, T. L. (1998). Intergroup competition and attitudes toward immigrants and immigration: An instrumental model of intergroup conflict. *Journal of Social Issues, 54*, 699–724.

Flege, J. E. (1984). The detection of French accent by American listeners. *Journal of the Acoustical Society of America, 76*, 692–707.

Flege, J. E. (1988). Factors affecting degree of perceived foreign accent in English sentences. *Journal of the Acoustical Society of America, 84*, 70–79.

Fleisher, B., Hashimoto, M., & Weinberg, B. A. (2002). Foreign GTAs can be effective teachers of economics. *Journal of Economic Education, 33*, 299–325.

Fuertes, J. N., Gottdiener, W. H., Martin, H., Gilbert, T. C., & Giles, H. (2012). A meta-analysis of the effects of speakers' accents on interpersonal evaluations. *European Journal of Social Psychology, 42*, 120–133.

Funkhouser, E., Pérez Sáinz, J. P., & Sojo C. (2002). *Research Network Working Papers*, Article Number R-437. Retrieved from http://www.iadb.org/document.cfm?id=788064.

Gallois, C., Ogay, T., & Giles, H. (2005). Communication accommodation theory: A look back and a look ahead. In W. Gudykunst (Ed.), *Theorizing about intercultural communication* (pp. 121–148). Thousand Oaks, CA: Sage.

Garcia, C. S. (2004). Contested discourses on national identity: Representing Nicaraguan immigration to Costa Rica. *Bulletin of Latin American Research, 23*, 434–445.

Giles, H. (1970). Evaluative reactions to accents. *Educational Review, 22*, 211–227.

Giles, H., & Johnson, P. (1981). The role of language in ethnic group relations. In J. C. Turner & H. Giles (Eds.), *Intergroup behavior* (pp. 199–243). Oxford, England: Blackwell.

Giles, H., & Johnson, P. (1987). Ethnolinguistic identity theory: A social psychological approach to language maintenance. *International Journal of the Sociology of Language, 68*, 69–99.

Giles, H., & Marlow, M. L. (2011). Theorizing language attitudes: Existing frameworks, an integrative model, and new directions. In C. T. Salmon (Ed.), *Communication yearbook* (Vol. 35, pp. 161–198). New York: Routlege.

Gluszek, A., & Dovidio, J. F. (2010a). The way they speak: A social psychological perspective on the stigma of nonnative accents in communication. *Personality and Social Psychology Review, 14*, 214–237.

Gluszek, A., & Dovidio, J. F. (2010b). Speaking with a non-native accent: Perceptions of bias, communication, and belonging. *Journal of Language and Social Psychology, 29*, 224–234.

Graddol, D. (2006). *English next: Why global English may mean the end of "English as a Foreign Language."* British Council, UK. Retrieved from http://www.britishcouncil.org/learning-research-english-next.pdf

Hakak, L. T., Holzinger, I., & Zikic, J. (2010). Barriers and paths to success: Latin American MBAs' views of employment in Canada. *Journal of Managerial Psychology, 25*, 159–176.

Hansen, K., Rakić, T., & Steffens, M. C. (2012). *To speak or not to speak? Expectancy violations and the interplay of accents and looks in impression formation.* Manuscript submitted for publication.

Hawkins, J. R. (2005). Language loss in Guatemala: A statistical analysis of the 1994 population census. *Journal of Sociolinguistics, 9*, 53–73.

Hornberger, N. H. (2000). Bilingual education policy and practice in the Andes-Peru, Ecuador, and Bolivia: Ideological paradox and intercultural possibility. *Anthropology and Education Quarterly, 31*, 173–201.

International Organization for Migration. (2010). *Facts and figures: The Americas.* Retrieved from http://www.iom.int/jahia/Jahia/about-migration/facts-and-figures/americas-facts-and-figures

International Movie Database (IMDB). (2012). *Bela Lugosi—biography.* Retrieved from http://www.imdb.com/name/nm0000509/bio

International Reading Association and the National Council of Teachers of English. (1996). *Standards for the English language arts.* Retrieved from http://www.ncte.org/library/NCTE-Files/Resources/Books/Sample/StandardsDoc.pdf

Kinzler, K. D., Shutts, K., DeJesus, J., & Spelke, E. S. (2009). Accent trumps race in guiding children's social preferences. *Social Cognition, 27*, 623–634.

Lev-Ari, S., & Keysar, B. (2010). Why don't we believe non-native speakers? The influence of accent on credibility. *Journal of Experimental Social Psychology, 46*, 1093–1096.

Lewis, M. P. (Ed.). (2009). *Ethnologue: Languages of the world* (16th ed.). Dallas, TX: SIL International. Retrieved from http://www.ethnologue.com/

Lindemann, S. (2011). Who's "unintelligible"? The perceiver's role. *Issues in Applied Linguistics, 18*, 223–232.

Linguistic Society of America. (2010). *Resolution on the Arizona teachers' English fluency initiative.* Retrieved from http://www.lsadc.org/info/lsa-res-arizona.cfm

Lippi-Green, R. (1994). Accent, standard language ideology, and discriminatory pretext in the courts. *Language in Society, 23*, 163–198.

Lippi-Green, R. (2012). *English with an accent: Language, ideology, and discrimination in the United States* (2nd ed.). New York: Routledge.

Lipski, J. (1991). Clandestine radio broadcasting as a sociolinguistic microcosm. In C. A. Klee, & L. A. Ramos-García (Eds.), *Sociolinguistics of the Spanish speaking world Iberia, Latin America, United States* (pp. 113–137). Tempe, AZ: Bilingual Press/Editorial Bilingüe.

MacIsaac, D. J., & Patrinos, H. A. (1995). Labor market discrimination against Indigenous people in Peru. *Journal of Development Studies, 32*, 218–233.

Mar-Molinero, C. (1995). Language policies in multi-ethnic Latin America and the role of education and literacy programs in the construction of national identity. *International Journal of Educational Development, 15*, 209–219.

Massini-Cagliari, G. (2004). Language policy in Brazil: Monolingualism and linguistic prejudice. *Language Policy, 3*, 3–23.

Mastro, D., & Behm-Morawitz, E. (2005). Latino representation on primetime television. *Journalism and Mass Communication Quarterly, 82*, 110–130.

Matsuda, M. J. (1991). Voices of America: Accent, antidiscrimination law, and a jurisprudence for the last reconstruction. *Yale Law Journal, 100*, 1329–1407.

Medeiros, A. L. (2006). *Sotaques na TV* [Accents on the TV]. São Paulo, Brazil: Annablume.

Milroy, J. (2001). Language ideologies and the consequences of standardization. *Journal of Sociolinguistics, 5*, 530–555.

Moseley, C. (Ed.). (2010). *Atlas of the world's languages in danger* (3rd ed.). Paris: UNESCO Publishing. Retrieved from http://www.unesco.org/culture/en/endangeredlanguages/atlas

Munro, M. J., Derwing, T. M., & Burgess, C. (2003). The detection of foreign accent in backwards speech. In M.-J. Sole, De.Recasens & J. Romero (Eds.), *Proceedings of the 15th International Congress of Phonetic Sciences* (pp. 535–538). Australia: Causal Productions.

Nielsen Company. (2011). *State of the media: March 2011 U.S. TV trends by ethnicity*. Retrieved from http://www.nielsen.com/content/dam/corporate/us/en/reports-downloads/2011-Reports/State-of-the-Media-Ethnic-TV-Trends.pdf

Niño-Murcia, M. (2003). 'English is like the dollar': Hard currency ideology and the status of English in Peru. *World Englishes, 22*, 121–141.

Padilla, A. M., Lindholm, K. J., Chen, A., Durán, R., Hakuta, K., Lambert, W., & Tucker, G. R. (1991). The English-only movement: Myths, reality, and implications for psychology. *American Psychologist, 46*, 120–130.

Patrinos, H. A. (1997). Difference in education and earnings across ethnic groups in Guatemala. *Quarterly Review of Economics and Finance, 37*, 809–822.

Patrinos, H. A., Velez, E., & Psacharopoulos, G. (1994). Language, education, and earnings in Asunción, Paraguay. *The Journal of Developing Areas, 29*, 57–68.

PEUL—Research Group on the Use of Language. (1991). Results of an integrated sociolinguistic study. *International Journal of the Sociology of Language, 89*, 25–46.

Piske, T., MacKay, I. R. A., & Flege, J. E. (2001). Factors affecting degree of foreign accent in an L2: A review. *Journal of Phonetics, 29*, 191–215.

Plaza Martínez, P. & Albó, X. (1989). Educación bilingüe y planificación lingüística en Bolivia [Bilingual education and linguistic planning in Bolivia]. *International Journal of the Sociology of Language, 77*, 69–91.

Preston, D. (2002). Identity and migration: Tarijeños and the Argentina experience. In D. Preston (Ed.), *La globalización y la movilidad de capital y mano de obra en América Latina rural* [Globalization and mobility of capital and labor in rural Latin America] (pp. 35-42). Retrieved from http://citeseerx.ist.psu.edu/viewdoc/download?doi=10.1.1.9.200&rep=rep1&type=pdf

Rajagopalan, K. (2005). Language politics in Latin America. *AILA Review, 18*, 76–93.

Rakić, T., Steffens, M.C., & Mummendey, A. (2011). Blinded by the accent! The minor role of looks in ethnic categorization. *Journal of Personality and Social Psychology, 100*, 16–29.

Ramos, J. M. (1997). Avaliação de dialetos brasileiros, o sotaque [Evaluation of Brazilian dialects, the accent]. *Revista de Estudos da Linguagem, 5*, 103–125.

Rivas, C. M. (2007). *Imaginaries of transnationalism: Media and cultures of consumption in El Salvador* (Doctoral dissertation). Retrieved from http://escholarship.org/uc/item/3cm8w99w.

Rubin, D. L. (1992). Nonlanguage factors affecting undergraduates' judgments of nonnative English-speaking teaching assistants. *Research in Higher Education, 33*, 511–531.

Santos Mota, K. M. (2002). A linguagem da vida, a linguagem da escola: Inclusão ou exclusão? Uma breve reflexão lingüística para não lingüistas [The language of life, the language of school: Inclusion or exclusion? A brief linguistic reflection for non-linguists]. *Revista FAEEBA, 11,* 13–26.

Scovel, T. (2000). A critical review of the critical period research. *Annual Review of Applied Linguistics, 20,* 213–223.

Segrest Purkiss, S. L., Perrewé, P. L., Gillespie, T. L., Mayes, B. T., & Ferris, G. R. (2006). Implicit sources of bias in employment interview judgments and decisions. *Organizational Behavior and Human Decision Processes, 101,* 152–167.

Shoemaker, A. (2011). Regionalism and cultural identity: English as the international language. *Antares, 5,* 20–37.

Spencer-Rodgers, J., & McGovern, T. (2002). Attitudes toward the culturally different: The role of intercultural communication barriers, affective responses, consensual stereotypes, and perceived threat. *International Journal of Intercultural Relations, 26,* 609–631.

Stephan, W. G., & Stephan, C. W. (2000). An integrated threat theory of prejudice. In S. Oskamp (Ed.), *Reducing prejudice and discrimination: The Claremont Symposium on applied psychology* (pp. 23–45). Mahwah, NJ: Erlbaum.

Target Group Index (TGI). (2009). *TGI global update.* Retrieved from globaltgi.com/knowledgehub/documents/TGIUpdate3.pdf

UNESCO. (2003). *Linguistic rights in national constitutions.* Retrieved from http://www.unesco.org/most/ln2nat.htm#With

US Equal Employment Opportunity Commission. (2012). *National origin discrimination.* Retrieved from http://www.eeoc.gov/laws/types/nationalorigin.cfm

Wated, G., & Sanchez, J. I. (2006). The role of accent as a work stressor on attitudinal and health-related work outcomes. *International Journal of Stress Management, 13,* 329–350.

CHAPTER THREE

Language Attitudes in Western Europe

TAMARA RAKIĆ & MELANIE C. STEFFENS

"Accent is the soul of a language; it gives the feeling and truth to it."
JEAN-JACQUES ROUSSEAU

Western Europe illustrates in an exemplary way that what counts as a language or a dialect, is very much a matter of ascriptions, ideology, and standardizations (see Dragojevic, Giles, & Watson, this volume). In the Western European context, comprising a great number of different languages at a rather limited geographical space, the linguistic situation reflects much of European history: It is filled with plenty of inconsistencies, disputes, and language-related movements. Indeed, language is often one of the main obstacles within the European Union. Even though there are 23 official languages and many materials are available in each of them, some countries have linguistic privileges because their language is defined as *lingua franca*, whereas others are required to accommodate to them. Both on the level of Western Europe and that of individual countries, there is a great plurality and blend of different languages and dialects each related to different social identities; therefore, interesting inter-language dynamics can be observed both within single countries or languages as well as between different countries. More specifically, across Western Europe many languages coexist that are not constrained to a country boundary, which makes the comparison and evaluation of different language forms and its speakers very interesting. What is merely a dialect in one country (e.g., "Moselfränkisch" in Germany) may be an official language in another (Luxembourg). Second, and in contrast, other countries have simultaneously different official languages that may be more or less restricted to geographical areas. Third, English as an official language is confined to the UK and Ireland (and Malta) geographically but its use as an international language makes it present in all other countries as well. Finally, illustrating language politics, in post-war Spain, the role of different official languages was lowered to dialects, with the exception of Castilian. Today, however, these other languages (e.g., Catalan) vindicate their significance and construe an important part of speakers' identity.

Should one define Western Europe as European Union or would a more objective, geographical approach be more suitable? In order to fully account for the complexity of languages' social meanings in the area, we opted for a mixed geo-political and historical approach. We will start out with a geo-political overview of the languages covered in this chapter, followed by a theoretical context for a better understanding of inter- and (intra) language dynamics. Subsequently, we will give an overview of the different topics that have been covered in language attitude studies concerning Europe. In spite of the differences between countries, several topics have been researched across them. These are attitudes towards foreign accents and towards dialects and regional accents. Minority languages have a special status in this regard. Moreover, there are studies on attitudes towards English as an international language. Another genuinely European topic is that of comparisons of same-language speakers across countries. Finally, we present some studies that have demonstrated effects of language stereotypes on performance and recall.

Overview of Language Varieties in Western Europe

Linguistic borders play an important role in the European context. Though we do acknowledge that there are no real monolingual communities in Europe, there are countries with officially only one majority language. Both Germany and France are monolingual countries with languages that benefit official status also in other countries with multiple official languages (i.e., Belgium and Switzerland). Germany has only one official language, the standard variety of German ("Hochdeutsch"). This, however, does not imply that there is no linguistic diversity within Germany or other German speaking countries, because of a multitude of dialects and accents. Conversely, German is officially spoken also in Belgium, Switzerland, and Austria, as well as in the South Tyrol region of Italy (for a comprehensive overview of German language varieties in and outside Germany, see Ammon, 1995). The situation regarding French is similar to German; it is an official language of a monolingual country (France) and officially spoken outside national borders, allowing for interesting within-language—between-countries comparisons. With regard to the standard varieties (i.e., French and German) there is however one difference: Standard French is also known as Parisian French, being geographically linked to the capital, whereas standard German is not associated with the capital. Another monolingual country is Greece. The Netherlands' official language is Dutch, with some recognized regional bilingual parts (e.g., Friesland, see Ytsma, 2011). Italy is officially monolingual, with some regional exceptions (e.g., German and Ladino in South Tyrol). However, there is a rich within-language variation, constituted by many dialects and accents (Cugno, 2008).

Turning to countries with multiple official languages in Western Europe, Malta is an example of a very small country with two official languages (Maltese and English). Additionally, Italian is present and relevant. The Maltese language (re)gained its official status recently. It is predominantly used in oral communication and to a much lesser extent in writing. The situation is very similar in tiny Luxembourg, where German and French are official languages in addition to Luxembourgish. Its neighbor, Belgium, is often referred to as the heart of Europe, as an example of a multilingual nation that in certain aspects serves as a model for the European Union. However, linguistically the situation in Belgium is anything but simple, and Belgium today appears more divided than unified by identity related issues (e.g., language, culture). As an example, for over a year after the last election, Belgium was without a government as the coalition could not agree upon such issues. The three official languages in Belgium barely coexist simultaneously in the same place. The only exception is Brussels, a bilingual city (for details on Belgium, see Mettewie & Janssens, 2011).

Sociolinguistically, Switzerland is a very interesting country allowing for different language-based comparisons; there are multiple official languages within the country, though actually the majority of population is monolingual (Garrett, 2010). Most of those languages are shared with other countries (i.e., Germany, France, and Italy). Hence status (and relative size) differences can be observed both within the country as well as compared to its neighbors.

English has a unique status within Europe, being an official language of the UK, Ireland, and Malta, but *de facto* present as an internationally recognized *lingua franca*. Wales is a small country next to England, and historically there has been much tension between the Welsh and English (Laugharne, 2011). Similarly, Scotland is not only isolated from England geographically, but mostly politically and linguistically. However, also within Scotland numerous accent varieties interact with the listeners' identity and evaluation of speakers. Today Ireland is predominantly an English-speaking country. However, Irish is still present and officially recognized as a language. In Ireland, even though relatively limited parts of the population are considered truly bilingual, the number of bilinguals is now increasing. Moreover, an increasing number of schools officially adopt bilingualism or predominantly the Irish language (Ó Laorie, 2011). The standard variety that is also an official language for the whole UK is referred to with different names: Received Pronunciation (R.P.), Queen's English, or BBC English. English can be regarded as a cradle of language attitude research. Some of the most influential theories (e.g., communication accommodation theory: Giles, 1973) have been developed in this context, and a great number of studies on language attitudes have been carried out (for comprehensive reviews, see Robinson & Giles, 2001).

Even though Spain could be in the same category as countries with multiple official languages, unlike Belgium or Switzerland these languages are not spoken in other European countries (with some minority exceptions). Historically, Spain was a multilingual country. However, after the beginning of Franco's regime in 1940 all languages except Castilian lost their official status and were banned from public life, being constrained to informal and private contexts such as family. This situation lasted until 1977 when political autonomy was granted to different "Comunidades Autónomas."

Theoretical Framework: Language Attitudes and Social Identity

Given this plethora of language situations, can some unifying theoretical frameworks be used to review the research findings? Language attitudes— the notion that language varieties can provoke an evaluative reaction—is probably as old as languages themselves. Among the aspects of communication that have been researched in studies on language evaluation (e.g., speech style, lexical diversity), accents have undoubtedly received most attention (Giles & Marlow, 2011). A main distinction is usually made between standard and nonstandard varieties. In some cases the former is associated with a high status origin (e.g., R.P. in Great Britain, Parisian French) whereas in others no such association exist (e.g., standard Italian), yet in any case the standard variety hides speakers' origin. In contrast, a nonstandard accent always reveals the origin of the speaker, whether from the same language community or not. Social identity theory (SIT: Tajfel & Turner, 1979) provides a suitable theoretical frame for our chapter, both with respect to speaker and listener; because it plays a central role in how different language varieties are being evaluated. Ethnolinguistic identity theory (ELIT: Giles & Johnson, 1981, 1987), drawing on SIT, has spelled out the language-identity bond (with a special emphasis on ethnicity). According to ELIT, language performs central psychological functions of positive social identity especially with regard to aspects concerning ethnicity. Therefore, it is not surprising that language is used as a very powerful cue to determine who is a member of the in- or out-group (Yzerbyt, Leyens, & Bellour, 1995). As an example, a recent study conducted in Germany confirmed that a speaker's accent is more important than appearance for categorizing people as Germans versus not (Rakić, Steffens, & Mummendey, 2011a). Specifically, while spontaneously categorizing target persons, participants attended significantly more to accent than to appearance: Interestingly, Standard German speakers [Italian accent speakers] were confused with one another irrespective of their typical Italian or German looks.

An essential part of ELIT is the concept of ethnolinguistic vitality (EV), determined by a combination of effects of demographics, institutional support (and control), and status. Demographics refer to the number of members of a language group as well as their distribution or concentration throughout a given community. Institutional support and control is the group's presence and support in political, media, educational institutions as well as the linguistic landscape. Finally the status (i.e., linguistic, social, and economic) and its perceived legitimacy are highly related to both demographics and especially institutional support. According to Giles, Bourhis, and Taylor (1977), ethnolinguistic vitality indicates the power that a given linguistic community has in order to appear as a distinctive social group. This in turn makes this group likely to behave as a collective entity in a distinctive and active way in intergroup encounters. EV, along with the group's perception of their subjective ethnolinguistic vitality (Bourhis, Giles, & Rosenthal, 1981), is essential in understanding intergroup attitudes especially with regard to second language learning as well as the use of code-switching strategies, which is, switching between two languages or accents (Sachdev & Bourhis, 1993). Consequently, in contexts where there is low EV, such as with the Irish language, negative attitudes toward learning other languages can be seen as protectionism of a group against other languages (e.g., English and French). This is not observed with high EV languages such as Catalan, for example (Lasagabaster & Huguet, 2011). Especially in a context of great linguistic diversity, as Europe, both identity and vitality issues linked to different languages shaped greatly the language attitudes presented below. Much more important than intrinsic factors that make some languages appear more likeable than others, are the social norms internalized at a very early age that guide perception and evaluations (e.g., Giles & Niedzielski, 1998).

In search, in part for, possible explanations for negative evaluations of nonstandard language varieties, communication accommodation theory (CAT) was developed (Shepard, Giles, & Le Poire, 2001). CAT accounts for the dynamics that occur in any given instance of communication and evaluation; especially with regard to speech: Does the speaker attempt to converge or diverge from the accent of the listener or the standard accent, following the norm to use standard language (cf. chapter 1, this volume, for a critical discussion)? On both sides, motivation as well as the interpretation of intentions of the other plays an important role.

Attitudes towards Foreign Accents

Research in several European countries has targeted attitudes towards foreign accents. A recent nationwide survey in Germany (Eichinger et al., 2009) has attempted to gather insights into language attitudes toward both regional (i.e., dialects) as well as foreign languages present through minorities in the country. Not surprisingly, the perceived beauty of a given accent is highly related to the overall positivity associated with a social group. Hence, even though phonetically French and Turkish share similar pronunciation patterns, the former is perceived as more pleasant and attractive. An explanation why for example Turkish accents in Germany are negatively evaluated is similar to the case of Portuguese in France (Koven, 2004). As Portuguese are perceived as a low-status group, they are usually evaluated negatively in France, and compared to standard French, their accent is regarded as inferior regarding competence and status.

In German speaking communities, accents are used to infer speakers' identity (e.g., Borčić & Wollinger, 2008), and foreign accents related to immigrant groups are especially negatively evaluated within Germany (Klink & Wagner, 1999). Similar findings are reported from the Netherlands, where Moroccan and Turkish are related to relatively prominent immigrant communities and to rather negative language attitudes (Nortier & Dorleijn, 2008). Conversely, also among immigrant groups, identity plays an important role in accommodation toward standard Dutch (Extra & Yagmur, 2010). Hence, while Moroccans identify strongly with their Islamic background, Turkish youth's cultural self-awareness is strongly linked to language practices, resulting in a major use of Dutch in everyday situations by Moroccans but not by Turkish immigrants. Similar studies with Greek immigrants to other countries have demonstrated that identity issues were strongly related to language practices and attitudes towards the language of the host country (e.g., Gardner-Chloros, McEntee-Atalianis, & Finnis, 2005).

Attitudes towards Dialects and Regional Accents

The linguistic situation of different countries today reflects much of the social practices and norms that have been accepted and transmitted. One way to gain insights on how they are adopted is to study children of various ages.

STUDIES WITH CHILDREN. Whereas developmental studies support the emergence of ethnolinguistic identities, their findings are inconclusive due to the different age groups studied in different language contexts. In a French study (Girard, Floccia, & Goslin, 2008), 5-6 year-old children were very good in between-language differentiation (i.e., native vs. foreign accent speech), though they seemed not to notice within-language differences (i.e., northern and southern accent French). Several explanations may account for this phenomenon; first, a foreign accent may vary more from non-foreign accent than different regional accents vary from one another. Second, at that age children start to develop their national identity, hence it may be more relevant to distinguish "us" versus "them" between languages than to distinguish within one's language. The effect diminishes with further development: Whereas regional differentiation increases, the differentiation between native and foreign remains persistent throughout lifetime.

Older children (aged 7–10 years) were able to differentiate and evaluate different varieties of Dutch, including one from Belgium (van Bezooijen, 1994); the results indicate an overall preference for standard Dutch over regional varieties, and interestingly the Belgian variety was not evaluated the most negatively. Overall, language attitudes seem to be transmitted automatically through socialization, with children demonstrating different patterns of evaluation of nonstandard varieties depending on their age (Giles et al., 1983). Welsh children at the age of 7 children clearly prefer they own accent and react negatively toward R.P., though by the age of 10 they show an evaluation pattern similar to adults (i.e., evaluating R.P. the best). Additionally, for Welsh pre-adolescents the language of testing influenced the evaluation of the Welsh accent: it was regarded as more selfish (in Welsh) and less intelligent (in English) (Price, Fluck, & Giles, 1983).

The bond between language and identity is complex, with the former being determined by the latter at the same time as identity development is influenced by language use and practices (Ender & Straßl, 2009). The possible implications of this relationship are especially visible with immigrant children in a dialect-speaking context of a host country such as Switzerland. These children may be forced to speak and adopt three languages at once, their native language (and first language), used to communicate with their parents, a German dialect that is used with peers, and standard German required at school. Unfortunately, communication norms in everyday life (i.e., the use of dialects) and institutional norms (i.e., the use of standard German) are conflicting, creating an ulterior barrier for immigrant children in securing their active role within society. In other words, it is the lack of identification possibility that makes standard language a tool to use at school, thus negatively influencing the motivation to learn it.

Teachers play an important role in the institutionalization of standard language and directly or indirectly transmit their norms and attitudes to children they teach. One study investigated the role of teachers in the promotion of standard German in regions where a strong dialect is spoken (Davies, 2000). The findings show that although teachers do not question their role in spreading the norm of standard German, the reality in the classroom indicates much less homogeneity than one would expect. Similar findings emerged in the context of Cyprus, where both Turkish and Greek are official languages (Sophocleous & Wilks, 2010), and the teachers display some ambiguities related to the use of the two varieties, standard Greek and the Cypriot-Greek dialect. Therefore, even though only standard Greek should be taught in the classrooms both teachers and children use both varieties. Also in this case, the influence of identity on teachers' as well as pupils' linguistic behavior and preferences is visible.

STUDIES WITH ADULTS. Throughout childhood, at different developmental stages, different aspects of language variation play important roles. Subsequently, in adulthood language attitudes remain rather stable and show a strong link to one's identity. How stable and persistent language attitudes are in society was shown recently in a comparison study between an early study by Giles (1970) and a relatively recent BBC survey (Garrett, 2010) of the English-language context. In brief, respondents from outside of England showed a clear own accent-bias. However, prestige was highest for the R.P., irrespectively of respondents' location. Therefore, in spite of their own-accent bias, nonstandard speakers adopt norms about the "proper" accent and its related status.

Participants in Dundee rated their own accent most favorably on status, employment and social attractiveness dimensions (Abrams & Hogg, 1987). Interestingly, the Glasgow accent was only devaluated when contrasted to the Dundee-accent but more positively evaluated in comparison with R.P., indicating clear ingroup favoritism of evaluators as well as their shifts in identification based on the comparison group. These results can be also interpreted in view of high subjective vitality and objective status that together promote accent loyalty.

Generally, the dynamics of identity and prestige issues are rather universal and not to be underestimated. As shown in a study confronting different regional accent variations by participants from Dublin (e.g., Edwards, 1977), though the Dublin accent speakers were evaluated worst on competence, at the same time they were evaluated highest on social attractiveness. Similarly, Masterson, Mullins, and Mulvihill (1983), looking at prestige and solidarity (comparable to competence and social attractiveness, respectively), found that own identity and background of listeners as well as the context of the evaluation play a crucial role in how given accents are evaluated.

Similar findings emerged in France, with high agreement that the Parisian French speakers are the most competent (Kuiper, 2005). In addition, for likeability a preference for one's own language variety over standard resulted in almost all cases. Furthermore there was a noticeable discrepancy between speakers' beliefs regarding the ability to speak accurate Parisian French; Parisian speakers ascribed themselves a much higher ability compared to nonstandard speakers, even though objectively the nonstandard speakers were very much able to adopt correctly the standard language (for attitudes toward language variations in France, see Paltridge & Giles, 1984).

A more provocative approach was taken in an attempt to confront slight regional differences of standard Dutch (Grondelaers, van Hout, & Steegs, 2010). Rather than assuming the existence of only one unique form in the whole country, it is argued that there is region dependent variability of the standard accent. Instead of being treated as regional accents, these slight accent variations start to be regarded as more or less accepted regional variations of standard Dutch. In that study, only authentic accent speakers were recorded and evaluated. Language attitudes were revealed by accent-type itself and by inter-individual speaker differences, as indeed participants were able to indicate speakers from the same regional variation. Demographics seem to play only a modest role regarding language attitudes and participants did not display own-group bias, probably due to the overall growing acceptance of regional differences.

Regional language variations are also very useful for studying social relations and stereotypes between different regions, because they can be varied without compromising ecological variety (e.g., as with the use of stereotypical visual features related to a given region). A recent empirical study in Germany shows how differentiated the evaluation of different regional accent speakers can be based on the dimensions that are asked (Rakić, Steffens, & Mummendey, 2011b). Specifically, all regional accent speakers were devalued on competence and hireability compared to standard German; however, with regard to the dimension "socio-intellectual status," Bavarian was rated as high as standard German. Typically, status evaluation follows closely that of competence (e.g., Fuertes et al., 2012); however, the stereotype linked to the Bavarian accent proved more important, the Bavarian dialect (and accent) is spoken proudly throughout different ranks of society. In other words, the high-perceived vitality of Bavarian appears to secure its high status even among out-group listeners.

In Italy, many dialects and regional forms seem to go through a sort of renaissance as they become more popular and used across different layers of society. Also in Italy, solidarity or identity is strongly linked to language use (i.e., pronunciation). In order to be fully accepted in any region as a community member it is important to sound local (Cavanaugh, 2005). Regional variations are especially relevant regarding the North-South division (e.g., Palomba & Maass, 1995). Some Italian studies have concentrated on the effects of code-switching and preferences between a certain Italian dialect and the standard variety (e.g., Sobrero, 1992), indicating context-dependent complex dynamics. Taken together, these findings demonstrate that language-based identity, linguistic vitality, and norms jointly determine how different accents are evaluated in different contexts.

Status Differences between Minority Languages

The division between dialects and minority languages is an artificial one. Some minority languages are similar to dialects in that they are related to a lower social status that negatively influences the evaluation of its speakers (for a Dutch example of the dialect-low SES relationship, see Kraaykamp, 2005). Often, the choice to speak this variety decreases with increased social status, for example, Frisian in Friesland, Netherlands (Ytsma, 2011; for evaluations of subjective ethnolinguistic vitality, see Ytsma, Viladot, & Giles, 1994). In addition, social attractiveness and less formality appear to be related to speaking the nonstandard language variety (Levin, Giles, & Garrett, 1994).

For languages that are an essential part of people's identities (e.g., for Welsh identity, see Bourhis, Giles, & Tajfel, 1973), it has been observed that, instead of an accommodation to another's speech, speakers diverge even more when their identity is threatened (Giles & Johnson, 1986; Bourhis, Giles, Leyens, & Tajfel, 1979). This phenomenon is observed with Dutch-speaking Belgians who occupy an interesting position in that they constitute the majority of the population in the country, but in Brussels, they are clearly in the minority (Deprez & Persoons, 1984). Their uncertain identity position was reflected in their clear-cut rejection of everything not corresponding to Flemish (or Dutch-speaking).

In Spain, the years of oppression before 1977 changed the linguistic map significantly, at least with regard to the vitality of different language communities (Ros, Cano, & Huici, 1987). Castilian has the highest status and vitality, followed by Catalan and Basque, with both Valencian and Galician being relatively low on both dimensions. This stratification is in part due to the type of population that speaks the different languages: Whereas Catalan is used by people in all strata of society, Galician or Valencian are rather constrained to rural areas and to lower status speakers. Different studies have investigated language attitudes towards different varieties; for example, concerning the Valencian language situation using student evaluators with different backgrounds (Ros, 1984). Both standard varieties (Valencian and Castilian) were regarded as superior compared to the respective nonstandard varieties on the dimensions of personal competence and social success. However, only the standard Castilian language was associated with high professional status (as compared to nonstandard speakers). Similar findings by Ferrer (2010) indicate that over time Valencian has maintained its official status though it has lost identity relevance, which has resulted in a diminishing number of speakers (possibly also due to the fading of conflict between Castilian, Catalan, and Valencian). In contrast, Catalan is still highly relevant for the social identification of its speakers. There is a large community of Catalan speakers including numerous publications, often written—ironically—in Castilian (e.g., Strubell i Trueta, 1984;

Viladot, Esteban, Nadal, & Giles, 2007). Moreover, Catalan speakers take much pride in their language and perceive high institutional support and status, generally conforming more objective vitality indicators (Ytsma et al., 1994).

Whereas the multilingual situation of Spain poses a challenge for the local population, it does so even more for immigrants (or visitors) faced with multiple new languages to deal with (e.g., Masgoret, 2006) that are important for integration, both on a social and professional level. Still different is the Basque country—a small language community at the border of Spain and France (Lasagabaster, 2011). Although an increasing number of the population, especially the young, is bilingual (Basque-Castilian), the Basque language it is not much used in everyday situations, where Castilian might be preferred. Nevertheless, Basque remains a strong factor for ingroup identification. In sum, these findings indicate that minority languages can have different status that may change with social movements and political contexts.

ATTITUDES TOWARDS ENGLISH AS AN INTERNATIONAL LANGUAGE. In the international context, attitudes toward English as a second language are mixed (Ferguson, 2009). In some cases (e.g., Italy) historically difficult relations have left a trace, making attitudes toward the learning of English ambivalent (Pulcini, 1997). Members of other language communities have also been reported to be reluctant to learn English, as even with a high mastery of the language accents still remain present, resulting in a negative evaluation of speakers. This, however, is also due in part to the amount of time spent using English as a second language (Flege, Frieda, & Nozawa, 1997) or general exposure via television or radio (Derwing & Rossiter, 2002).

In Malta, even though English as an official language is ascribed higher professional status (because it is essential for professionals); it is often evaluated negatively and as snobbish when used in informal contexts (Caruna, 2011). On the contrary, both Maltese and Italian are evaluated higher on social attractiveness (e.g., Sciriha, 2001).

Comparisons of Same-Language Speakers across Countries

As language plays such an important role in social identity, the comparison with same language countries can provide interesting insights into asymmetrical attitudes. The evaluation of French varieties as spoken in France, Belgium, and Switzerland has been compared. The French perceived their language competence as much higher than that of French-speaking Belgians and Swiss. Interestingly, this view was shared by those groups (Yzerbyt, Provost, & Corneille, 2005). Simultaneously, a compensation mechanism revealed higher warmth ratings for Belgians and Swiss as compared to French. Other studies have found such a compensation mechanism under identity threat; that is, when one's social identity distinctiveness is compromised. In one such study (Master et al., 2010), French-speaking and German-speaking Swiss showed opposite patterns in the evaluation of dominance and arrogance of French and Germans. Both indicated higher dominance for the respective same language country, but not higher arrogance for the respective minority-speaking group. Probably due to the relative within-country size and status difference, French-speaking Swiss perceived German-speaking Swiss to be more dominant than vice versa. A similar, but stronger pattern was found regarding the arrogance evaluation. French-speaking Swiss perceived themselves similar to the French both generally and linguistically, though at the same time affectively they did not like such a resemblance (for similar findings also in the Swiss context see van Oudenhoven, Selenko, & Otten, 2010).

This ambivalent attitude of the French-speaking Swiss towards the French can be explained by identity threat that is caused by perceived similarity with the French that at the same time offers support for their lower status in Switzerland. Quite the reverse pattern was true for German-speaking Swiss. Whereas generally they did perceive positive similarity with the Germans, this was not the case once linguistic similarity was assessed, indicating the need to positively distance themselves from Germans. It is worth observing however that there are objectively big differences between Swiss German and the German spoken in Germany. Whereas this might account for part of the findings, it still leaves room for an influence of subjective evaluation that serves as an identity regulation tool. Historically the perceived relation of German-speaking Swiss and Germans is rather difficult (Hogg, Joyce, & Abrams, 1984). Generally, the Swiss have tried distancing themselves from Germans, which is visible in the use of Swiss German as well as a higher solidarity evaluation of Swiss German speakers over standard German speakers. In contrast, no such distinction was made regarding status, with both being equally high, especially if the evaluation occurred in a formal context.

Effects of Language Stereotypes on Performance and Recall

We present two studies demonstrating the pervasive role of language identities by showing effects on linguistic performance and recall. Identification plays an important role for German speaking Italians in South Tyrol, and as such, they are subject to negative effects of stereotype threat, the phenomenon of underperforming at a given task as a paradoxical result of worrying about confirming a negative stereotype linked to one's social identity. Italian native speakers underperformed in a German test (their second language) when reminded of the negative stereotype concerning the linguistic competences of their group (Paladino et al., 2009). Interestingly the same was true if they simply believed that their social group (i.e., the Italian-speaking community) occupies a lower status in the region.

The Irish identity is strongly embedded within language, especially in view of the history and British occupation (Ó Riagáin, 2007). This provides an interesting example of how different language varieties can make listeners' identity more salient and consequently change the recalling of certain information (Cairns & Duriez, 1976). During the time of disturbances in Northern Ireland among Catholic and Protestant schoolchildren, after ensuring the comprehension of different accent types (i.e., Belfast, Dublin, or R.P.), the children listened to a text recording made in one of three accents. Afterward they were asked to recall some information heard as well as answer some identity related questions ("Which country do you live in?"). After exposure to an R.P. accent Catholic children scored significantly lower on the recall test than Protestant children or other Catholic children being exposed to a Belfast accent. In contrast, Protestant children's performance dropped only after a Dublin accent exposure. Similarly, Catholic children were more prone to saying that they live in Ireland, and Protestants in Northern Ireland, after exposure to an R.P. speaker. Therefore, for Catholic children the R.P. was strongly linked to negative attitudes toward everything English, and thereby hindered their recall and increased identification with Ireland (and the Irish). Hence, even though attitudes were not explicitly measured, they were demonstrated through identification and attention.

Conclusion

The aim of this chapter was to give an overview of attitude-related research concerning the plurality of languages, dialects, and accents that simultaneously coexist in Europe, offering insights into the linguistic map of Western Europe. The whole of Eastern Europe is missing, not for lack of interest, but rather for lack of research. Maybe in the next edition these countries and linguistic communities will also be appropriately represented.

Generally, people hold rather negative attitudes toward nonstandard language varieties. Interestingly, this is usually a shared view among standard and nonstandard speakers. With some exceptions a standard accent gains on prestige (status) and competence whereas a nonstandard one gains on social attractiveness (solidarity)—though this (especially for the latter) depends on the evaluator's identification. However, the high status and competence of the standard variety can produce a backlash effect when they are perceived as too snobbish.

In view of the increasing population mobility, which is one of the leading principles of Europe, an ever growing number of immigrants is faced with having to learn a new language, often very different from their native one, and even at a high level of proficiency an accent is hard (if not impossible) to lose. The result is that those nonstandard speakers will probably never be acknowledged as ingroup members, with all the negative consequences related to this (Gluszek & Dovidio, 2010). Issues of language discrimination are central and sadly present (Ng, 2007).

One of the biggest challenges of Europe to this day is the multilingualism of its constituent countries on one hand, and the relatively small proportion of multilanguage populations on the other. Additionally, there are a large number of issues concerning minority languages in many countries. Often, the struggle to keep them alive comes at the cost of actively engaging in finding a solution to achieve a truly multilingual community. Possible reasons are found in many examples covered in this chapter, often related to ethnolinguistic identity. Unfortunately, language has been used throughout history as a means of oppression. Though this should not be an issue anymore, historical fear prevails. It is not far-fetched to assume that if someone feels pressured to adopt another language, this is also seen as a social-identity threat—and it is well known that social identity is essential to humans. Hence rather than imposing languages, the plurality we have to express our thoughts, feelings, and culture should be celebrated. Learning a new language does not mean losing one's identity but rather expanding it to a new horizon (e.g., Rubenfeld et al., 2006).

As we have seen, paradoxically multilingual countries rarely have multilingual populations. An interesting fact we could not cover regards different national language policies regarding foreign language movies or programs. Many countries prefer dubbing, even though exposure promotes second language learning (Dewaele, 2002). Especially regions fighting for their own minority language rights are often internationally disadvantaged, as those resources are usually subtracted from learning foreign languages. An additional problem is subtle implicit division among languages—those worthy of being learned as a second language and those less prestigious.

What future directions should the research field pursue? One possible direction could be a shift toward a more dynamic model, taking into account different (linguistic and cultural) contexts and motivations in interpersonal communication; finding the balance between facilitation of between language communications without compromising the existing multitude of different languages. What possible intervention could be developed to promote language diversity as a positive societal attribute? These are some questions that may receive attention in the years to come, as the interest on language attitudes continues to grow and the fertile ground of (Western) Europe's many linguistic communities only waits for its moment to be taken into consideration.

Notes

Writing of this chapter was supported by grants of German Research Foundation to the first author (DFG; RA 2203/1-1) and the second author (DFG; Ste 938/10-1). The authors would like to thank Howie Giles and Bernadette Watson for valuable comments on an earlier draft of this chapter.

References

Abrams, D., & Hogg, M. A. (1987). Language attitudes, frames of reference, and social identity: A Scottish dimension. *Journal of Language and Social Psychology, 6,* 201–213.

Ammon, U. (1995). *Die deutsche Sprache in Deutschland, Osterreich und der Schweiz: Das Problem der natinalen Varietäten* [The German language in Germany, Austria and Switzerland: The problem of national varieties]. Berlin: de Gruyter.

Borčić, N., & Wollinger, S. (2008). Deutschland, Österreich, Luxemburg und die Schweiz: Identität und Sprachpolitik [Germany, Austria, Luxemburg and Switzerland: The identity and language politics]. *Informatologia, 41,* 156–160.

Bourhis, R. Y., Giles, H., Leyens, J. P., & Tajfel, H. (1979). Psycholinguistic distinctiveness: Language divergence in Belgium. In H. Giles & R. N. St. Clair (Eds.), *Language and social psychology* (pp. 1–20). Oxford: Blackwell.

Bourhis, R. Y., Giles, H., & Rosenthal, D. (1981). Notes on the construction of a 'subjective vitality questionnaire' for ethnolinguistic groups. *Journal of Multilingual and Multicultural Development, 2,* 145–155.

Cairns, E., & Duriez, B. (1976). The influence of speaker's accent on recall by Catholic and Protestant school children in Northern Ireland. *British Journal of Social and Clinical Psychology, 15,* 441–442.

Caruna, S. (2011). Language use and language attitudes in Malta. In D. Lasagabaster & Á. Huguet (Eds.), *Multilingualism in European bilingual contexts: Language use and attitudes* (pp. 184–207). Clevedon, UK: Multilingualism Matters.

Cavanaugh, J. R. (2005). Accent matters: Material consequences of sounding local in northern Italy. *Language and Communication, 25,* 127–148.

Cugno, F. (2008). Dialetti e lingue minoritarie nell'Italia contemporanea [Dialects and minority languages in contemporary Italy]. *Rapid Research Letters, LIII,* 157–186.

Davies, W. V. (2000). Linguistic norms at school: A survey of secondary-school teachers in a central German dialect area. *Zeitschrift für Dialektologie und Linguistik, 67,* 129–147.

Deprez, K., & Persoons, Y. (1984). On the ethnolinguistic identity of Flemish high school students in Brussels. *Journal of Language and Social Psychology, 3,* 273–296.

Derwing, T. M., & Rossiter, M. J. (2002). ESL learners' perceptions of their pronunciation needs and strategies. *System, 30,* 155–166.

Dewaele, J.-M. (2002). Psychological and sociodemographic correlates of communicative anxiety in L2 and L3 production. *International Journal of Bilingualism, 6,* 22–38.

Edwards, J. R. (1977). Students' reactions to Irish regional accents. *Language and Speech, 20,* 280–286.

Eichinger, L. M., Gärting, A. K., Plewnia, A., Roessel, J., Rothe, A., Rudert, S., Schoel, C., Stahlberg, D., & Stickel, G. (2009). *Aktuelle Spracheinstellungen in Deutschland* [Contemporary language attitudes in Germany]. Mannheim, Germany: Institut für Deutsche Sprache.

Ender, A., & Straßl, K. (2009). The acquisition and use of German in a dialect-speaking environment: Facets of inclusion and exclusion of immigrant children in Switzerland. *International Journal of Applied Linguistics, 19*, 173–187.

Extra, G., & Yagmur, K. (2010). Language proficiency and socio-cultural orientation of Turkish and Moroccan youngsters in the Netherlands. *Language and Education, 24*, 117–132.

Ferguson, G. (2009). Issues in researching English as a lingua franca: A conceptual enquiry. *International Journal of Applied Linguistics, 19*, 117–135.

Ferrer, R. C. (2010). Changing linguistic attitudes in Valencia: The effects of language planning measures. *Journal of Sociolinguistics, 14*, 477–500.

Flege, J. E., Frieda, E. M., & Nozawa, T. (1997). Amount of native-language (L1) use affects the pronunciation of an L2. *Journal of Phonetics, 25*, 169–186.

Fuertes, J. N., Gottdiener, W., Martin, H., Gilbert, T. C., & Giles, H. (2012). A meta-analysis of speakers' accents on interpersonal evaluations. *European Journal of Social Psychology, 42*, 120–133.

Gardner-Chloros, P., McEntee-Atalianis, L., & Finnis, K. (2005). Language attitudes and use in a transplanted setting: Greek Cypriots in London. *International Journal of Multilingualism, 2*, 52–80.

Garrett, P. (2010). *Attitudes to language*. Cambridge, UK: Cambridge University Press.

Giles, H. (1970). Evaluative reactions to accents. *Educational Review, 22*, 211–227.

Giles, H. (1973). Accent mobility: A model and some data. *Anthropological Linguistics, 15*, 87–105.

Giles, H., Bourhis, R. Y., & Taylor, D. M. (1977). Towards a theory of language in ethnic group relations. In H. Giles (Ed.), *Language, ethnicity and intergroup relations* (pp. 307–348). London: Academic Press.

Giles, H., Harrison, C., Creber, C., Smith, P. M., & Freeman, N. H. (1983). Developmental and contextual aspects of children's language attitudes. *Language and Communication, 3*, 141–146.

Giles, H., & Johnson, P. (1981). The role of language in ethnic group relations. In J. C. Turner & H. Giles (Eds.), *Intergroup behavior* (pp. 199–243). Oxford: Blackwell.

Giles, H., & Johnson, P. (1986). Perceived threat, ethnic commitment, and interethnic language behavior. In Y. Y. Kim (Ed.), *Interethnic communication: Current research* (pp. 91–116). Thousand Oaks, CA: Sage Publications.

Giles, H., & Johnson, P. (1987). Ethnolinguistic identity theory: A social psychological approach to language maintenance. *International Journal of the Sociology of Language, 68*, 69–99.

Giles, H., & Marlow, M. L. (2011). Theorizing language attitudes: Past frameworks, an integrative model, and new directions. In C. Salmon (Ed.), *Communication yearbook* (Vol. 35, pp. 161–197). Thousand Oaks, CA: Sage.

Giles, H., & Niedzielski, N. (1998). German sounds awful, but Italian is beautiful. In L. Bauer & P. Trudgill (Eds.), *Language myths* (pp. 85–93). Harmondsworth, UK: Penguin.

Girard, F., Floccia, C., & Goslin, J. (2008). Perception and awareness of accents in young children. *British Journal of Developmental Psychology, 26*, 409–433.

Gluszek, A., & Dovidio, J. F. (2010). The way they speak: A social psychological perspective on the stigma of nonnative accents in communication. *Personality and Social Psychology Review, 14*, 214–237.

Grondelaers, S., van Hout, R., & Steegs, M. (2010). Evaluating regional accent variation in standard Dutch. *Journal of Language and Social Psychology, 29,* 101–116.

Hogg, M. A., Joyce, N., & Abrams, D. (1984). Diglossia in Switzerland? A social identity analysis of speaker evaluations. *Journal of Language and Social Psychology, 3,* 185–196.

Klink, A., & Wagner, U. (1999). Discrimination against ethnic minorities in Germany: Going back to the field. *Journal of Applied Social Psychology, 29,* 402–423.

Koven, M. (2004). Transnational perspectives on sociolinguistic capital among Luso-Descendants in France and Portugal. *American Ethnologist, 31,* 270–290.

Kraaykamp, G. (2005). Dialect en sociale ongelijkheid: Een empirische studie naar de sociaaleconomische gevolgen van het spreken van dialect in de jeugd. *Pedagogische Studiën, 82,* 390–403.

Kuiper, L. (2005). Perception is reality: Parisian and Provençal perceptions of regional varieties of French. *Journal of Sociolinguistics, 9,* 28–52.

Lasagabaster, D. (2011). Language use and language attitudes in the Basque country. In D. Lasagabaster & Á. Huguet (Eds.), *Multilingualism in European bilingual contexts: Language use and attitudes* (pp. 164–183). Clevedon, UK: Multilingualism Matters.

Lasagabaster, D., & Huguet, Á. (2011). *Multilingualism in European bilingual contexts: Language use and attitudes.* Clevedon, UK: Multilingual Matters.

Laugharne, J. (2011). Language use and language attitudes in Wales. In D. Lasagabaster & Á. Huguet (Eds.), *Multilingualism in European bilingual contexts: Language use and attitudes* (pp. 164–183). Clevedon, UK: Multilingual Matters.

Levin, H., Giles, H., & Garrett, P. (1994). The effects of lexical formality and accent on trait attributions. *Language and Communication, 14,* 265–274.

Masgoret, A. M. (2006). Examining the role of language attitudes and motivation on the sociocultural adjustment and the job performance of sojourners in Spain. *International Journal of Intercultural Relations, 30,* 311–331.

Masterson, J., Mullins, E., & Mulvihill, A. (1983). Components of evaluative reactions to varieties of Irish accents. *Language and Speech, 26,* 215–231.

Matser, C., van Oudenhoven, J. P., Askevis-Leherpeux, F. O., Florack, A., Hannover, B., & Rossier, J. M. (2010). Impact of relative size and language on the attitudes between nations and linguistic groups: The case of Switzerland. *Applied Psychology: An International Review, 59,* 143–158.

Mettewie, L., & Janssens, R. (2011). Language use and language attitudes in Brussels. In D. Lasagabaster & Á. Huguet (Eds.), *Multilingualism in European bilingual contexts: Language use and attitudes* (pp. 164–183). Clevedon, UK: Multilingualism Matters.

Ng, S. H. (2007). Language-based discrimination: Blatant and subtle forms. *Journal of Language and Social Psychology, 26,* 106–122.

Nortier, J., & Dorleijn, M. (2008). A Moroccan accent in Dutch: A sociocultural style restricted to the Moroccan community? *International Journal of Bilingualism, 12,* 125–142.

Ó Laorie, M. (2011). Language use and language attitudes in Ireland. In D. Lasagabaster & Á. Huguet (Eds.), *Multilingualism in European bilingual contexts: Language use and attitudes* (pp. 164–183). Clevedon, UK: Multilingualism Matters.

Ó Riagáin, P. (2007). Relationships between attitudes to Irish, social class, religion and national identity in the Republic of Ireland and Northern Ireland. *International Journal of Bilingual Education and Bilingualism, 10,* 369–393.

Paladino, M.-P., Poddesu, L., Rauzi, M., Vaes, J., Cadinu, M., & Forer, D. (2009). Second language competence in the Italian-speaking population of Alto Adige/Südtirol: Evidence for linguistic stereotype threat. *Journal of Language and Social Psychology, 28,* 222–243.

Palomba, E., & Maass, A. (1995). *Spontaneous categorization along invisible cues: The effects of accent and attitude position on memory.* Unpublished Manuscript. University of Padova, Padova, Italy.

Paltridge, J., & Giles, H. (1984). Attitudes towards speakers of regional accents of French: Effects of regionality, age and sex of listeners. *Linguistische Berichte, 90,* 71–85.

Price, S., Fluck, M., & Giles, H. (1983). The effects of language of testing on bilingual pre-adolescents' attitudes towards welsh and varieties of English. *Journal of Multilingual and Multicultural Development, 4,* 149–161.

Pulcini, V. (1997). Attitudes toward the spread of English in Italy. *World Englishes, 16.1,* 77–85.

Rakić, T., Steffens, M. C., & Mummendey, A. (2011a). Blinded by the accent! The minor role of looks in ethnic categorization. *Journal of Personality and Social Psychology, 100,* 16–29.

Rakić, T., Steffens, M. C., & Mummendey, A. (2011b). When it matters how you pronounce it: The influence of regional accents on job interview outcome. *British Journal of Psychology, 102,* 868–883.

Robinson, W. P., & Giles, H. (Eds.). (2001). *The new handbook of language and social psychology.* Chichester, UK: John Wiley & Sons.

Ros, M. (1984). Speech attitudes to speakers of language varieties in a bilingual situation. *International Journal of the Sociology of Language, 47,* 73–90.

Ros, M., Cano, J. I., & Huici, C. (1987). Language and intergroup perception in Spain. *Journal of Language and Social Psychology, 6,* 243–259.

Rubenfeld, S., Clément, R., Lussier, D., Lebrun, M., & Auger, R. (2006). Second language learning and cultural representations: Beyond competence and identity. *Language Learning, 56,* 609–631.

Sachdev, I., & Bourhis, R. Y. (1993). Ethnolinguistic vitality: Some motivational and cognitive considerations. In M. A. Hogg & D. Abrams (Eds.), *Group motivation: Social psychological perspectives.* (pp. 33–51). Hemel Hempstead, UK: Harvester Wheatsheaf.

Sciriha, L. (2001). Trilingualism in Malta. *International Journal of Bilingual Education and Bilingualism, 4,* 23–37.

Shepard, C. A., Giles, H., & Le Poire, B. A. (2001). Communication accomodation theory. In W. P. Robinson & H. Giles (Eds.), *The new handbook of language and social psychology* (pp. 33–56). Chichester, UK: John Wiley.

Sobrero, A. A. (1992). Alternanza di codici, fra italiano e dialetto: Dalla parte del parlante. In A. A. Sobrero (Ed.), *Il dialetto nella conservazione: Ricerche di dialettologia pragmatica* (Vol. 7, pp. 11–30). Lecce, Italy: Dipartimento di Filologia Linguistica e Letteratura dell'Università di Lecce.

Sophocleous, A., & Wilks, C. (2010). Standard modern Greek and Greek-Cypriot dialect in kindergarten classroom interaction: Teachers' and learners' language attitudes and language use. *Language, Culture, and Curriculum, 23,* 51–69.

Strubell i Trueta, M. (1984). Language and identity in Catalonia. *International Journal of the Sociology of Language, 47,* 91–104.

Tajfel, H., & Turner, J. C. (1979). An integrative theory of intergroup conflict. In W. G. Austin & S. Worchel (Eds.), *The social psychology of intergroup relations* (pp. 33–47). Monterey, CA: Brooks-Cole.

van Bezooijen, R. (1994). Aesthetic evaluation of Dutch language varieties. *Language and Communication, 14*, 253–263.
van Oudenhoven, J. P., Selenko, E., & Otten, S. (2010). Effects of country size and language similarity on international attitudes: A six-nation study. *International Journal of Psychology, 45*, 48–55.
Viladot, M. A., Esteban, M., Nadal, J. M., & Giles, H. (2007). Identidad, percepción de vitalidad etnolingüística y comunicación intergrupal en Cataluña. *Revista de psicología social aplicada, 17*, 223–247.
Ytsma, J. (2011). Language use and language attitudes in Friesland. In D. Lasagabaster & Á. Huguet (Eds.), *Multilingualism in European bilingual contexts: Language use and attitudes* (pp. 144–163). Clevedon, UK: Multilingualism Matters.
Ytsma, J., Viladot, M. A., & Giles, H. (1994). Ethnolinguistic vitality and ethnic identity: Some Catalan and Frisian data. *International Journal of the Sociology of Language, 1994*, 63–78.
Yzerbyt, V., Leyens, J.-P., & Bellour, F. (1995). The ingroup overexclusion effect: Identity concerns in decisions about group membership. *European Journal of Social Psychology, 25*, 1–16.
Yzerbyt, V., Provost, V., & Corneille, O. (2005). Not competent but warm...really? Compensatory stereotypes in the French-speaking world. *Group Processes and Intergroup Relations, 8*, 291–308.

CHAPTER FOUR

Language Attitudes in the Nordic Countries

TORE KRISTIANSEN

The term *Nordic countries*, as used in this chapter, refers to the five sovereign states of Denmark, Norway, Sweden, Iceland, and Finland—including the Åland islands in the Baltic Sea with an autonomous status within the Finnish state—as well as Greenland and the Faroe Islands in the North Atlantic Ocean with an autonomous status within the Danish state. In English, *Scandinavia* may be a more commonly used name for this part of the world (perhaps with only vague ideas of what territories are included?). As used within the area itself, and in this chapter, Scandinavia is taken to encompass only Norway, Sweden, and Denmark without the North Atlantic territories; the wider area, to be covered in this chapter, is known as the Nordic countries, or rather just *The North (Norden)*.[1]

Three different language families are represented among the traditional populations in the Nordic countries. Greenlandic is an Eskimo-Aleutic language, while Finnish and Sámi belong to the Finno-Ugric branch of the Uralic language family, without being mutually intelligible. Icelandic, Faroese, Norwegian, Swedish, and Danish are all varieties of the North Germanic branch of the Indo-European language family. The North Atlantic varieties—Icelandic and Faroese—have undergone relatively little change since the time of the common Old Norse language (i.e., the Viking Age), and are to some degree mutually intelligible, although more in writing than speech. In contrast, the Scandinavian varieties—Norwegian, Swedish, and Danish—have changed away from the common origin to such a degree that mutual intelligibility with the North Atlantic varieties came to an end hundreds of years ago. However, as they changed in the same direction, there is still a high degree of mutual intelligibility between the Scandinavian varieties.

These languages cover a vast gamut in terms of numbers of users. Approximate numbers are: Swedish 9.5 million, Danish 5.5 million, Finnish 5.5 million, Norwegian 5 million, Icelandic 300,000, Faroese 60,000, Greenlandic 55,000, and Sámi 25,000. Other languages with many users and a long tradition in the Nordic countries include varieties of Romani and sign language. From the 1960s onwards, increased immigration from all over the world has brought the number of languages spoken in the Nordic area into the hundreds.

In order to understand the very different language-ideological 'climates' that are found in the Nordic countries, it is crucial to realize that only Denmark and Sweden have always been politically independent states—and that they have ruled over the other countries for centuries. Norway, including its North Atlantic territories, came under Danish rule from the end of the 14th century. As a consequence of defeat and victory in the Napoleonic wars, Norway (but not the North Atlantic territories) came under Swedish rule in 1814, and obtained full independence only in 1905. Iceland voted for full independence from Denmark in 1944 (Denmark was occupied by Germany under WWII, Iceland by first British and then U.S. troops), while the Faroe and Greenlandic populations have had home rule systems since 1948 and 1979, respectively (and permanent debates about whether to go for full independence or not).

The Swedish king ruled over Finland from the 12th century until 1809, when Sweden had to cede Finland and Åland to the Russian tsar as another offshoot of the Napoleonic wars. After more than one century as an autonomous Grand Duchy of Russia, Finland declared its full independence in the wake of the October 1917 revolution in Russia, while Åland, with its Swedish-language population in the Gulf of Bothnia between Sweden and Finland, was granted home rule status within the new Finnish republic in 1921.

From the beginning of times, the indigenous people of the area, the Sámi people, was the heavily losing part in the conflict with the continually northwards-expanding newcomers. No official geographic delimitation of their country Sápmi exists, and the area they inhabit includes parts of Norway, Sweden, Finland, and the Russian Kola peninsula. Only in recent decades have the states which house Sámi populations began recognizing them and granting them political rights as a people or nation, including the creation of Sámi parliaments in Finland (1973), Norway (1987), and Sweden (1993).

The fundamental language-ideological issue raised in all of the socio-historical contexts outlined above is: *which language is the best?* People and communities face language issues in terms of *good or bad*, and find solutions, which can be described and compared as ideological stances on what I shall call the dimension of *purism*.

Forms and degrees of purism underlie and unite the three ideologies to be addressed in the chapter: *standard language ideology, nationalist ideology*, and *nativist ideology* (see Dragojevic, Giles, & Watson, this volume).

Standard Language Ideology (SLI) in the Nordic Countries

Adhering to a well-known tripartite methodological approach to the study of language attitudes, I first characterize 'purism' in the Nordic communities as expressed or revealed in 'societal treatments' of language (in official politics, education, and media), and then extend the emerging picture by adding knowledge drawn partly from responses to *direct* questioning about language (in interviews or questionnaires), partly from reactions to language in *indirect* questioning (of the kind which can be obtained in speaker evaluation experiments: SEEs).

Societal Treatments of the 'Linguistic Norm and Variation' Issue[2]

The Nordic communities' very different histories in terms of domination and subordination have resulted in very different ideological profiles with regard to how the issue of 'linguistic norm and variation' is treated in official language politics and important institutions of societal life. In the wake of the Renaissance/Reformation, when new understandings and beliefs, and new technology (book printing), led to new views in the domain of language, the choice of an endoglossic (national) variety to replace exoglossic (foreign) standards as the best language was on the agenda only in the politically independent states of Denmark and Sweden. In the countries under foreign rule, the construction of an endoglossic standard became an issue in connection with later aspirations for political independence, beginning with the nationalist upheavals in the 19th century.

In 17th century's Denmark and Sweden, it was a matter of course that the best language was spoken in the capital cities by educated people at the court and in academia. The ideological force at work in this first step of standardization, in which one particular variety is selected and all others excluded, is internal *functional* purism: only one variety is seen as appropriate for use in public functions. Or put the other way round: the community needs one and only one variety for use in public functions. This way of thinking is still seen as natural and beyond discussion in Denmark and Sweden (as perhaps in most comparable communities). The same holds true of efforts that belong under internal *formal* purism, that is, efforts to codify and cultivate the standard without including features from other endoglossic varieties. Likewise, the standard language has had a self-evident monopoly position in schools and media. Thus, centuries of undisputed SLI have led to the establishment of strong standard languages in Denmark and Sweden—strong both in the sense of allowing for little variation in terms of linguistic features, and in the sense of having acquired a hegemonic position in public use, and a general acceptance in the population as the 'best language'. This situation was largely reached for written standards at the end of the 18th century—at which time the contours of spoken standards also developed, while the general spread of standard speech in the population is a much later, post-WWII, phenomenon.

When 'the language issue' came on the national liberation agenda in the middle of the 19th century, two different roads to a Norwegian written standard were followed. The 'revolutionary' road was to discard the Danish-influenced variety spoken by the capital city upper class, and instead construct the written norm based on features that were shared by 'genuine' Norwegian dialects spoken by common people in the countryside. The 'reformist' road was to select the capital city upper-class variety as basis, not for creating a new written norm but for making changes in the Danish written norm, which continued to be used in Norway even if the country had come under Swedish rule (as above). Thus, Norway at the beginning of the 20th century entered its new era as an independent nation with two closely related written languages, which had been accorded equal status in an 1885 Parliamentary Act.

Throughout most of the 20th century, the state pursued a policy of creating one written norm by allowing for many variants in both existing norms, which made them 'overlap'. The idea was that subsequent elision of non-overlapping forms would eventually result in only one written norm, of the rigid and stable kind that everyone else has. An increasingly strong opposition to this 'merging' road towards one Norwegian standard, especially from the 'reformist' camp in the 1950s, prompted the state to retreat, and eventually to a formal abandonment of the 'merger' politics at the beginning of the 21st century. A whole century of 'language battle', in which all camps had the same aim of creating a 'normal' European state with a 'normal' standard language, culminated in the unique situation that there was still no single Norwegian standard. These two closely related official written norms, Nynorsk (the 'revolutionary' solution) and Bokmål (the 'reformist' solution) both include extensive systems of variants, which reflect differences in spoken varieties. Arguably, this situation is a main reason why today's Norway is characterized by a strong dialect ideology rather than a strong SLI. Dialectal diversity is present and accepted as the normal state of affairs in all public domains: in schools, in media, in Parliament.

As with Norway, efforts to create a Faroese standard written norm were a mid-19th century 'national liberation' project. However, unlike Norway, there was no endoglossic upper-class (Danish-influenced) spoken variety to take into consideration as basis for the norm. However, the Faroes were (and are) characterized by dialectal diversity, so the selection of one dialect over the others was an option. The alternative, which was the chosen solution, was to construct the orthography as an 'impartial super-structure' on the dialectal diversity. This approach yielded a strongly etymologizing orthography, which in writing removed some of the distance that had developed to Icelandic in speech. Subsequently, formal purism has been adopted; few changes have been made to the original orthography. Hence, a considerable gap between the spoken and written forms of words persists in Faroese. This has been seen as a reason why there is much tolerance of dialectal variation and few signs of an emerging spoken standard. The relatively recently established broadcast media (radio 1957, TV 1984) use dialects and have abandoned initial attempts at developing a standard reading pronunciation (Hansen, Jacobsen, & Weyhe, 2003).

As is well known, a remarkably strong oral and written literary tradition developed early in Iceland. An already existing spoken standard, developed as part of a common Norwegian-Icelandic oral tradition, seems to have been the basis for the 12th century codification of the written norm, which has remained largely stable since then. The same seems to be true of the spoken language. Thus, it is a true peculiarity of Icelandic that the language (or rather the Icelandic population) has not developed any dialects to talk about during its 1100 years on the North Atlantic island. The sociolinguistic reasons for this are debated and shall not preoccupy us here. There is no doubt, however, that a very strong SLI has developed in Iceland since the 19th century, in which reference to the literary heritage plays an important role, but the foundational element of this ideology is external purism (which we get back to below). Nevertheless, it is possible to give an example of internal phonetic variation and possible change in Icelandic, which was actually eliminated by purist intervention. A tendency to merge mid-high and mid-low front vowels started in the 19th century and was widespread in Iceland in the first half of the 20th century. It may have been a characteristic of casual speech rather than of geographical or social varieties, and was fought in public discourse and in schools as *flámæli* ('slack-jawed speech'). Sociolinguistic research in the 1980s showed that it was virtually extinct (Árnason, 2011).

Finnish dialects fall into two categories: western and eastern. When the Reformation gave birth to the first texts written in Finnish, the 'naturally' selected basis was the southwestern dialects, as the capital city and religious centre was the southwestern town of Åbo (Turku in Finnish). Little beyond religious texts was written in Finnish until the national awakening in the 19th century, at which time the western dialects were judged to be 'corrupted' (by Swedish influence), and many features of the 'purer' eastern dialects were included in the norm as the written language was elaborated to suit all societal domains. Finnish is often mentioned as an example of a language with a phonetic orthography. Even if dialectal variation is taken into account, it seems that phoneme-grapheme correspondences are simpler in Finnish than in most languages, and a 'speech-should-copy-writing' ideology has been strong in Finnish public life (Nuolijärvi & Vaattovaara, 2011). The same kind of ideology applies also to the spoken standard of Finland Swedish. "[T]he general rule is that if you are educated, you should speak as you read" (Östman & Mattfolk, 2011, p. 78), or perhaps rather speak-as-you-spell. In terms of phonology, this ideology gives a spoken standard, which is easily discernible from Sweden Swedish (and often lauded by other Scandinavians, in particular Danes, as easily understandable, exactly because 'words are pronounced as they are spelled'). However, the leading principle of Finland-Swedish language politics is to insist on Sweden Swedish as the norm for Swedish spoken in Finland. Underlying this insistence is a fear that the Finland-Swedish language, which is said to host over 80 countryside dialects (*ibid.*), will have no future if the spoken standard is allowed to diverge too much from the language used in Sweden.

Greenlandic is divided into three main dialects: eastern, western, and northern. Writing came with the missionaries in the 18th century. The first systematic orthography, created in the middle of the 19th century, was instrumental in the development of a relatively rich production of texts in Greenlandic language. This writing was based on the western dialects around the capital city of Nuuk, but because the orthography was built on the morphemic principle, it was largely a 'superstructure' above phonetic variation. However, as the orthography's distance from spoken language made it difficult to learn to use correctly in writing, a new orthography, based on the phonemic principle, was introduced in 1973. The notion of a spoken standard is associated with Nuuk speech.

The Sámi language is also divided into three main dialects: eastern, central, and southern, each of them with many subdivisions. Six different orthographies exist. However, the great majority of Sámi-speaking people speak a central variety known as North Sámi, for which a common orthography (developed by the Sámi Language Council in the 1970s and accepted by the Nordic Sámi Conference) has been used in Norway, Sweden, and Finland since 1979. This has allowed for the development of a written language, which is an essential precondition for the legislative and institutional support that has developed for North Sámi in particular in recent decades, including considerable progress in the essential domains of education and media.

Social Purism in Responses to *Direct* Questioning

A question about preferences regarding language in radio and TV was included in a representative telephone survey conducted by professional opinion institutes in seven Nordic communities (as part of the MIN project, more below). People expressed their feelings about *use of common everyday language instead of standard lan-*

guage by radio and TV employees, choosing between five options from 'very positive' to 'very negative'. The results in terms of means on a five-point scale rank the communities as follows: NORWAY (1.79) > FINNISH-LANGUAGE FINLAND (2.14) > SWEDEN (2.34) / FAROES (2.42) > DENMARK (2.54) > SWEDISH-LANGUAGE FINLAND (2.82) > ICELAND (3.07); differences are statistically significant except for Sweden/Faroes.

As all of the communities except Iceland came out on the positive side of the scale's midpoint (3), the result indicates a general rejection of the idea that the broadcast media journalists should conform to a standard norm. In accordance with general expectations, the use of 'common everyday language' in radio and TV was more acceptable to younger people (the significant dividing line being the age of 60)—again with the exception of Iceland, where the younger generations were more negative than the 60+ generation and, thus, testified to the exceptional nature and strength of Icelandic SLI.

The same relative positivity with regard to (one's own) local speech also emerges in results from 'label ranking', a method for direct questioning which has been widely used by Danish and Norwegian sociolinguists with an interest in the role of attitudes in language variation and change. When young Danes rank—in terms of 'own liking'—a list of 'variety names' covering the whole country, the average result for any audience in any Danish site shows the same evaluative hierarchy: the local variety comes out in top position, followed by the variety of the local big city, and with the standard variety *rigsdansk* in third position. The traditional depreciation of Copenhagen working class speech is reproduced, as *københavnsk* appears further down in the rankings (with the modification that 'local patriotism' secures top position for *københavnsk* in Copenhagen itself, and second position on the island of Sealand where Copenhagen is the local big city). This pattern indicates that the youngsters have appropriated SLI, but also that it is overshadowed by 'local patriotism'. As *københavnsk* may be equated with 'modern' Copenhagen speech, *rigsdansk* with 'conservative', the evaluative hierarchy is (1) LOCAL > (2) CONSERVATIVE > (3) MODERN.

Furthermore, as the traditional Danish dialects are disappearing, because the younger generations replace all 'local' features (except for some prosodic 'coloring') with features from Copenhagen speech, and from its 'modern' variety more than from its 'conservative' variety—yielding the vitality hierarchy (1) MODERN > (2) CONSERVATIVE > (3) LOCAL—we note that the evaluative hierarchy turns the vitality hierarchy upside down, and that it seems to falsify any hypothesis one might have about a cause–effect relationship between language attitudes and ongoing language change, an issue returned to below.

A project on 'dialect change processes' (http://folk.uib.no/hnohs/DEP/) is in progress in the western part of Norway, the Nynorsk core area, where the position of the traditional dialects may be even stronger than elsewhere in the country. Recall that Norway in general, in contrast to Denmark, has very vital dialects and no undisputed spoken standard. The dialect labels to be ranked by the informants in this project covered the whole country and included, in all six research sites, labels for the three locally relevant categories which can be generalized as the NATIONAL CENTRE (Oslo), REGIONAL CENTRE, and RURAL DISTRICT varieties; 'centre' and 'district' changing with the change of research site. As with Denmark, the youngsters ranked their own variety (whether rural district or regional centre) in first position, while the national centre variety in most cases came out last. Comparing these evaluative patterns with descriptions of language change in the same communities, Sandøy (forthcoming) concludes that the performed 'local patriotism' does not seem to have any bearing on the youngsters' use of language.

Social Purism in Responses to *Indirect* Questioning

Evaluative patterns obtained in direct questioning represent 'overt' attitudes. People are aware of giving away attitudes towards linguistic varieties or variants as they respond; the attitudes are *consciously offered*. This will normally be the case also in SEEs, even in cases where the questioning is purely indirect in the sense that it addresses speaker qualities only, and no speech qualities. Regardless of whether the technique used is 'matched guise' or 'verbal guise' (see Dragojevic et al. and Davies and Bentahila, this volume, for an elaboration of these methods), it would indeed be strange if people did not become aware of the purpose of the experiment—that is, 'measurement' of language attitudes—as long as the stimulus speakers represent saliently different varieties (whether languages, dialects, or accents). It is our experience, however, that respondent 'innocence' (non-awareness) can be maintained if the variation represented by the stimulus speakers does not go beyond the variation which occurs in the everyday speech of the community under study, and if the 'measurement' instrument (i.e., the questions asked) does not direct attention to language. Thus, on the assumption that 'covert', *subconsciously offered* attitudes may be different from 'overt' attitudes and have another relation to language change, several Nordic projects on language change have included SEEs that have been carefully designed and administered so as to secure the non-salience of language, and thus avoid arousal of respondent 'suspicion'. (See Kristiansen, 2010, for a discussion of the use of SEEs in variationist sociolinguistics, and with respect to Labov's work in particular.)

Studies of this kind in Denmark since the late 1980s have found a radical and consistent effect of changing the 'response condition' from awareness (label ranking) to non-awareness (SEE). While assessment in the 'awareness' condition yields the ranking (1) LOCAL > (2) CONSERVATIVE > (3) MODERN, assessment in the 'non-awareness' condition yields the ranking (1) MODERN > (2) CONSERVATIVE > (3) LOCAL (with the specification that MODERN does particularly well on the evaluative dimension of 'dynamism', while CONSERVATIVE does as well or better along the evaluative dimension of 'superiority'). Most importantly, while the former hierarchy contradicts the general patterns of language change, the latter does not. This finding has led the ongoing Danish LANCHART project (Language Change in Real Time, http://www.lanchart.hum.ku.dk) to hypothesize that 'covert' attitudes are a main driving force in language change, decisively involved in language change processes in ways that 'overt' attitudes are not (for an overview of this research, see Kristiansen, 2009)

The LANCHART approach to conceptualization and operationalization of the conscious/subconscious distinction was adopted in the project on 'dialect change processes' in Western Norway (see above). SEE assessments in the six research sites resulted in all combinations of first, second, and third position for the speech varieties of NATIONAL CENTRE, REGIONAL CENTRE, and RURAL DISTRICT. Comparisons of the 'overt' and 'covert' evaluative patterns show Norway to be similar to Denmark in that 'awareness vs. non-awareness' yields very different results. In contrast to Denmark, there is no straightforward correspondence between 'covert' evaluative patterns and language change patterns. Sandøy (forthcoming) preliminarily concludes that there is no clear influence of 'covert' social values on language change in Norway.

Nationalist Ideology in the Nordic Countries

Some degree of external (national) purism is often involved in the construction of a standard language. Where the peril or bad influence is thought to come from varies with the socio-historical conditions. While very different, on the one hand, because of the historical relationships of domination and subordination dealt with above, these conditions may, on the other hand, be assumed to be similar in the present-time era of general globalization and anglification. The section on 'social treatments' is therefore divided here into treatments first of traditional external influence, and then English influence.

Treatments of Traditional External Influence

In the case of Denmark and Sweden, 'purifying' efforts were important elements in the historical process of language standardization from the 16th through to the 19th century, directed against Latin, French, and German. The history is particularly complicated in the case of the German influence in Denmark which—besides being very strong in its Hanseatic Low German shape in the Middle Ages (as in the Nordic area in general)—continued for centuries in its High German shape as important parts of the country's cultural and administrative elite, including some of the kings, did not speak Danish. Many of them had their roots in the German-speaking duchies of Schleswig and Holstein, which, at that time, formed part of the Danish kingdom. German influence in this sense was largely brought to an end in the decades around 1800. However, it is part of the picture that the only reform of Danish orthography in the 20th century was passed in 1948, three years after the end of WWII and German occupation. Doing away with capital first letters in nouns and introducing the letter å, the reform was clearly anti-German and pro-Scandinavian in nature.

As a consequence of the historical eastwards dominance by Sweden, mainland Finland has two official languages: Finnish and Swedish. While Swedish had been the administrative language until 1809, Finnish gradually obtained a stronger official position as the Russian tsar instigated a series of legislative efforts, which in 1863 put Finnish on an equal footing with Swedish "in all matters of immediate significance for the genuine Finnish population." From this time on, Finnish was rapidly developed as a language suitable for use in all domains of society, in competition both with attempts at Russification and with Swedish, which kept its dominant position at the higher levels of administration and education for some time into the 20th century.

While Finnish is the first language of the vast majority of the population, Swedish is the first language of a minority—steadily decreasing in terms of percentage (less in terms of numbers), from about 13 percent in 1900 to about 5 percent today (some 265,000 people)—and is an obligatory school subject for Finnish-language pupils. A number of Finnish municipalities in the coastal areas where Swedish is commonly spoken, including the capital Helsinki (Helsingfors in Swedish), either has Swedish as their administrative language or are bilingual. In Åland, which always was Swedish-speaking, Swedish is the only official language, and spoken today by 94 percent of the island's 28,000 inhabitants. As the norm for Swedish spoken in Sweden is also adopted as norm for Swedish spoken in Finland (see above), the rather strong external purism of Finland-Swedish language politics is directed against fennicisms (and is therefore not a 'national purism' in the usual sense).

The westwards dominance of Denmark resulted in strong influence from Danish in Norway, the Faroes, Iceland and Greenland. Even the spoken languages were heavily influenced in parts of the societies. In Greenland, the Danish colonization, beginning in the 18th century, represented an ever stronger-growing threat to the Greenlandic language until the ideological changes of the 1960–70s that led to the establishment of Home Rule in 1978. Greenlandic was now to become the main language, while Danish would remain an important language of learning and general use. In a 2009 Act that established Greenlandic self-government, Greenlandic is said to be the official language, while no mention is made of a role for Danish in Greenland. In practice, Danish continues to play an important role in administration and higher education. Some 5,000 people in Nuuk, a third of the town's population, are Danes who speak little or no Greenlandic.

In the Faroes, Iceland and Norway as well, the aim and consequences of the efforts to elaborate and implement endoglossic standard languages have been to gain domains of usage away from Danish. In the Faroes, Danish is still an official language beside Faroese, and Danish is learned by everyone in school, but recent decades have seen the status and strength of Faroese grow immensely in all domains of the society. The influence of Danish in Icelandic society had been decreasing and was reduced to nothing after the vote for full independence in 1944. Since then, Danish has been taught in school as an obligatory foreign language.

As for Danish in Norway, perhaps the most spectacular effort to oust its influence is the Norwegian Parliament Act of 1878 that forbad teachers to correct their pupils' dialects. This meant, in particular, that there should be no exercises in reading aloud with a Danish pronunciation. It was to be the burden of the teachers to adapt their language to that of the children; and not the burden of the children to adapt to a both socially and nationally alien norm.

Since then this principle has been reconfirmed by Norwegian authorities several times and is still in force. With regard to the written language, it is possible to insist, as some do, that Bokmål (the result of the 'reformist road', see above) is a Dano-Norwegian language, linguistically and/or ideologically. Otherwise, the role of Danish writing came to an end in Norwegian society with the 'norwegianization' of the Danish orthography from the beginning of the 20th century.

Ousting of Danishisms has been a favorite activity among language cultivators. A notorious example of this in Norway is the purist engagement with a number of morphological affixes (which linguistically speaking are Germanisms, and a testimony to the heavy impact of Low German on Danish and North Germanic more generally in the Middle Ages). The taboo on these affixes in Nynorsk is strong (although the orthographic norm has been loosened somewhat) and is known as the ideological 'illness' of *anbehetelse* (composed of the affixes *an-* , *be-*, *-het*, *-else*). These affixes have also been a target for codifiers of Faroese (Hansen et al., 2003). Whereas Nynorsk and Faroese purism against '*anbehetelse* words' and other Danishisms exemplifies *specific* purism, Icelandic purism stands out by having developed into *general* purism in the 20th century, meaning that all alien linguistic material is targeted, irrespective of source and kind.

Based on general acquaintance with their traditional language politics, linguists agree on what the 'purism-profile' of the Nordic countries looks like (from 'laissez-faire' to 'purism'): DENMARK—SWEDEN—SWEDISH-LANGUAGE FINLAND—FINNISH-LANGUAGE FINLAND—NORWAY—FAROES—ICELAND (e.g., Vikør, 1993).

The Influence of English

In Iceland, the massive presence of British and U.S. soldiers in the 1940s motivated strongly expressed warnings against the influence from English. In the post-WWII era, the accelerating influence from English as 'the language of globalization' has become a focus of much public concern in all of the Nordic area, involving, from the 1990s onwards, linguists and politicians.[3] Some talk about English influence in terms of threat: English conquers domains and becomes the dominating language in higher education, media, and business life, and the national language is invaded by English words. Others focus on the advantageous bilingualism that follows with the omnipresence of English, and point out that today's import of English words is nothing in comparison with the medieval massive import from Low German. One of Denmark's political parties has even proposed to make English an official language in Denmark.

Under the pressure of increasing English impact on both language and society, extensive official reports have resulted in governmental statements and parliamentary acts in several of the Nordic communities. Even in Denmark and Sweden, where the status of Danish and Swedish as 'national languages' always has been so self-evident that official statements to that effect never have been an issue, governmental statements appeared in 2009 (in Sweden with the status of a parliamentary Act). These statements refrain from talking about official languages, but use formulations like "Danish shall continue to be the society-and-culture-sustaining language in Denmark," and "Swedish is the principal language in Sweden."

A notion of 'parallel language use' has been largely embraced in the national policies, as well as in a *Declaration on a Nordic Language Policy* adopted by the Nordic Council of Ministers in 2006. The most advanced developments and implementations of this notion so far are to be found within the domain of higher education.[4] Since 2008, Copenhagen University has housed a Centre for Internationalization and Parallel Language Use (CIP), and a professorship in this field since 2011. At CIP's homepage (http://cip.ku.dk/english), one can read that "[t]he use of parallel languages refers to a situation in which two languages are considered equal in a particular domain, and where the choice of language depends on what is deemed most appropriate and efficient in a specific situation." A more internationally oriented centre for research of Cultural and Linguistic Practices in the International University (CALPIU), based at Roskilde University, states on its home page (http://imw.ruc.dk/calpiu/calpiu) that "[...] many voice their fear that English might change its role from the universal contact language to the dominant language in Danish universities. Within CALPIU, it is assumed that internationalization is about the relationship between many cultures within the same educational institution, and about the possibility of practicing diversity as a resource in education."

The notion of 'parallel language use' is likely to develop as an important ideological construction under late-modern conditions of language use, even though understanding of it tends to vary quite considerably. While governmental statements talk of 'parallel language use' with the perspective of strengthening the competitive capacities of the national language, CIP scholars have pointed out that Copenhagen University approaches the 'parallel language use' issue from the perspective of strengthening the English-language capacities of the institution.[5] It should be added that English-language spoken media like films and TV programs are never dubbed in the Nordic countries (only for children). The language-ideological consequences are considerable. In addition to the amount of status gained by being the 'default language' of the globalized media universe, the omnipresence of English-in-its-varieties in films and popular culture has the effect of familiarizing the Nordic populations with the social values that are stereotypically associated with these varieties. Young Danes' SEE reactions to varieties of English have been found to be largely in harmony with native stereotypes, in spite of limited ability to consciously recognize the varieties. As a possible explanation, it was suggested that "[…] the subjects possess some kind of stored, subconscious information based on previously acquired, media-transmitted stereotypes" (Ladegaard, 1998, p. 269).

National Purism in Responses to Direct Questioning

In the MIN telephone survey, representative samples of the populations answered the same five questions about their attitudes towards the influence of English. Four questions addressed people's attitudes at an 'abstract' level, asking in general terms about the acceptability or desirability of (i) using English words in the national language, (ii) creating new national words as a remedy, (iii) having English as the common mother-tongue for all human beings, (iv) using English as the workplace language in national enterprises. The fifth question moved the attitudes-towards-English issue to a more 'concrete' level by presenting three pairs of words—made up of an English word (*email, bodyguard*, and *design*) and a 'synonym' from the respondent's national language—and asking for a preference judgement. The similarity of the result-patterns allowed the researchers to combine results from the 'abstract' and 'concrete' levels and obtain a ranking of the communities in terms of 'general overt English-positivity': (1) DENMARK > (2) SWEDEN > (3) NORWAY / SWEDISH-LANGUAGE FINLAND > (4) FINNISH-LANGUAGE FINLAND / FAROES > (5) ICELAND.

This result is surprising in its similarity with the linguists' 'purism profile' above. The only difference is that the linguists have overestimated Norwegian purism—which probably happens because Nynorsk is likely to be more salient in linguists' minds than Bokmål when purism is on the agenda. When he includes both Norwegian languages, Vikør's ranking actually looks like this: DANISH—SWEDEN SWEDISH—BOKMÅL—FINLAND SWEDISH—FINNISH—NYNORSK—FAROESE—ICELANDIC (Vikør, 2010). Thus, the surprising and highly interesting finding is that telephone-interviewed representative samples of the Nordic populations reproduce the relative degree of purism, which, according to linguists, characterizes their language-politics traditions. What does that mean? It must mean that a community's degree of purism is present in its public discourse in a way that makes it readily available to individuals who are asked a series of questions about their attitudes to English. Nevertheless, it remains a mystery how this degree of purism emerges as an average score that is 'right' relative to the average scores of the other communities. The mystery is not lessened when we take into account that the Nordic 'purism profile' results from socio-historical conditions that reigned long before English became the external 'threat'.

National Purism in Responses to Indirect Questioning

In order to find out whether these degrees of purism would emerge also in subconsciously offered attitudes, the MIN project elicited reactions to English-influenced language in a SEE, which used the matched-guise technique (see Dragojevic et al., this volume) and was designed and administered to prevent informants from becoming aware of the purpose. It was not possible to make the samples representative in the same way as in the telephone survey, but about 600 listener-judges were recruited in each community with the aim of obtaining a socially broad sample. The matched-guise voice had 6–7 English features in her 'English' version and none in her 'National' version. Much effort was put into making the English coloring of the text 'the same' in all languages. Three filler voices had various combinations of the English features. In all seven communities, the five voices (four speakers) were women aged around 30, and they spoke for about 50 seconds each. Audiences were told that a radio station was interested in their help in choosing between five applicants for a position as newsreader. The applicants had been given the same short text from a news agency. Their task had been, during ten minutes, to make whatever changes they wanted to the text and prepare for reading it aloud. The text itself was taken from a Danish newspaper and dealt with an issue—online shopping—that made the use of some English words seem 'natural'. In brief, this whole cover story was aimed at construing a plausible situation for five slightly different performances of the same text. The performances were assessed from 'not at all' to 'very much' on eight seven-point scales representing (what was assumed to be) positive personality traits. Finally, the applicants were to be ranked from one to five according to their suitability for the job.

In Iceland and the Faroes, the SEEs did not succeed in the crucial sense that informants remained unaware of what it was all about. To a lesser extent, this problem also occurred in Finnish-language Finland. It may well be that experiments of this kind simply cannot be constructed and administered so that informants remain unaware in more purist communities—at least not as long as English words are involved and the context of use to be considered is news-reading on the radio. In the four Scandinavian-language communities, the non-awareness condition was upheld during data collection, and the obtained evaluations can be regarded as subconsciously offered.

The results for Denmark showed a strong favoring of the National guise on all evaluative items. Favoring of the National guise was also true for Sweden—but far less so with regard to items that normally are said to reflect competence and status (*ambitious, intelligent, independent, efficient*) than with regard to items that are assumed to reflect sociability and solidarity (*pleasant, trustworthy, interesting, relaxed*). In contrast, Swedish-language Finland and Norway showed a tendency to upgrading the English guise in comparison with the National guise. In Swedish-language Finland, the English guise was judged more *efficient* and *interesting*; in Norway, it was judged more *ambitious, independent* and *relaxed*.

Two mean values, one for the National guise and one for the English, were calculated for each community by adding the values for all eight personality items and dividing by eight. The difference between the two mean values was taken as a measure of relative 'English-positivity' in the communities. Based on this difference the communities rank as follows, from more to less English-positivity: (1) SWEDISH-LANGUAGE FINLAND/NORWAY > (2) SWEDEN > (3) DENMARK. Compared with the differences in 'overtly' expressed purism (above), this ranking in terms of 'covertly' expressed attitudes to the influence of English turns the language-ideological world, at least the Scandinavian-language part of it, upside down. Just as with social purism (as revealed in the Danish and Norwegian studies), it is clear that national purism may be very different depending on whether attitudes are consciously or subconsciously offered. It is less clear to what extent it can also be claimed that subconsciously offered attitudes towards English correspond better to changes in use. However, in some MIN analyses of English use in the Nordic countries—for example, figures for frequency of English words in newspapers, and figures for increase in this frequency from 1975 to 2000 in particular—Norway does come out on top. In other words, there are data from both use and 'covert' ideology, which indicate that the Norwegian community is more open to English influence than what is recognized in 'overt' ideology.

Nativeness Ideology in the Nordic Countries

A third ideological approach to 'best language' moves the issue from language to speaker and construes native-like competence as 'good' and non-native-like competence as 'bad'.

The conception of language excellence in terms of nativeness is well known, of course, from teaching and learning of foreign languages in school (i.e., after appropriation of one's native language/s). In the case of English, as the main foreign language to be appropriated in all Nordic countries today, 'native-like' is likely to become a difficult notion as acquaintance with other varieties than 'The Queen's English' increases through travelling and media exposure. So far, however, Danish and Norwegian SEE results indicate that the notion of 'best language' is still largely associated with upper-class British English.

Underpinned by discourses about language heritage and authenticity, the ideology of nativeness, crudely stated, holds that the best (old, original, genuine) language has been saved by, and has to be learned from, the 'true natives'—alias linguistically 'unspoiled' peasants living far away from the language-mixing of the urban foreign-influenced social upper-class. While there is no doubt that the belief in a 'native linguistic purity' in this sense has played an important mobilizing role in the various political liberation movements (both national and social in nature) in the Nordic area, it is also true that linguistically more 'spoiled' parts of the populations often have felt the requests for native-like competence by language gatekeepers to be frustrating and de-mobilizing.

It should be added that requests for native-like competence do not necessarily pull together with social or national purism. It is a well-known phenomenon in the Nordic countries that local dialect-speaking communities guard their linguistic borders by powerful social psychological 'mechanisms', on two fronts. That is, while community members become targets of general ridicule if they 'betray their roots' by trying to speak 'proper' (Norwegian has a special, deprecating word—*knot* /kno:t/—for such linguistic behavior), 'proper'-speaking new arrivals run the risk of receiving the same treatment if they try to speak like the locals.

Lately, the ideology of nativeness has acquired new prominence because of immigration.

Indeed, another important motivation behind the last decade's efforts to formulate official language politics in the Nordic countries, besides the influence from English, has been the growth in numbers of languages—to some 200—spoken by the various immigrant groups that have arrived since the 1960s. Including children of foreign-born parents, the immigrant parts of the populations today make up 17 percent in Sweden, 10–11 percent in Denmark, Norway, and Iceland, and 4 percent in Finland. The *Declaration on a Nordic Language Policy* (from 2006) explicitly states that "[t]he use of parallel languages does not only involve English; it must also be applied to the languages of the Nordic countries."

The principle of parallellingualism is spelled out, partly to mean that speakers of the traditional Nordic languages must be secured the language rights they are entitled to by the *Nordic convention on language* (in existence since 1981), and partly to mean that Nordic residents with a non-Nordic first language should be provided thorough instruction in the country's 'society-sustaining language', on the one hand, and the opportunity to use and develop their own mother tongue on the other. In another paragraph on multilingualism, the declaration calls it a responsibility to world society to see to it that languages that are not national languages anywhere (like Sámi, for instance) continue to live and develop, and that all minority languages can continue to exist.

Ideological differences do exist, both between and within the Nordic countries, with regard to political intentions as well as implementations in this domain—not least with regard to the crucial issue of mother-tongue education—but overall there can be no doubt that the 'social treatment' of minority languages (old and new) has changed dramatically for the better in a few decades. The background is the general 'upgrading' of native and minority peoples and cultures in dominating western thinking from the 1960–70s onwards. Prior to that time, governmental policies adopted the 'civilatory' approach of replacing the traditional minority languages Greenlandic, Sámi, Romani, and Sign Language with the respective majority languages. Another matter is whether this change in official social treatment is reflected in the thinking of majority lay people.

The question has been raised with regard to Sámi in connection with a case from the Northern Norwegian city of Tromsø, where a recent proposal to make Sámi an official city language beside Norwegian provoked very strong negative reactions from majority citizens. It has been argued that these reactions reveal that the traditional stigmatization of all things Sámi is still very much alive in the majority population, which fears to be seen as Sámi if their city were to become officially bilingual in Norwegian and Sámi. Likewise, in the case of majority speech with 'outlandish colorings', it seems that little has changed for the better when one learns that speakers with non-native accents quite generally have been found to be downgraded in SEEs in comparison with speakers who display native or native-like competence.

There may be room for hope, though. Having found in their data that "[t]here is a clear general tendency to connect 'good' Danish with 'native' Danish," Jørgensen and Quist (2001, p. 52) stress that this tendency is less strong among their younger respondents, and conclude that "[t]he underlying criticism levelled at the educational system, and the vast majority of those involved in public discussion about language, with their uniformly excessive emphasis on native, national standard Danish, is good news for the Danish language" (*ibid.*, p. 55). Or, rather, if we follow Jørgensen and his collaborators in their subsequent dismissal of the entire idea that languages can be delimited and counted, and instead found our theorizing on notions of *polylingualism* and *languaging* (Jørgensen, 2010), the good news is for *languagers*, in Denmark and elsewhere. Indeed, if it is possible for even Danish purism to be undermined by late-modern conditions for language use, the language-ideological future seems generally open.

Conclusion

Whether conceived of in a social, national, or native perspective, notions of linguistic 'purity' are based on the assumption that it is possible (and important) to delimit varieties on linguistic grounds and define what belongs to a variety and what does not. This view is being seriously challenged by the use of language, which is found among youth in many contemporary multicultural urban environments. Sociolinguistic studies in such environments are relatively well developed in Scandinavia (see Quist & Svendsen, 2010). Most work in this field adopts qualitative approaches in ethnographic type studies of social meaning-making in interactions and falls outside the scope of this chapter. I want to stress as my view, however, that research programs which integrate ethnographic and survey approaches will be important in future language-ideological studies of the 'mechanisms' of language variation and change (Maegaard, 2010, reports from such a study in Copenhagen).

Dialectologists have always known, of course, that clear border lines are hard to spot in the reality of language use, and that all varieties are socially constructed, ideologically 'imagined' entities—with particularly strong institutional support in the case of 'national languages' (the dialects with an army and navy). Somewhat paradoxically, perhaps, I take it that the chapter's account of the various Nordic efforts to construct a 'best language' undermines the very idea that it is in the nature of language to be delimited and kept 'pure'.

Notes

1. Vikør (2004) is a discussion of the problem with the terms *Nordic* and *Scandinavian*. Throughout the chapter, references will be restricted to English-language literature.
2. There is a vast literature about the languages and language communities in the Nordic area. The standard English-language introduction is Haugen (1976). (We may recall that Haugen's foundational work in the field of 'Language Planning' was an analysis of the 'language struggle' in Norway; Haugen, 1966.) Vikør (1993, and later editions) is an eminent textbook with lots of information on all aspects of the Nordic languages. Of particular relevance to the per-

spective of this chapter is Vikør, 2000). Several edited volumes contain articles on language standardization in Nordic communities; e.g., Bandle et al. (2002–2005); Deumert & Vandenbussche (2003); Kristiansen & Coupland (2011).
3. Most of this literature is in Nordic languages, including 13 Novus Press volumes so far from the pan-Nordic MIN project. For an English-language presentation of MIN results, see Kristiansen & Sandøy (2010), which also offers reviews of reports from other investigations of the English influence in Denmark, Sweden and Norway. The MIN quantitative attitudes studies are heavily drawn on in the present article. For English-language articles based on data from some of the many qualitative MIN interviews, see Östman & Thøgersen (2010); Thøgersen (2010).
4. In addition to presenting academic articles on the use of English in Danish Universities, Harder (2009) offers a direct flavour of the argument about the issue by including a series of 'position statements' by major participants in the debate.
5. Thøgersen and Hultgren personal communication; Hultgren (forthcoming) is an analysis of Danish university policies in this domain.

References

Árnason, K. (2003). Icelandic. In A. Deumert & W. Vandenbussche (Eds.), *Germanic standardizations: Past to present* (pp. 245–279). Amsterdam: Benjamins.
Bandle, O. et al. (Eds.). (2002-2005). *The Nordic languages. An international handbook of the history of the North Germanic languages, I-II*. Berlin: Walter de Gruyter.
Deumert, A., & Vandenbussche, W. (Eds.). (2003). *Germanic standardizations: Past to present*. Amsterdam: Benjamins.
Hansen, Z. S., Jacobsen, J. i L., & E. Weyhe, E. (2003). Faroese. In A. Deumert & W. Vandenbussche (Eds.), *Germanic standardizations: Past to present* (pp. 157–191). Amsterdam: Benjamins.
Harder, P. (Ed.). (2009). English in Denmark: Language policy, internationalization and university teaching. Thematic issue of *Angles on the English-Speaking World*, Vol. 9. Copenhagen: Museum Tusculanum Press.
Haugen, E. (1966). *Language conflict and language planning: the case of modern Norwegian*. Cambridge, MA: Harvard University Press.
Haugen, E. (1976). *The Scandinavian languages. An introduction to their history*. London: Faber & Faber.
Hultgren, A. K. (forthcoming). Whose Parallellingualism? Overt and Covert Ideologies in Danish University Language Policies. *Multilingua*.
Jørgensen, J. N. (2010). *Languaging. Nine years of poly-lingual development of young Turkish-Danish grade school students*. [Copenhagen Studies in Bilingualism, The Køge Series. Vol. K15-K16]. Copenhagen: Copenhagen University Press.
Jørgensen, J. N., & P. Quist (2001). Native speakers' judgements of second language Danish. *Language Awareness, 10*, 41–56.
Kristiansen, T. (2009). The macro-level social meanings of late-modern Danish accents. *Acta Linguistica Hafniensia, 41*, 167–192.

Kristiansen, T. (2010). Attitudes, ideology and awareness. In R. Wodak, B. Johnston, & P. Kerswill (Eds.), *The Sage handbook of sociolinguistics* (pp. 265–278). Los Angeles, CA: Sage.

Kristiansen, T., & Coupland, N. (Eds.). (2011). *Standard languages and language standards in a changing Europe*. Oslo: Novus Press.

Kristiansen, T., & Sandøy, H. (Eds.). (2010). The linguistic consequences of globalization: The Nordic countries. *International Journal of the Sociology of Language, 204*.

Ladegaard, H. J. (1998). National stereotypes and language attitudes: The perception of British, American and Australian language and culture in Denmark. *Language and Communication, 18*, 251–274.

Maegaard, M. (2010). Linguistic practice and stereotypes among Copenhagen adolescents. In P. Quist & B. A. Svendsen (Eds.), *Multilingual urban Scandinavia. New linguistic practices* (pp. 189–206). Bristol, UK: Multilingual Matters.

Nuolijärvi, P., & Vaattovaara, J. (2011). De-standardisation in progress in Finnish society? In T. Kristiansen & N. Coupland (Eds.), *Standard languages and language standards in a changing Europe* (pp. 67–74). Oslo: Novus Press.

Östman, J.-O., & Mattfolk, L. (2011). Ideologies of standardization: Finland Swedish and Swedish-language Finland. In T. Kristiansen & N. Coupland (Eds.), *Standard languages and language standards in a changing Europe* (pp. 75–82). Oslo: Novus Press.

Östman, J.-O., & Thøgersen, J. (2010). Language attitudes and the ideology of the Nordic. *International Journal of the Sociology of Language, 204*, 97–127.

Quist, P., & Svendsen, B. A. (Eds.). (2010). *Multilingual urban Scandinavia: New linguistic practices*. Bristol, UK: Multilingual Matters.

Sandøy, H. (forthcoming). Driving forces—in the Norwegian perspective. In T. Kristiansen & S. Grondelaers (Eds.), *Experimental studies of changing language standards in contemporary Europe*. Oslo: Novus Press.

Thøgersen, J. (2010). Coming to terms with English in Denmark: discursive constructions of a language contact situation. *International Journal of Applied Linguistics, 20*, 291–325.

Vikør, L. S. (1993; new editions 1995 and 2001). *The Nordic languages: Their status and interrelations*. Oslo: Novus Press.

Vikør, L. S. (2000). Northern Europe: languages as prime markers of ethnic and national identity. In S. Barbour & C. Carmichael (Eds.), *Language and nationalism in Europe* (pp. 105–129). Oxford, UK: Oxford University Press.

Vikør, L .S. (2004). Scandinavia vs. Norden. *Scandinavian Review*, summer, 40-45.

Vikør, L. S. (2010). Language purism in the Nordic countries. *International Journal of the Sociology of Language, 204*, 9–30.

CHAPTER FIVE

Language Attitudes in the Maghreb Countries of North West Africa

EIRLYS E. DAVIES & ABDELALI BENTAHILA

In the Maghreb countries of Morocco, Algeria, and Tunisia, language issues are an everyday concern. In daily life people may move back and forth between acquired and learned languages, dialect and standard, ancestral and outsider's languages. Behind these conscious and unconscious choices lie attitudes, proclaimed in the press or harbored almost unawares: attitudes to languages themselves as objects, to the peoples and individuals who use them, and to the worlds to which they offer access. And the way the Maghrebis perceive other individuals or groups, or react to others' messages, is undoubtedly affected by the language varieties used by these others.

Language ideology in the region, as in the rest of the Arabic-speaking world, has for many centuries been marked by the Arabic diglossia which is often cited as a textbook example of the opposition between a high variety, highly codified and endowed with considerable prestige, and a low variety, generally disparaged and ill-defined (Ferguson, 1959a). On the one hand is what Arab scholars refer to as *fusha*, a term which covers both Classical Arabic, the vehicle of the Koran and the sacred language of Islam, and the formal written variety in use today, for which Western researchers commonly use the label Modern Standard Arabic (MSA). This high variety, learned only through formal education, contrasts with the various colloquial dialects of Arabic, acquired as mother tongues and used in everyday interaction, which possess no standardized written form. Yet despite this sharp contrast, it must be admitted that the ordinary citizen of the region quite happily uses the term *arabiyya* to cover all these varieties. At some level, then, despite the very different attitudes they may inspire, the colloquials, the variety used in literature and the media, and the Koranic variety are all felt to constitute one and the same language.

The various colloquial varieties of Arabic are associated with national and regional groupings. In addition, sizable numbers of inhabitants (estimated by various sources at between 20% and 40% of the population of Morocco and Algeria, along with an insignificant 1% of Tunisians) still speak the Hamito-Semitic language that Western researchers refer to as Berber, a name rejected by the language's users, who call themselves Imaghizen and prefer to label their language Tamazight or Amazigh (which we will therefore use below). This was the original language of the region before the Arabs arrived in the seventh century, but its speakers, once converted to Islam, gradually underwent Arabization until today only pockets of Amazigh speakers remain, most of them concentrated in isolated mountainous areas of Morocco and in Kabylia and the Saharan regions of Algeria, and speaking dialects which are not entirely mutually intelligible (which means that their users may need to resort to colloquial Arabic as a lingua franca).

Added to this are further complications deriving from the presence in North Africa today of outsiders' languages: the language of the French colonizers, who occupied all three countries for varying periods of time, and to a lesser extent that of the Spanish, who occupied certain areas of Morocco. More than half a century after the French left, and following decades of language planning policies aimed at eradicating their language, French remains the usual medium for science, technology, business and financial activities, as well as an everyday medium of communication for many people.

In this chapter, we have judged it most convenient to look in turn at attitudes to each variety (*fusha*, colloquial Arabic, Amazigh, French, and code-switching), and then to examine some evidence for how people are perceived when using different languages. We shall refer to studies carried out during the last few decades, from the early years after independence to recent years, noting historical and geographical contrasts where these are evident, and considering the possible implications of recent changes and current trends.

Existing Studies and Limitations

Discussion of language attitudes in the Maghreb is nothing new. Questions relating to diglossia, the special status of *fusha* and the inferior status of the dialects have been addressed for centuries by Arab scholars. On the other hand, studies concerned with the vernaculars and with the other languages used in the Maghreb are more recent and have largely been framed within the Western scientific tradition, with most published works being in French or English. These have looked at users' attitudes to the languages themselves and the ways they are used, and their opinions as to the roles the languages should play in various domains, such as education and literature. However, before looking at some of these studies, it seems important to point out a few of the limitations of the work carried out to date. A first remark concerns the methodology adopted. Some studies have looked mainly at the publicly expressed attitudes put forth in the media, by educationalists or language planning commissions. Others have sought to elicit laypersons' views, typically using questionnaires and/or interviews. The pitfalls of such methods are well-known; leading questions may push informants to make claims that would not otherwise have occurred to them, or oblige them to select between alternatives none of which really corresponds to their own view. The questions asked are also often very broad and encourage sweeping responses, whereas attitudes may be highly context-dependent. Interpreting remarks is often difficult because of the lack of precise terminology in general use. For instance, discussions often refer simply to Arabic, without indicating whether *fusha* or Colloquial Arabic is intended; it is worth noting, for example, that the constitutions of the various countries identify their official language as simply *arabiyya*.

Informants may also be unable or unwilling to give accurate information. Their claims about their proficiency and language habits may be influenced by emotion and concern for image. For instance, Maamouri (1998, p. 33) refers to the "attitudinal blindness in favor of fusha" which leads people to claim it as their language, even though it has no native speakers. Activists may claim to speak Amazigh even though their knowledge of it is very limited, while others who learned it as their first language prefer to deny this inheritance. On the other hand, of course, these very discrepancies in informants' responses may be very revealing of underlying attitudes. Conscious of this, Bentahila and Davies (1989) deliberately used a vague expression in asking Moroccan informants which language they considered to be "their own language," with varied and quite striking results, some of which will be mentioned below.

Another factor influencing the plausibility of data collected is the background of the researchers, who may be members of the speech community under investigation or foreign academics, often using the region as a source of material for a doctoral thesis. While insiders may possess greater insight into the situation, they sometimes have a personal axe to grind, or let their emotional involvement in a particular issue cloud their discussion. Outsiders might be expected to be more objective, but they are often ill equipped to handle delicate social interactions or to interpret what they observe, and, more seriously, they may not be aware of these shortcomings. While some respondents may view foreign interviewers with distrust, declining to answer frankly, others may offer totally inaccurate information because they are eager to paint a rosy picture of their society, or simply enjoy misleading over-inquisitive foreigners.

Some of these problems may be avoided via the use of more indirect methods of extracting information about possibly unconscious language attitudes, such as the matched guise technique, which investigates the way individuals' language choices affect the ways they are perceived by others. However, so far there have been relatively few studies of this type. There are also other as yet poorly explored avenues which might shed light on language attitudes. One such is the investigation of the linguistic landscapes of Maghrebi cities: the way the various languages are used in street signs, names of shops, notices, etc.

A further problem relates to the types of informant chosen. Academics, particularly foreign ones with few contacts outside the university, have frequently exploited the captive pool of informants formed by their own students. There is nothing intrinsically wrong with this, provided the results obtained are then presented as representing the views of this particular group; but all too often the responses are discussed as if they were representative of broader sections of society. But the attitudes of university students of English, or of those pursuing graduate studies in the USA, for instance, cannot be assumed to be shared by other sectors of Maghrebi society.

One final reservation about previous discussions of the language situation is related to the fact that all across the region things are changing fast. The past few decades have seen dramatic developments in population movements, levels of literacy, educational policies, political and ideological positions, and, most recently, the move towards greater democracy. Clearly, then, the findings of an attitudinal study conducted twenty or thirty years ago cannot be taken as representative of the contemporary situation. Walters (2003) is at pains to trace changes in the Tunisian language situation over recent decades; yet we frequently note the tendency, especially in general surveys of the sociolinguistics of the region, to cite older studies as if their results were still valid today. To cite just one example, Serson (2003, p. 73) quotes a 1968 observation about the instrumental value placed on French in Morocco without even raising the question of its current validity.

In what follows, we will attempt to set the various studies referred to within their historical contexts and where possible to relate their findings to the situation in which they were obtained. Given the limitations noted above, however, our survey may in some parts be more of an indication of what needs to be researched than an affirmation of what is already established.

Attitudes to the High Variety of Arabic

A saying of the Prophet Mohammed declares that Arabic is the language of heaven, and over the centuries there have always been plenty of scholars to sing its praises as the most beautiful, pure and perfect tongue; Ferguson (1959b) accordingly cites this belief in the inherent superiority of *fusha*, aesthetically and linguistically, as the first of his "myths about Arabic." Added to this came its political status as a unifying force holding together the Arab nation, well traced by Suleiman (2003), who shows how "formulations of Arab nationalism, whether embryonic or fully fledged in character, are invariably built around the potential and capacity of Arabic in its standard form to act as the lynchpin of the identity of all those who shared it as their common language" (p. 224).

Following independence, the Maghrebi states found themselves with education systems highly reliant on French. Seeking to affirm a united Arab identity and eradicate the traces of the colonizer, all three put in place programs aimed at gradually replacing French by MSA in their education and administration systems. Executed with varying degrees of rapidity and thoroughness, and often advancing in a two steps forward, one step back fashion, these policies have now produced curricula where Arabic is the medium of instruction throughout primary and secondary education, though French has still been maintained as a medium for higher education in such domains as science, technology, and business.

However, ideological concerns have sometimes been an obstacle to *fusha*'s evolution. Concern to preserve the language's "purity" and awareness that its prestige springs from its links with a distant past have made many reluctant to accept diachronic changes which would be taken for granted in other languages. The use of MSA in the domains of science and technology has been held up by arguments over the correct ways of coining new terminology, and protests at foreign borrowings which are thought to threaten the integrity of the language. Attempts to ensure consistent terminological usage across the Arab world, through the work of language academies, have had limited success. Regional differences inevitably emerge; indeed, Maamouri suggests that there are "as many fushas as there are Arab countries" (1998, p. 36). Moreover, despite the talk of Arabic as a symbol of Arab unity, in actual practice MSA does not always prove to be a convenient lingua franca, either within the Maghreb or across its borders. A Moroccan and a Tunisian may still find it easier to converse in French than in MSA, while an Algerian and an Iraqi may find English the most convenient choice.

Today, despite the undeniable prestige attached to *fusha*, its status is still in some ways paradoxical. The illiterate and poorly educated still represent substantial proportions of the population of the Maghreb; UNESCO's Institute for Statistics gives recent literacy rates for adults over fifteen of 77.6% for Tunisia (2008), 72.6% for Algeria (2006), and only 56.1% for Morocco (2009). The illiterate do not understand or use MSA, although they can of course recite Koranic passages learned by heart. But at the other extreme, many in the upper echelons of society also lack proficiency in MSA; large numbers of those now in positions of authority pursued their studies via the medium of French, and even today the elite frequently opt to place their own children in foreign-run schools, even though this choice may mean they will not achieve proficiency in MSA. This fact in itself speaks volumes about the ambivalence of current attitudes to *fusha:* while it may be glorified as an object, it is not always valued as a tool.

On an individual level, too, some naturally resent the pressure placed upon them to handle this language with particular respect. Edward Said's recollection of his experience of learning MSA in Egypt will certainly be echoed by many Maghrebis: "The atmosphere of rote learning, taught by lamentably ungifted and repressive teachers and clergymen, and a sort of 'it's good for you' attitude, against which I was in perpetual rebellion, undermined the project altogether" (Said, 2002, p. 228). In addition, the constant preoccupation with using MSA correctly, reflected in the way people enjoy pointing out grammatical errors by eminent figures (something noted by Maamouri, 1998, p. 39), makes some self-conscious and even reluctant to use it.

Attitudinal surveys have elicited varied responses. Bentahila's (1983) Moroccan subjects, consulted for their views about Classical Arabic, Moroccan Arabic and French, tended to voice the established ideological positions, with a significant majority choosing Classical Arabic as the most beautiful and richest language. Interestingly, this variety was judged far less practical than either colloquial Arabic or French, yet at the same time it was also named as the language Moroccans should use above all—the contrast between ideal and reality appearing again here. Likewise, a strong identification with the language may be expressed even by those who do not master it well. And Bentahila and Davies (1989) found even native speakers of Amazigh, some of whose parents did not know any Arabic, nevertheless claiming Arabic as their own language, and even in some cases as the language of their ancestors; in these cases ideas of Islamic and national identity seem to take priority over ethnic and linguistic affiliations.

On the other hand, Saad (1992) found clear divisions between his Algerian student informants, with those claiming Amazigh as a home language displaying consistently negative attitudes to both Arabic and Arabization programs, whereas the others expressed positive attitudes to Arabic as a language but negative ones to the Arabization policy. And more recently, among Bektache's (2009) informants, university students from the Amazigh-speaking Bejaia region of Algeria, 55% chose Amazigh as their preferred language while only 4% chose Arabic, with 95% expressing dissatisfaction with their country's language policy. In Algeria maybe more than in Morocco, promotion of Arabic seems to be perceived as oppression of Amazigh, thanks perhaps to its very radical language laws which for some time required only Arabic to be used in all administrative and associative domains, including all public meetings and even street signs. But other factors may also come into play. Brahimi and Owens (2000) found that among their Algerian informants, Amazigh-speakers expressed significantly less favorable attitudes to MSA and to Arabization than did native speakers of Arabic; but these attitudes also seemed to relate to place of residence, with Amazigh-speakers living in Arabic-speaking areas expressing feelings closer to those of the Arabic speakers with regard to the political status of MSA.

Such background differences between the informants used in the various published studies make it very difficult to collate their findings, but it would be interesting to trace the evolution of attitudes as the Arabization process has advanced, and compare the feelings of those who have been subject to it to those who have not. One might imagine that the new cohorts of Arabized students would not see French as important in the way their bilingual parents might; on the other hand, by making a high degree of proficiency in French relatively rare in the younger generation, the implementation of Arabization may, ironically enough, have made French proficiency even more highly prized and sought after.

What is clear is that, where Arabic is concerned, ideological positions and practical needs do not always coincide. It is of course easy to assign others to a possibly monolingual future for the sake of some abstract principle when one is oneself already a proficient bilingual (Berger, 1998); it is less easy to be convinced in the rightness of a solely Arabic-medium education if one knows that this leads to a serious disadvantage on the job market, as Mansouri (1991) claimed was the case in Algeria. Accordingly, many people endorse Arabization as an affirmation of national identity, yet as individuals still wish to profit from the advantages of a bilingual education (indeed, some of the architects of Arabization programs famously placed their own children in private or foreign schools to ensure they would receive instruction in French, adopting the strategy of "elite closure" (Bentahila, 1983; Benrabah, 2007)). Because of such conflicting feelings, it may be quite difficult to gain true insights into current attitudes to the high variety of Arabic. Direct questioning may well extract from informants statements of what they think they ought to feel; their innermost feelings may appear confused and inconsistent even to themselves.

Attitudes to Colloquial Arabic

While *fusha* is traditionally admired, the colloquial varieties of Arabic are regularly denigrated, the assumption being that they have suffered degradation over the centuries (a view traced by Eisele, 2003 and Suleiman, 2004). García Sánchez (2010) recounts how an Arabic teacher working with children of the Moroccan community in Spain talks "condescendingly" (p. 193) of his pupils' home variety of Arabic, describing it as "backward" (p. 183) and deploring the fact that it is so far removed from *fusha* (p. 179).

However, despite this kind of rhetoric, people may well be very much attached to their own dialects, and take a positive attitude to those who use the same dialect. While MSA retains its special status as an overarching symbol of Arab identity, prestige varieties seem to be emerging from among the dialects. According to Walters (2003), the Tunis variety is becoming a regional standard for Tunisia, while Miller (2004) makes a similar claim for the Casablanca variety in Morocco.

The attitudes of users of one dialect to other Arabic dialects also merit investigation. Satellite television is now a feature of life even in remote villages, and while the globalized Arabic TV networks might be seen as a force bringing the various Arabic-speaking communities closer together, they have also had the effect of making people more aware of the extent to which their own dialect differs from others. Ibrahim (2000) reports that her Moroccan informants rated Egyptian Arabic as more beautiful than Moroccan Arabic, but Walters (2007) suggests that these informants may have been influenced by the Egyptian nationality of the researcher; further research is needed here.

The importance of colloquial Arabic as a spoken ingroup marker is suggested by some researchers' findings that Westerners' use of the dialect is not always welcomed. Walters (1996), exploring the extent to which Anglophone wives of Tunisians acquire Tunisian Arabic, noted that some husbands clearly were not keen for their wives to learn to speak Arabic, and that some women felt that educated Tunisians were uncomfortable speaking Arabic to them, preferring to use French. The strong local connotations of such colloquial dialects may mean that outgroup members who try to use them are perceived as intruders. And in the European diaspora, despite the fact that colloquial Arabic is not highly valued by the wider community, second and third generation Maghrebi immigrants have tended to cling to their colloquial dialects as strong identity markers, even if they have only limited mastery of them (Abu Haidar, 1994). Alongside this identification with colloquial Arabic by those of North African origin, however, we may also note a more surprising use of this language as an identity marker.

For in Europe today there is also an interesting trend towards the espousal of elements of the Maghrebi colloquial dialects by urban youths who are not of Maghrebi origin. Nortier and Dorleijn (2008) report on what they call "Moroccan-flavored Dutch," a recently emerged ingroup variety used in Dutch cities by youths of varied origins (Turkish, Moroccan, Surinamese, and even native Dutch), which features Dutch spoken with a Moroccan accent and certain non-standard grammatical features, together with the insertion of Moroccan Arabic fillers, interjections, and certain grammatical morphemes. Rather than signaling Moroccan identity, this variety is now a marker of solidarity between multiethnic youth groups. This trend could be taken as an instance of the tendency towards more dynamic, less deterministic relations between language, ethnicity and identity explored by Rampton (1995, 2006). It provides an interesting example of how conditioned attitudes are by context; the symbolic value of Moroccan Arabic for these users in the Netherlands is far removed from its significance in its original homeland.

While speech in colloquial Arabic may thus be a strong marker of ingroup identity, the idea of writing it, at least in public discourse, has until very recently been met with fierce resistance. Just one example is the suggestion, proffered by Nafusa Said (reported by Eisele, 2003), that the idea of writing colloquial Arabic comes from foreigners plotting to undermine the status of *fusha* and thereby threaten the unity and cultural legacy enshrined in this variety. Foreign educationalists have long expressed concern about the problems faced by Maghrebi children beginning school, who are not taught to write and read the colloquial variety they have already acquired at home, but are instead expected to master the new syntax, lexis and phonology of MSA at the same time as they take their first steps towards literacy. There have therefore been calls for initial literacy to be taught in colloquial Arabic rather than MSA (see, for instance, Daniel & Ball, 2010; Maamouri, 1998; Salmi, 1987), but these have had little effect, since any such move would involve far more than merely replacing MSA materials with dialectal ones: it would have to overcome deeply entrenched attitudes towards the roles of the two varieties. Many would be outraged to find their children learning to write a dialect which in their view does not deserve to be written; for instance, when a French school in Morocco decided to offer a course in Moroccan Arabic for pupils having difficulty with the usual MSA course, their parents protested vehemently. The issue also arises in immigrant contexts, where parents are often adamant that the so-called home language programs offered by schools should in fact teach their children a language which is no one's home language: the prestigious *fusha* which the parents themselves do not know. García Sánchez (2010) quotes the *fqih* who teaches *fusha* in one Spanish school as asserting that only this variety can give the children a strong sense of identity and high self-esteem. Symbolic values here seem to take precedence over practical communicative needs.

On the other hand, outside the education system, people do on occasion incorporate colloquial Arabic into their private written correspondence. For instance, Belnap and Bishop (2003) report that Arab students in the USA, including Moroccans, claim to use Colloquial Arabic when writing to their families, and suggest that this trend is accelerating. However, there would seem to be a big difference between this use of the colloquial, in what is after all private, personal interaction, and another, more recent phenomenon: the deliberate incorporation of colloquial Arabic into public written discourse. On advertising billboards in Moroccan cities today, we can now read words and phrases plucked straight from the colloquial variety, written in Arabic script or, even more surprisingly, transliterated in the Roman alphabet. Walters (2003) reports the same trend in Tunisia. Twentieth century would-be modernizers of Arabic, like Salama Musa and Abdulaziz Fahmi, called in vain for a shift to the Roman alphabet; but now this shift seems to be being executed without much comment by young people who have never even heard of these earlier campaigns.

The source of such innovation seems to lie, not in intellectuals' arguments about the priority of the mother tongue or in foreigners' attempts to destroy Arab unity, but rather in changes in the wider environment. It springs from the rapid spread of information technologies which have opened up new possibilities for communication and at the same time imposed limitations on their exploitation. People now write emails and cell phone text messages to convey things they would earlier have expressed orally, whether face to face or by phone. Consequently, phone calls in colloquial Arabic have been replaced by text messages which are also composed in colloquial Arabic; and Arabic speakers, faced with computer keyboards and cellphones which do not provide for the composition of messages in the Arabic script, have simply devised a way of writing their Arabic messages using Roman script together with certain numerals (see Atifi (2003) on this trend in Moroccans' contributions to internet forums, and Yaghan (2008) on the same trend among Jordanians). Apart from these practical motivations, this strategy also seems to provide young people with an ingroup style which older people may find it difficult to decipher, and it may also have something of a liberating effect, offering as it does a way of writing that is far removed from the weighty prescriptions attached to other writing in Arabic.

The fact that the trend now seems to be spreading beyond personal, computer-mediated communication to more public discourse, as the billboards demonstrate, raises further questions. After centuries when the use of correct standard Arabic was considered essential in any written message that was meant to be taken seriously, the public's reactions to the new advertisements featuring written colloquial Arabic are certainly worth investigation. Things are moving fast, and for the moment it is perhaps not yet clear whether it is a change of attitude which has made possible this change of usage, or whether the change of usage is bringing in its wake a change of attitude.

Attitudes to Amazigh

Shifts of attitude may also be under way with regard to Amazigh, long seen as relevant only as a home language, associated with remote rural regions and illiteracy. While Colloquial Arabic, as part of the continuum referred to as *arabiyya*, still retains associations with Islam, Amazigh has no such religious associations, nor was it ever much used in writing. Following independence, it received little or no recognition from governments more concerned with affirming their countries' unity and Arab identity; the Arabization programs which sought to eradicate French also left no room for Amazigh.

A number of studies have reported an ongoing language shift away from Amazigh in Morocco. Bentahila and Davies (1992) identified a common pattern of shift over two generations, where older Amazigh monolinguals had bilingual children and non-Amazigh speaking grandchildren, and more recently El Kirat El Allame (2007) reports on "the deliberate non-transmission of the Amazigh language to the younger generations" (p. 710). Hoffman (2006) shows how, with the migration of men to cities where Arabic is spoken, Amazigh has become more and more restricted to the women left behind in remote villages. As for attitudes to this loss, Bentahila and Davies (1989, 1992) found some evidence that the loss of the Amazigh language was not experienced as a loss of Amazigh identity; 15% of the Amazigh speakers they questioned chose to describe themselves as Arabs, 30% said they considered Arabic rather than Amazigh to be their own language, and 20% said they did not wish their children to learn Amazigh. El Kirat El Allame (2007) reports that her informants considered the abandonment of Amazigh "an efficient solution" (p. 711), and concludes that "the Amazigh people are not proud of or satisfied with their social identity" and show "indifference and lack of concern towards the Amazigh identity and language" (p. 713). Indeed, anthropologists working in the post-independence era were at pains to point out that the division between Arabs and Imaghizen had never been clear-cut or based on language (Gellner, 1973), and that the categories were not seen as mutually exclusive (Rosen, 1973). On the other hand, Brahimi and Owens (2000) obtained different findings from their Algerian study; a large majority of their Amazigh-speaking informants said that all Imaghizen should learn Amazigh, and they found no evidence of large-scale shift. Moreover, some researchers have argued that knowledge of the Amazigh language is an essential element in Amazigh identity (El Aissati, 2001).

This view has led many educated Amazigh speakers to join militant activist groups, and these are beginning to obtain results. In 2002 Algeria declared Tamazight a national language alongside Arabic, and since then the language has begun to be taught in schools in its heartland areas, and promoted by an academy and the High Commission for Amazighity, set up in 2007. A similar institution, the Royal Institute of Amazigh Culture (IRCAM), was set up in Morocco in 2001, along with a program for the teaching of Amazigh in primary schools, and in 2011 Morocco's new constitution finally assigned Amazigh the status of an official language beside Arabic.

There is an interesting contrast between the two countries' strategies: Algeria has focused more on teaching the language at university level, and in the areas where most Amazigh speakers live, while Morocco has started with the early years of primary school and opted for a nationwide program, albeit one which is still far from being implemented. Significantly, King Mohammed VI of Morocco recently described Amazighity as being "the common heritage of *all* Moroccans" (italics ours), thus presenting it as a unifying element (speech on March 9, 2011). In contrast, Berger (1998, p. 45) points to the "numerous internal cultural splittings" that have resulted from the tendency to classify Algerians into Arabophones and Amazighophones, and similar observations are made by Abu Haidar (2000) and Benrabah (2004). It remains to be seen what attitudinal consequences these contrasting policies will have.

So far, the implications of these changes for the heartland speakers of Amazigh seem not to have been much explored. The activists who have adopted Amazigh as a political cause seem to be seeking power for a language whose value for its native speakers is as a symbol of solidarity. These native speakers might even feel uneasy that the language which for them represents home, family, and intimacy is now being studied by outsiders. Hoffman (2006) stresses the gulf that exists in Morocco between the activists, mostly educated urban-dwelling males, and the illiterate women living in isolated villages who actually form the heart of the Amazigh language community. These women were not consulted by the decision-makers in the capital who claim to speak for the Imaghizen people, but their reactions to recent developments certainly deserve to be investigated.

The choice of a standardized writing system for Amazigh has also aroused fierce debate. The Moroccan authorities have opted to use Tifinagh, an alphabet based on an ancient North African script, rather than using the Arabic script, hitherto adopted by many non-militant writers, or the Roman alphabet, most used by groups outside Morocco (Pouessel, 2008). Some see this choice as a highly symbolic affirmation of Amazigh's specificity and its pre-Islamic presence in the region, others consider it divisive, since Algeria's Imaghizen have not adopted this alphabet, and still others suspect that using this little-known script will, in the end, only serve to marginalize material written in it. In practical terms, the decision requires children to learn three different alphabets (Arabic, Tifinagh, and French) in their first years of schooling. And for the rural Amazigh speakers, it would seem to represent yet another hurdle; they may already have struggled to attain a certain level of literacy in Arabic, yet now, if they wish to read and write Amazigh, they will have to start again and learn a totally different writing system.

Once again, there seem to be conflicts between ideologies and people's individual needs. And once again, we have a situation in flux which deserves much more careful investigation. In the space of a few years, Amazigh has gone from being the home language of a minority, used in a very limited range of domains, and not known at all by the majority of the population, to a language with official status, now actively promoted and developed and taught as a subject in the state education system. It remains to be seen whether these changes will bring in their wake corresponding changes of attitude.

Attitudes to French and to the Mixing of Arabic and French

French and its relationship to Arabic have been a major focus of discussion both by specialists interested in language attitudes and by lay commentators, who exhibit varying degrees of objectivity and emotion. The historical associations of French with the colonizer are still being evoked, but at the same time its role as a medium of wider communication is also appreciated.

Nowhere has hostility to the use of French has been expressed with more violence than in the debate over Francophone writers. Novelists and poets who opted to publish in French rather than Arabic following independence have regularly been reviled, insulted, and accused of treachery and of "cultural bastardy" (Armitage, 2000, p. 44) for choosing to create literature in the colonizer's language. Some have paid the ultimate price; during the 1990s many Francophone Algerian writers were brutally murdered by Islamist extremists, as were many teachers of French. And yet here again perceptions are contradictory; while those writing in French rather than Arabic are often accused of being subjugated to the colonizer, others have claimed that writing in French rather than Arabic is a kind of liberation, since it allows them to address subjects and feelings which could not acceptably be expressed in Arabic. Armitage (2000) suggests that this may be particularly true for women writers. Déjeux and Mitsch (1992) quote Moroccan author Tahar Ben Jelloun's remarks to this effect, while Tageldin (2009) quotes similar observations by Algerian woman writer Assia Djebar.

Yet while people may consider the writing of literature in French as an act of betrayal, there is no doubt that the ability to communicate effectively in French is seen as a great personal asset. French is often described as a scar left by colonization, but the grandchildren of those who fought in the resistance movement against the French are now queuing up at private language centers to embrace it and all it can offer them. Alongside the views of those like Mansouri (1991, p. 161), who concludes that "the existence of a Western language in an Arabic and Islamic society, as with French in Algeria, is bound to create socio-cultural cleavages," we may set those of the many who feel that the continued presence of French in the Maghreb is a source of enrichment and an added value for its societies. Indeed, such divergent views may be expressed by the same individual on different occasions. Nor is there anything to stop individuals judging that what is not good for society as a whole may nevertheless be a source of personal gain to themselves and their children.

In fact, while the role of French in administration and education is now very much reduced, there are far more speakers of French in the Maghreb today than there were during the colonization period (thanks to population growth and the spread of education to all social strata). Benrabah (2007) cites recent surveys showing increases in the proportion of Algerian over-sixteens who can speak French, which now exceeds 60% (though it should be noted that these polls seem to have relied on self-ascription), and more than three quarters of his respondents believed that French would continue to maintain its place in Algerian society.

Questionnaires asking directly for attitudes to French have often found it to be highly valued. For instance, Bentahila's (1983) informants rated it more lively, versatile and modern than either high or low varieties of Arabic, and a large majority wanted their children to master it. Much more recently, Benrabah (2007) suggests that the bitter associations of French with colonization are weakening for younger Algerians, and that now that the status of Arabic in Algeria is secure, people are paradoxically more ready to embrace French, since it is no longer seen to pose a threat to their identity. He found that most schoolchildren in his Algerian study still did not want French to be replaced by Arabic. Similarly, Marley (2005) claimed that most of her Moroccan teacher informants wanted a return to French for all science teaching (though paradoxically a majority of these also expressed support for the Arabization policy). Again, however, it is important to recognize that attitudes to French may vary considerably between different sectors of the population; for instance, Maamouri (1998) claimed that total Arabization would be welcome to rural populations, who saw French as an unnecessary obstacle, but would be opposed by urban dwellers, who saw a command of French as a great asset on the job market. Incidentally, while we do not have space here for a detailed look at attitudes in North-West Morocco to Spanish, another ex-colonizer's language, we may note in passing Sayahi's (2005) conclusion that this language also continues to be used and appreciated there because of its economic value.

In everyday conversation among Maghrebis, French is often intermingled with colloquial Arabic in a style featuring extensive code-switching. This style is marked by certain distinctive switch patterns not attested in other communities, which have therefore attracted considerable attention from code-switching researchers, and which are seen as highly emblematic of their users' North African identity (Bentahila, Davies, & Owens, forthcoming). Arabic-French code-switching thus serves as a strong ingroup marker, as researchers have repeatedly noted (Walters, 1996; Boumens & Caubet, 2000). It has therefore been exploited as an expression of Maghrebi identity in artistic expression like popular song lyrics, where it has also been shown to contribute aesthetic and rhetorical effects (Bentahila & Davies, 2002; Davies & Bentahila, 2006, 2008). Yet despite its evident usefulness and effectiveness as a vehicle for ingroup exchanges, explicitly expressed attitudes to this code-switching seem to be almost universally negative. Criticisms of the style can often be read in the media, and Bentahila's (1983) informants described it as a mark of ignorance, carelessness, laziness or even psychological problems.

The Influence of Language Choice on Perceptions of Speakers

The studies reported on so far have concentrated mainly on examining explicitly affirmed attitudes, and we have repeatedly noted the inconsistencies and conflicts between these proclaimed attitudes. There have also been a few attempts to investigate whether the language used may impact the outlook an individual adopts on other issues. Bentahila (1983), using a completion test, found that bilingual informants expressed more westernized views of the world when completing statements in French, and more traditionally Islamic ones when completing them in Arabic. Coffman (1992) concluded from his study at the University of Algiers that students pursuing their studies in Arabic were more likely to express sympathy with Islamist positions: "Arabization is a cause of greater Islamization" (p. 188). A final issue concerns the way language attitudes may affect the way people react to the language choices of their fellows. This has been investigated using the matched guise technique, which offers a means of accessing possibly unconscious language attitudes.

In an early study, Bentahila (1983) asked Moroccan bilingual informants to evaluate the Moroccan Arabic and French guises of three bilingual speakers, and found that overall the French guises were judged more important, educated, and modern than the Arabic ones. The contrast was not as simple as this, however, since judgments varied considerably depending on the type of accent used. The speaker whose accent in French approximated to that of a native French speaker was also judged significantly more intelligent, honest, entertaining and less religious in French than in Arabic, whereas the one using a heavily Moroccan-accented French which identified him as a native of Fez was not assigned significantly higher status in this guise; he was in fact perceived as significantly more intelligent in his Arabic guise.

A second matched-guise test avoiding Fez-accented speakers was then carried out. Here the three speakers' French guises were likewise rated more highly on status traits (intelligent, educated, rich, important, and modern); they were also judged more likeable, sociable and entertaining, and less religious than when they spoke Arabic. Again, the higher ratings for status straits were not significant in the case of a speaker with a markedly Moroccan accented French. Clearly, not all French speakers were judged equally.

While Bentahila's (1983) matched guise tests were carried out thirty years ago, a decade later, Belazi (1991) obtained quite similar findings with Tunisian informants, using Tunisian Arabic and French guises. In his study, the Arabic guises were more highly evaluated for religiosity, conservatism and nationalism, the French ones for status traits (including important, educated, modern, and intelligent). Moreover, he also found that the speaker with a more "French" accent in French was more highly evaluated for status traits than the other two. Belazi concludes that in fact it is not merely *fusha* which is associated with religion; even the colloquial dialects bear these connotations when contrasted with French.

In an attempt to investigate perceptions of code-switching, as contrasted with use of a single language, Bentahila (1983) conducted a further matched guise test, comparing three guises each for two speakers: Arabic-French code-switching, only French and only Arabic. The contrast between the French and Arabic guises observed in the earlier tests was replicated again here. But the code-switching guises were judged significantly less favorably than either the French or the Arabic guises on both status and solidarity traits, being perceived as less intelligent, educated, important, competent and eloquent, but also as less sociable, self-confident and likeable. The negative views on code-switching elicited via direct questioning thus appear again when investigated more indirectly. The fact that speakers were seen as less patriotic and more influenced by colonization when using code-switching than when speaking Arabic seems unsurprising; but their code-switching guises also received much lower ratings than the purely French guises for these two traits. This was perhaps related to a feeling that those who used code-switching were displaying carelessness and a lack of respect for any language, or were actually incapable of keeping the two languages separate, (Walters (1996), in fact, claims that educated Tunisians find it difficult to avoid French-Arabic code-switching (when conversing with peers), Conversely, those holding forth exclusively in French were thought to possess a certain mastery over the colonizers' language and were making a deliberate choice to use it, for their own ends.

More recently, Lawson and Sachdev (2000) carried out a matched-guise test with Tunisian informants, using samples from one male and one female speaker, each of whom provided five separate guises, speaking in MSA and English as well as in Tunisian Arabic, French and French-Arabic code-switching. In keeping with the results of the earlier studies, they found the foreign language guises (English and French) rated higher for modernity and the Arabic ones rated higher for religiousness and traditionalism. They also found that for both the male and the female speaker, the code-switching guise was evaluated less highly on both status and solidarity traits.

However, a difference emerged between the two speakers. The female's other guises were perceived similarly in all respects, but in the case of the male speaker, the Tunisian Arabic guise was judged most favorably, on both status and solidarity traits. Lawson and Sachdev (2000) suggest that these findings may indicate that the diglossic opposition between high and low varieties of Arabic is not reflected in attitudes, and that Tunisians may now be taking increasing pride in their own colloquial variety of Arabic.

There would in fact seem to be something of a problem in using a matched guise test to compare MSA, associated only with highly formal contexts, with colloquial Arabic, still less with a code-switching variety. Very few people can actually spontaneously produce purely MSA discourse (as opposed to a mixture of colloquial and MSA); the MSA guise would therefore doubtless sound like a prepared speech, whereas the code-switching guise would suggest carefree spontaneity. It seems difficult to see how these guises could really be considered to be "matched" in such a study; they would evoke entirely different contexts and motives as well as possibly different personalities.

Lawson and Sachdev's (2000) study is further complicated by the fact that three different languages were randomly used to elicit the judgments of the informants, all university students of English (and therefore not necessarily representative of any larger group). Those who were asked to respond in English exhibited a difference of attitude, in that they took a less negative view of both code-switching guises than those responding in Arabic or French. This finding is interesting in itself, but overall the large number of variables in this study (speakers of two sexes, each using five different guises, and judged by informants using three different languages) makes the interpretation of the results quite complex.

One observation that can be drawn from a comparison of these three studies is that while the 1983 and 1991 studies both found French guises to be associated with greater prestige, this contrast does not emerge in the 2000 study. If this difference is confirmed, it might reflect shifting attitudes to French, possibly related to changes in the language situation brought about through the Arabization process.

However, even these limited studies are enough to suggest that generalizations about "French" are dangerous; for the Maghrebis' French is not a monolithic entity, any more than is their Arabic. The impression given by speaking French may depend on the proficiency of the person using it, and on the proficiency of the observer. Thus, we saw that Bentahila's (1983) and Belazi's (1991) bilingual informants took French-accented French as a mark of education, but were not so impressed by users of heavily local-accented French. In fact, the use of French by persons with limited knowledge of it may be met with denigration or even ridicule by speakers that are more fluent. On the other hand, these same persons might manage to give an impression of sophistication among people with even less knowledge of French than themselves. Since the implementation of Arabization, there are now relatively few Maghrebis who learned French from the French; it would therefore be interesting to see if these distinctions are still significant for the younger generation today.

The possibility of a gender difference suggested by the tendency to favor the male but not the female speaker's Tunisian Arabic guise over all the others also needs further examination. However, caution is certainly needed in attributing differences of judgment solely to a contrast of language, for, as Bentahila's (1983) and Belazi's (1991) results suggested, perceptions might depend on not only the language used, but also on the particular dialect or accent featured in the guise. This may evoke varying reactions in the judges (whose own background may prove relevant here). Ultimately, we must recognize that an artificial situation where people are asked to evaluate an individual's personality solely based on the way s/he speaks may well elicit stereotyped or even caricatural judgments, which would not be made in a real-life situation. Further investigation is therefore needed before anything more than tentative comments can be made.

Conclusion

The survey offered here has perhaps served more to illustrate the difficulty of making firm pronouncements about language attitudes than to present a clear picture of the situation in the Maghreb over the last few decades. Our conclusions therefore include several caveats. It is important to avoid sweeping generalizations about attitudes, for these may be highly context-dependent, influenced by a number of separate factors; attempts to identify neat patterns all too often lead to oversimplification. It is essential to recognize the difference between public pronouncements and private feelings, between accepted ideologies and individual interests. The symbolic values attached to Arabic, the colonialist overtones clinging to French may be proclaimed in debate; but they may ultimately have very little to do with the individual's covert attitudes to the languages. People are capable of holding contrasting or even apparently contradictory attitudes to language issues and their behavior and declarations cannot always be taken as evidence for their attitudes.

Language attitudes in the Maghreb are a function of many factors. Some aspects of the situation have been affected by centuries of cultural heritage, some by deliberate internal language planning policies, and some by globalized trends such as developments in communication technology. The last fifty years have seen many fluctuations in the roles and perceptions of the various languages, and more changes seem to be on the way. The home language of isolated rural communities is suddenly being promoted as a national language; the hated language of the colonizers is perhaps more of an asset than ever before in a fiercely competitive job market. The reviled colloquial variety is invading the sphere of public writing; and representing Arabic using the Roman alphabet no longer seems to be a taboo. It remains to be seen what impact other factors, such as higher literacy rates, shifting political allegiances, changes in international relations and greater democracy, may have upon this language scene in the coming years. What is clear is that current language attitudes in the Maghreb offer many very interesting avenues of research.

References

Abu Haidar, F. (1994).Language and loyalty: The case of Algerian immigrants' children in France. In Y. Suleiman (Ed.), *Arabic sociolinguistics: Issues and perspectives* (pp. 43–56). Richmond, UK: Curzon Press.

Abu Haidar, F. (2000). Arabization in Algeria. *International Journal of Francophone Studies, 3,* 151–163.

Armitage, A. (2000). The debate over literary writing in a foreign language: An overview of francophonie in the Maghreb. *Alif: Journal of Comparative Poetics, 20,* 39–67.

Atifi, H. (2003). La variation culturelle dans les communications en ligne: Analyse ethnographique des forums de discussion marocains. *Langage et Société, 104,* 57–89.

Bektache, M. (2009) Contact de langues: Entre compétition des langues et enjeux interculturels à l'Université de Béjaia. *Synergies Algérie, 8,* 91–105.

Belazi, H. M. (1991). *Multilingualism in Tunisia and French/Arabic code-switching among educated Tunisian bilinguals.* Doctoral dissertation. Ithaca, NY: Cornell University Press.

Belnap, R. K., & Bishop, B. (2003).Arabic personal correspondence: A window on change in progress? *International. Journal of the Sociology of Language, 163,* 9–25.

Benrabah, M. (2004). Language and politics in Algeria. *Nationalism and Ethnic Politics,10,* 59–78.

Benrabah, M. (2007).Language maintenance and spread: French in Algeria. *International Journal of Francophone Studies, 10,* 193–215.

Bentahila, A. (1983). *Language attitudes among Arabic-French bilinguals in Morocco.* Clevedon, UK: Multilingual Matters.

Bentahila, A., & Davies, E. E. (1989). On mother and other tongues: The notion of possession of a language. *Lingua, 78,* 155–181.

Bentahila, A., & Davies, E. E. (1992). Convergence and divergence: Two cases of language shift in Morocco. In W. Fase, K. Jaspaert, & S. Kroon (Eds.), *Maintenance and loss of minority languages* (pp. 197–210). Amsterdam: John Benjamins.

Bentahila, A., & Davies, E. E. (2002). Language mixing in rai music: Localization or globalization? *Language and Communication, 22,* 187–207.

Bentahila, A., Davies, E. E., & Owens, J. (forthcoming). Codeswitching and related issues involving Arabic. In J. Owens (Ed.), *Oxford handbook of Arabic linguistics.* Oxford, UK: Oxford University Press.

Berger, A. E. (1998). Algeria in other(s)' languages: Toward a rethinking of Algeria's linguistic predicament. *Parallax,4,* 43–46.

Boumens, L., & Caubet, D. (2000). Modelling intrasentential codeswitching: A comparative study of Algerian/French in Algeria and Moroccan/Dutch in the Netherlands. In J. Owens (Ed.), *Arabic as a minority language* (pp. 113–180). Berlin: Mouton de Gruyter.

Brahimi, F., & Owens, J. (2000).Language legitimization: Arabic in multiethnic contexts. In J. Owens (Ed.), *Arabic as a minority language* (pp. 405–446). Berlin: Mouton de Gruyter.

Coffman, J. M. (1992). *Arabization and Islamization in the Algerian university.* Doctoral dissertation. Stanford, CA: Stanford University Press.

Daniel, M. C., & Ball, A. (2010). The Moroccan educational context: Evolving multilingualism. *International Journal of Educational Development, 30,* 130–135.

Davies, E. E., & Bentahila, A. (2006). Code switching and the globalization of popular music: The case of North African rai and rap. *Multilingua, 25,* 367–392.

Davies, E. E., & Bentahila, A. (2008). Code-switching as a poetic device: Examples from rai lyrics. *Language and Communication, 28,* 1–20.

Déjeux, J., & Mitsch, R. H. (1992). Francophone literature in the Maghreb: The problem and the possibility. *Research in African Literatures, 23,* 5–19.

Eisele, J. (2003). Myth, values, and practice in the representation of Arabic. *International Journal of the Sociology of Language, 163,* 43–59.

El Aissati, A. (2001). Ethnic identity, language shift and the Amazigh voice in Morocco and Algeria. *Race, Gender and Class, 8,* 57–69.

El Kirat El Allame, Y. (2004). *The lexical and morphological structure of the Beni Iznassen Amazigh language in a context of language loss.* Doctoral dissertion. Rabat, Morocco: Mohamed V University.

El Kirat El Allame, Y. (2007) Language shift: Amazigh. In K. Versteegh (Ed.), *Encyclopedia of Arabic language and linguistics* (Vol. 2, pp. 702–716). Leiden, The Netherlands: Brill.

Ferguson, C. (1959a). Diglossia. *Word, 15,* 325–340.

Ferguson, C. (1959b). Myths about Arabic. *Monograph Series on Languages and Linguistics 12,* 75–82. Washington, DC: Georgetown University Press.

García Sánchez, I. (2010). The politics of Arabic language education: Moroccan immigrant children's language socialization into ethnic and religious identities. *Linguistics and Education, 21,* 171–196.

Gellner, E. (1973). Introduction. In E. Gellner & G. Micaud (Eds.), *Arabs and Berbers: From tribe to nation in North Africa* (pp. 11–21). London: Duckworth.

Hoffman, K. E. (2006). Berber language ideologies, maintenance, and contraction: Gendered variation in the indigenous margins of Morocco. *Language and Communication, 26,* 144–167.

Ibrahim, Z. (2000). Myths about Arabic revisited. *Al-Arabiyya, 33,* 13–28.

Lawson, S., & Sachdev, I. (2000). Code switching in Tunisia: Attitudinal and behavioral dimensions. *Journal of Pragmatics, 32,* 144–167.

Maamouri, M. (1998). Language education and human development: Arabic diglossia and its impact on the quality of education in the Arab region. *Mediterranean Development Forum, September 3–6,* 1998, Marrakech, Morocco. Accessed 11 Nov 2011.citeseerx.ist.psu.edu/viewdoc/download?doi=10.1.1.125.

Mansouri, A. (1991). *Algeria between tradition and modernity: The question of language.* Doctoral dissertation. Albany: State University of New York.

Marley, D. (2005). From monolingualism to multilingualism: Recent changes in Moroccan language policy. In J. Cohen, K.T. McAlister, K. Rolstad, & J. MacSwan (Eds.), *ISB4: Proceedings of the 4th international symposium on bilingualism* (pp. 1487–1500). Somerville, MA: Cascadilla Press.

Miller, C. (2004) Variation and change in Arabic urban vernaculars. In M. Haak, K. Versteegh, & R. Dejong (Eds.), *Approaches to Arabic dialects: Collection of articles presented to Manfred Woidich on the occasion of his sixtieth birthday* (pp. 177–206). Amsterdam: Brill.

Nortier, J., & Dorleijn, M. (2008). A Moroccan accent in Dutch: A sociocultural style restricted to the Moroccan community? *International Journal of Bilingualism, 12,* 125–142.

Pouessel, S. (2011). Écrire la langue berbère au royaume de Mohamed VI : Les enjeux politiques et identitaires du tifinagh au Maroc. *Revue des Mondes Musulmans et de la Méditerranée.* Accessed 11 November 2011. http://remmm.revues.org/index6029.html

Rampton, B. (1995). *Crossing: Language and ethnicity among adolescents.* London: Longman.

Rampton, B. (2006). Language and ethnicity at school: Some implications from theoretical developments in sociolinguistics. *Langageetsociété, 116,* 51–71.

Rosen, L. (1973). The social and conceptual framework of Arab-Berber relations in central Morocco. In E. Gellner & G. Micaud (Eds.), *Arabs and Berbers: From tribe to nation in North Africa* (pp. 155–173). London: Duckworth.

Saad, Z. (1992). *Language planning and policy attitudes: A case study of Arabization in Algeria.* Doctoral dissertation. New York: Columbia University Teachers College.

Said, E. W. (2002). Living in Arabic. *Raritan, 21,* 220–236.

Salmi, J. (1987). Language and schooling in Morocco. *Educational Development 7,* 21–31.

Sayahi, L. (2005). El español en el norte de Marruecos: Historia y análisis. *Hispanic Research Journal, (6),* 195–207.

Serson, W. J. (2003). *Le rôle sociolinguistique du français au Maroc.* Master's dissertation. Ottawa: Carleton University.

Suleiman, Y. (2003). *The Arabic language and national identity.* Washington, DC: Georgetown University Press.

Suleiman, Y. (2004). *A war of words: Language and conflict in the Middle East.* Cambridge, UK: Cambridge University Press.

Tageldin, S. M. (2009). Which *qalam* for Algeria? Colonialism, liberation and language in Djebar's L'amour, la fantasia and Mustighanimi's Dhakirat al-jasad. *Comparative Literature Studies, 46,* 467–497.

UNESCO Institute of Statistics. (2009). *National adult literacy rates.* Accessed 13 March 2012. http://stats.uis.unesco.org/unesco/TableViewer/tableView.aspx?ReportId=210

Walters, K. (1996). Gender, identity, and the political economy of language: Anglophone wives in Tunisia. *Language in Society, 25,* 515–555.

Walters, K. (2003). Fergie's prescience: The changing nature of diglossia in Tunisia. *International Journal of the Sociology of Language, 163,* 77–109.

Walters, K. (2007). Language attitudes. In K. Versteegh (Ed.), *Encyclopedia of Arabic language and linguistics* (Vol. 2, pp. 650–664). Leiden, the Netherlands: Brill.

Yaghan, M. A. (2008). "Arabizi": A contemporary style of Arabic slang. *Design Issues, 24,* 39–52.

CHAPTER SIX

Language Attitudes in Southern Africa

DESMOND PAINTER & JOHN DIXON

St. Clair (1982) observed that in order to understand current language attitudes we must '...reach back into the past and investigate the social and political forces operating within the history of a nation.' In this vein, we begin by noting that language has long acted as a significant marker of difference and domination in southern Africa. Indeed, it has assumed a central position alongside race, ethnicity, class, nationality and gender in the sociopolitical history of the region. However, language has also been more than simply one element among others in the colonial index of human differences. Political differentiation and mobilization in southern Africa has often placed language in *constitutive* relationships with other components of colonial boundary drawing and subjectification, such as 'race' and 'ethnicity'.

Indeed, colonial encounters have always and everywhere relied heavily on language as both a dimension of the definition of otherness and, importantly, as an instrument of rule. The study, mastery and management of indigenous languages came to play an important epistemological as well as political role in most colonial societies (Cohn, 1996; Errington, 2008; Gilmour, 2006). The story of southern Africa, from colonialism to apartheid and beyond, could thus easily be told from the vantage point of linguistic difference and differentiation. Such a language history of the region would be a story of misunderstanding and translation, of language hierarchies, shift and attrition; in other words, a story about how language was affected by colonial encounters. It would also be a story of linguistic nationalisms, racializing language ideologies and, in these early decades of the twenty-first century, of radical linguistic diversity and emerging struggles over language rights in new polities; a story, in short, of how language has affected politics, identities and social relations during and after colonialism. Significantly, indigenous languages in southern African countries have remained both numerically prevalent and ethnolinguistically 'vital' (cf. Giles & Johnson, 1981). At the same time, however, the erstwhile colonial languages remain politically and economically hegemonic; that is, they still function as languages of power, status, aspiration and upward mobility (Mazrui & Mazrui, 1998).

It is against this complex sociopolitical background that we assess the development and current state of the study of language attitudes in southern Africa in this chapter. Although a comparatively under developed area of inquiry, research on language attitudes in the region has accumulated steadily since the 1970s. The majority of research has been conducted by social psychologists and sociolinguists based in the Republic of South Africa; however, in recent years, important work has also emerged within a number of other southern African societies. Our emphasis here, however, will at times seem biased in favor of developments in South Africa. The reason for this is straightforward, reflecting the distribution of social science production in the region and our own greater familiarity with developments in this particular country.

The chapter has three objectives. First, we discuss how language attitudes have been ideologically intertwined with a variety of political projects in southern Africa, ranging from colonial rule to the racial divisions of the apartheid state to the contradictions of postcolonial transformation. Second, we review the broad interdisciplinary field of language attitude research in Southern Africa, outlining its central research objectives and priorities, assumptions about the nature of ethnolinguistic landscapes and subjectivities, methodological perspectives, and key findings. In so doing, we show how the study of language attitudes has functioned as a critical lens through which to view problems of ethnic and racial discrimination. Finally, looking to the future, we outline some ways in which research on language attitudes might be developed in order to capture the complex, rapidly changing, ethnolinguistic contexts of post-apartheid society.

Language and Politics in Southern Africa: Situating Language Attitudes

Although the study of language attitudes was only systematized as an area of social science enquiry as recently as the early 1960s (Bradac, Cargile, & Hallett, 2001), human societies have always ascribed meaning and value to linguistic differences—to how speech patterns within and between social groups differ and what these differences might signify. An obvious example is the word 'barbarian', derived from the Ancient Greek word 'barbaros', which is said to have an onomatopoetic origin (Joseph, 2004). This word negatively represented the *sound* of the foreigner's speech, which was portrayed as devoid of communicative sense and animalized in order to regulate those who used such speech beyond the threshold of the human. The word came to be used more generally in many languages to indicate lack of civilization.

This is the case also in southern Africa, where expressions of what today would be called language attitudes are as old as the colonial record itself. When Portuguese sailors first rounded the Cape, and encountered the local Khoikhoi, they described the indigenous languages in harsh, often dehumanizing terms. In fact, representations of Khoikhoi and other indigenous languages became a regular feature of writing about the Cape from the early sixteenth century onwards. John Davys commented, as early as 1598, that 'their words are for the most part inarticulate, and, in speaking, they clocke with the Tongue like a brood Hen, which clocking and the words are both pronounced together, verie strangely' (as cited in Gilmour, 2006, p. 16). John Milward offered a very similar 'observation' in 1614: 'These people are most miserable, destitute of religion in any kind, as farre as we can perceive, and of all civility; their speech is a chattering rather than language' (p. 15). In 1634, the traveler Thomas Herbert described Khoikhoi languages as 'rather apishly than articulately sounded' (p. 16); and in 1694, Jean-Baptiste Tavernier wrote: 'when they speak they fart with their tongues in their mouths' (as cited in Mostert, 1992, p. 67).

This pattern of representation of linguistic difference was not restricted to the Khoikhoi or, for that matter, to southern Africa. The denigration of indigenous, non-European languages became a pervasive feature of colonial discourse and a significant ingredient in the denigration of indigenous peoples as such. During the eighteenth and early nineteenth centuries, through the labor of comparative philologists, anthropologists and missionaries, the study of language directly contributed to the objectification of the idea of humanity into an abstract scientific category. At the same time, however, through the study language origins and the demarcation of families of language, it supported the construction of taxonomies of increasingly naturalized kinds within the broader category of the human. In other words, language prepared the ground for and occupied the position biology would later play in theories of race and the development of scientific racism: it was conceived as the decodable record, the 'DNA' as it were, that defined humanity as a category whilst also revealing its internal differentiations and hierarchies of development. Importantly, recent studies in the history of scientific racism confirm that early observations of southern African indigenous peoples played a significant role in the overall development of a European discourse of race (Hudson, 2004).

It is unsurprising, then, that critiques of colonialism often highlight language ideologies and communicative practices. Frantz Fanon, for example, 'ascribes a basic importance to the phenomenon of language' (2008, p. 8). He gives three reasons for this emphasis, all of which are crucial for a historical contextualization of the study of contemporary language attitudes in postcolonial settings. The first concerns the linguistic *consequences* of colonial racism: indigenous languages were viewed through racist lenses and thus became objects of contempt. The second concerns the linguistic *dimensions* of colonial racism. Unlike other cultural attributes that were subjected to racist devaluation (e.g., dress and religious beliefs) language mediated encounters between colonizer and colonized and thus became a principal site for the enactment of processes of misrecognition and dehumanization. The third concerns the status afforded European languages in the colonies. More than simply languages of administration and power, European languages became the yardsticks of 'civilization', for as Fanon recognised (p. 8), the colonial subject 'will be proportionately whiter—that is, he will come closer to being a real human being—in direct ratio to his mastery of the [colonial] language.'

> Every colonized people—in other words, every people in whose soul an inferiority complex has been created by the death and burial of its local cultural originality—finds itself face to face with the language of the civilizing nation; that is, with the culture of the mother country. The colonized is elevated above his jungle status in proportion to his adoption of the mother country's cultural standards. He becomes whiter as he renounces his blackness.... (Fanon, 2008, p. 9)

In other words, for Fanon, as for Aimé Césaire, Steve Biko and other critics of colonialism, indigenous populations were not only subjected to material domination, but also to the psychological effects of cultural alienation as well (Hook, 2004). The pervasiveness of negative European representations of colonial subjects and indigenous cultural practices fuelled feelings of cultural inferiority and affected social aspirations within the colony. This, in turn, had profound consequences for the development of colonial and postcolonial language attitudes and practices. On the one hand, the loss of language amounts to a loss of conceptual power; that is, of the power to name and define oneself and the world. In this regard, 'loss' does need not be taken literally: it is enough for indigenous languages to be devalued to the point where negative ideas about their nature and utility become a pervasive ideology and become internalized by its speakers. On the other hand, the adoption of European languages by colonial subjects can be seen as a practical necessity that in time assumed a psychological dimension. Languages such as French and English were perceived to offer more than mere social mobility; they held out the promise of cultural salvation, which, as Fanon (2008) pointed out, took the form of an alleviation of *blackness*.

However, this was almost always a false promise. To some extent, of course, by crossing the 'soft' boundaries of language some individuals were able also to cross the 'hard' boundaries of power and status (c.f. Banks, 1987). However, European languages remained codified in terms of race and class, and the social mobility they offered was always limited (Djité, 2008; Mazrui & Mazrui, 1998). Racial discrimination was not annulled by language accommodation but instead reproduced, in finer grained forms, via the stigmatization of black accents. The European language thus became another site where difference could be registered and targeted by discriminatory practices. Furthermore, indigenous languages were not simply disregarded in the colonial societies of southern Africa. On the contrary, they were often incorporated into colonial strategies of rule, and thus became essential components of the governmental rationalities according to which colonial subjects were rendered visible and could be codified, demarcated, divided, managed and addressed as learners, laborers, ethnic and racial subjects within the colonial setup. In fact, the reduction of colonial speech continua to the abstract categories of languages (standardized written forms) in southern Africa never simply represented existing ethnolinguistic landscapes and identities. Languages and ethnicities were 'invented' by missionaries and colonial linguists in southern Africa, and corroborated through the creation of literary cultures and publics, generally in the interests of various forms and phases of Western influence and domination (Harries, 1995; Makoni, 1994).

This was especially true in the case of apartheid South Africa. According to Alexander and Heugh (2001, p. 19): 'Apartheid language policy, like apartheid policy generally, was calculated to bring about and entrench divisions among black people and their total subjugation....' Apartheid, in other words, not only defined, imposed and regulated a division between white and black, but also differentiated between different categories of black—and it did this primarily in terms of 'ethnicity' (Worden, 1994). Ethnicity, in turn, could most precisely be defined in relation to *language*. Apartheid thus incorporated the language categories established during the colonial era into an ideological vision of parallel ethnolinguistic nationalisms (Alexander, 2002). Indeed, in the words of the so-called 'architect of apartheid', the early apartheid era prime minister H.F. Verwoerd, 'Africans who speak different languages must live in separate quarters...' (as cited in Alexander, 1989, p. 21). The notion of the 'mother tongue' was thus given an ideological value in apartheid South Africa, which was similar to but also deepened the colonial pattern evident in the rest of southern Africa. Indeed, many considered the apartheid state's promotion of indigenous languages as media of instruction in schools, for example, as 'an attempt to retribalize black South Africans' (Reagan, 2002, p. 422).

Consequently, colonial and apartheid language politics has had a significant impact on attitudes towards both colonial and indigenous languages in the region. Critics like Ngũgĩ wa Thiong'o (1986) may have advocated the inversion of colonial language relations and considered the empowerment of indigenous language as essential for 'decolonizing the mind', but for many others indigenous languages had been tainted by their incorporation into colonial strategies of subjectification and rule. These languages, too, could be seen as instruments of cultural alienation; as colonial constructs that needed to be 'disinvented' instead of uncritically embraced (Makoni & Pennycook, 2004). Indeed, political elites in southern Africa frequently favored the former colonial languages as official instruments of postcolonial nation building (Djité, 2008). Accepting the hegemony of European languages in this manner may have reflected elite class interests and lubricated neocolonial relations between the new states and their erstwhile colonial masters (Mazrui, 1997). Yet European languages were also considered by some as ethnically neutral enough to defuse intergroup tensions and consolidate political community.

In South Africa, for example, English was regarded by many in the liberation struggle as an 'unmarked code for intercultural and interethnic communication' (Kamwangamalu, 2001, p. 87)—the almost obvious vehicle for black solidarity, transcendence of apartheid ethnic divisions, and post-apartheid nation-building (Alexander, 1989; Ridge, 2000). It also, increasingly, became the symbol of economic mobility; and, in recent years, of the particular expressions of subjectivity and social aspiration associated with neoliberal globalization:

> English became all the more desirable, seen by many as the magic key to socio-economic advancement and power. In contrast, indigenous languages were regarded by many of their own speakers as worthless because of their functional limitations with regard to access to participation and mobility in wider society. (De Klerk, 1999, p. 312)

The high status of English—not only economically but politically as well—in South Africa has further been bolstered by the association of apartheid with the Afrikaans language (Van Rensburg, 1999). Whereas Afrikaans was increasingly perceived during the twentieth century as the language of Afrikaner Nationalism, apartheid bureaucracy and police brutality, English became associated with liberal values, social mobility and internationalization (Kamwangamalu, 2002). However, ironically, the political ascendancy of Afrikaans during the apartheid era was itself achieved via collective resistance to imperial aggression. Afrikaner nationalism developed partly in response to the Anglicization of the Cape Colony and imperial British interventions in the Boer Republics, Transvaal and Orange Free State, during the late nineteenth century (Giliomee, 2004). At the time, Afrikaans was considered little more than a crude, lowly patois, hardly the vehicle of a powerful form of settler nationalism. Consider the following description in the *Cape Monitor* in 1875:

Afrikaans cramps your thoughts. It impedes your energies. It brings the blush to every modest woman's cheeks and makes the educated recoil with disgust too often. It corrupts the morals of your children and befouls their innocent expressions. (As cited in Beukes, 2007, p. 248)

Interestingly enough, such negative, often racialized, perceptions of Afrikaans were not restricted to the English elite. It was also shared by early Afrikaner political leaders, many of whom considered the language nothing more than a lowly derivative of Dutch. It was only on the back of successive language movements and much agitation by Afrikaner ethnic entrepreneurs that Afrikaans was embraced as a symbol of the emergent white nationalism and a means of white social mobility (Giliomee, 2004). The development of Afrikaans institutions, dictionaries and literature elevated the language to an essential component of the political economy and cultural politics of Afrikaner nationalism. Apartheid South Africa became a bilingual state, and eventually Afrikaans was also enforced as a language of instruction at black schools. The latter policy led directly to the Soweto youth uprisings in 1976 and a hardening of negative perceptions about Afrikaans, especially amongst black South Africans (De Klerk, 2002).

In order to become such an important ideological component of Afrikaner nationalism and white subjectivity in South Africa, the origins of Afrikaans had to be distorted quite radically (Roberge, 1990). Rather than a creole language emerging from contact between settlers and indigenous peoples, official histories of Afrikaans in the twentieth century had to present the language as 'racially pure'. Afrikaans had to be rehabilitated as a *white* language and the varieties spoken by colored and black communities (who still account for the majority of speakers of the language) accorded a lower status. According to Marks and Trapido (1987, p. 17) 'purged of its lower class and "Colored" associations', Afrikaans could become a symbol of a modernizing Afrikaner identity. Esterhuyse (1986), for example, studied the ideological representation of colored varieties of Afrikaans in language textbooks used in South African schools during the apartheid era. His study revealed a denial of the creole origins of Afrikaans, as well as the pervasive inferiorization (and frequently infantalization) of colored varieties of the language.

In recent years, Afrikaans language activists in South Africa have responded to the perceived loss of status of Afrikaans in a post-apartheid context where 11 languages have official status, but where English is becoming increasingly hegemonic (Louw, 2004). Such activism is sometimes regarded as a neo-nationalist attempt on the part of white Afrikaner elites to bolster their cultural and economic power, especially in institutions such as universities (Kriel, 2006). However, there are also indications that Afrikaans is being appropriated by colored language and social activists, a process which seems to challenge the historical relationship between Afrikaans and whiteness (Webb, 2010).

Language activism on behalf of indigenous African languages has been less visible than in the case of Afrikaans, but is certainly not insignificant. Unlike Afrikaans, however, African language activism is not aimed at maintaining linguistic privilege, but to urge government and speakers of African languages to empower languages that have historically been underdeveloped. One can expect debates about the status of African languages to become increasingly important sites of struggles over class, culture, national identity, and the meaning of modernization in South Africa and other southern African countries.

Studying Language Attitudes in Southern Africa

In the preceding sections, we have argued that language has played a significant political role during the history of colonialism in general and in southern Africa in particular. We have also highlighted some of the consequences of colonial language practices, especially in relation to definitions and performances of race and racism, for intergroup relations and social mobility in postcolonial societies. Language is certainly an abiding issue in these societies—not simply due to the administrative demands of language policy and planning in multilingual settings, but also because of the role it has played in the reproduction of colonial identities, relationships, and patterns of inequality.

Given this, the social psychology of language is a surprisingly underdeveloped field of study in southern Africa. Existing research has originated mainly in the Republic of South Africa, yielding a small, relatively fragmented, literature (Louw-Potgieter, 1991; Painter, 2006) that rather lacks in theoretical coherence or sustained areas of specialization. There is, however, a growing body of southern African work emerging in neighboring disciplines, including sociolinguistics, the sociology of language, applied linguistics and education studies. Researchers in these fields increasingly pay attention to the social psychological significance of language in the management of intergroup relations, the negotiation of racial, ethnic and class identities, and the reproduction of social inequalities. In this regard, the social psychological concept of language attitudes has been fruitfully employed in a variety of research programmes.

Making Sense of the Accented Other

Internationally, the empirical study and theoretical refinement of language attitudes, which could be defined as 'the perceptual and attitudinal significance of details of language' (Sanders, 2005, p. 177), maintains its central position in the social psychology of language and adjacent disciplines (e.g., Bayard, Weatherall, Gallois, & Pittam, 2001; Bradac & Giles, 2005). The study of accent evaluation, in particular, has highlighted the pernicious nature of class, ethnic and racial stereotyping across diverse societies, revealing how speech characteristics may mark category distinctions and facilitate a negative evaluation of speakers who use non-standard language forms (e.g., Bishop, Coupland, & Garrett, 2005; Coupland & Bishop, 2007; Dixon & Mahoney, 2004). Indeed, according to Bradac and Giles (2005, p. 208), 'the study of attitudes toward accents and dialects and the attendant judgments of speakers who use them is the most enduring topic in the language-attitudes research tradition.'

Relatively few studies of accent evaluation have been conducted in southern Africa. In one of the earliest, Vorster and Proctor (1976) investigated black attitudes to 'white languages' (English and Afrikaans) and their speakers in South Africa. Using the matched guise technique, Vorster and Proctor asked Xhosa-speakers to rate white Afrikaans- and English-speaking South Africans on a number of variables. They found that English was judged more favorably than Afrikaans as a language, and that English-speakers were perceived as better looking, of a higher social standing, and friendlier than Afrikaans-speakers. Dixon, Tredoux, Durrheim, and Foster (1994), asked white, English-speaking South African students to make attributions of guilt after hearing a recording of a colored Afrikaans-speaking criminal suspect being interrogated by a white English-speaker. In this study, suspects who converged to English were rated as significantly less guilty than those who diverged to the Cape Afrikaans dialect. They also found that suspects accused of blue-collar crimes were more often considered guilty than those accused of white-collar crimes.

Tarnished by History? Attitudes Towards Afrikaans

Both of the abovementioned studies reveal the stigmatization of Afrikaans, especially in relation to more favorable perceptions of English, but in contrasting ideological contexts. In Vorster and Proctor's (1976) study, conducted at a time of mounting black resistance to Afrikaner rule, Afrikaans was clearly associated by blacks with white power and racism. In Dixon et al.'s (1994) study, by contrast, a non-standard variety of Afrikaans was used as the basis of racial and class discrimination. In other words, the studies reveal how different varieties and accents of Afrikaans have different 'ideological values' (cf. Coupland & Bishop, 2007).

Unfortunately, we do not know if black attitudes towards Afrikaans have changed significantly since the demise of apartheid or indeed, if the ideological values associated with different speech styles *within* the broader Afrikaans speech community have shifted. These are areas that require further research. Anecdotal evidence suggests a destigmatization of all varieties of Afrikaans. In the post-apartheid era, much emphasis has been placed on the deracialization of the language and the need to forge an inclusive Afrikaans speech community (Webb, 2010). However, whether or not this is the case and whether or not it reflects a significant repositioning of different varieties of Afrikaans in relation to race, ethnicity and class remains to be seen. Our own view is that Afrikaans may well be regarded more positively now that the language has lost much of its political and administrative functions, but this also means that non-Afrikaans speakers increasingly view the language less favorably as a language of learning and teaching at schools and universities (Van der Walt, 2006; Verhoef & Venter, 2008). Furthermore, even though Afrikaans still has important identity functions for significant numbers of especially working class and rural colored Afrikaans-speakers, this does not always translate into identification with white Afrikaans speakers. As a respondent in a qualitative study by Dyers (2008, p. 52; see also Dyers, 2004) expresses it: 'We don't actually speak proper Afrikaans. We speak Cape Afrikaans, a mixture of English and Afrikaans.'

In the Shadow of English? Attitudes Towards Indigenous African Languages

Attitudes towards indigenous African languages are equally complex and equally in need of further research. In their studies of language attitudes in the Eastern Cape province of South Africa, De Klerk and Bosch (1993, 1994) used the matched guise technique to explore Xhosa-speakers' evaluations of the languages and speech styles of a region in which Xhosa, English and Afrikaans are all widely spoken. Their participants rated Xhosa more favorably when it was spoken in a Xhosa accent than when it was spoken in English or Afrikaans accents. Rated as languages, however, both English and (surprisingly) Afrikaans were evaluated more positively than Xhosa. A similar pattern has emerged in research conducted in schools and tertiary institutions in South Africa, which suggests that black South African students favor English over African languages as media of learning and teaching (Aziakpono & Bekker, 2010; Bangeni & Kapp, 2007; Dalvit & De Klerk, 2005; Moodley, 2010; Van der Walt, 2006). Ngidi (2007) argued that this preference for English is frequently based on social aspirations: 'Learning isiZulu will not give a highly paid job because these days you need to speak English if you want a highly paid job' (p. 119).

However, it remains a matter of some debate whether the privileging of English over African languages is driven by purely pragmatic interests or whether it results from a devaluation of these languages by their own speakers. In a study of attitudes towards African languages as media of learning and teaching amongst Xhosa-speakers in Grahamstown, South Africa, De Klerk (2000) found that her (mostly middleclass) participants were all motivated to send their children to English medium schools. Whilst parents generally gave pragmatic reasons for choosing English, such as economic benefits and better equipped English schools, the study also revealed negative evaluations of African languages as such. Quite a number of respondents felt that Xhosa had no future role in South Africa and that it would eventually die out. Others saw it as a language that might survive in private domains, but would lose its public and institutional currency.

At the same time, other researchers suggest that the utilitarian choice for English is context-specific and that African languages retain value as markers of identity and media of social intercourse. Finchelescu and Nyawose (1998), for example, analyzed a focus group discussion with Zulu students in the Western Cape about their perceptions of the post-apartheid South African language policy. Although English was positively regarded as a national language and a language of economic opportunity, Zulu was strongly embraced as a symbol of cultural identity and belonging. In this regard, Dyers (2008) suggested that language shift towards English is more marked in middle-class, upwardly mobile black and mixed-race families than in working class, rural communities, where communal ties and ethnic identities are typically stronger. De Kadt (2005) likewise showed how different groups of Zulu speakers invest the language with different identity values and use it for various forms of intra-group distinction. Furthermore, a recent study of language attitudes and practices in multilingual schools indicated that the use of "African languages by learners enables them to insert new identities into this space and interrupt the exclusive power of English" (Ndlangamandla, 2010, p. 61).

Friend or Foe? The Complexities of Attitudes Towards English

Although English as such is generally accorded positive values, especially in relation to its perceived facilitation of nation building, modernization and economic mobility (e.g., Makalela, 2004; Smit, 1996), this does not mean all varieties of English are valued equally. Far too little research has been conducted in southern Africa on the ideological values of different English varieties and speech styles. In this regard we concur with Wiebesiek, Rudwick, and Zeller (2011): 'A promising possibility for future research is an examination of the positioning of different varieties of English in a context of increasing deracialization in many facets of life in South Africa.' Of course, it would be equally relevant to explore the positioning of English (along with the other languages) in relation to *continuing* practices of racialization. Wiebesiek, Rudwick, and Zeller researched attitudes towards 'Indian English' in South Africa. In their study, young, educated Indian South Africans acknowledged the existence of an Indian variety and role it plays within the Indian community, but distanced themselves from its use. Moodley (2010), in turn, studied black South African attitudes towards Indian English. The Indian variety was likewise judged negatively, and significantly, it was done so by invoking an explicitly *white* standard. As one participant in this qualitative study noted: 'they use words incorrectly, like "come quickly quickly." White people don't do this' (p. 118). Furthermore, the research suggested that speaking the Indian variety may expose one to discrimination: 'Even the lecturers, Indian lecturers, they speak faster than English speakers, so they confuse us, and we chose to have white English speaking lecturers rather than Indian, because we don't understand Indian lecturers' (p. 118).

Smit and Verhoef (2003) explored black teachers' attitudes towards black varieties of English in South African classrooms. They set out to determine whether assessments of the quality of a student writing task would be affected by the variety of English the work was presented in, but their findings were inconclusive. One of the reasons for this may be that so-called 'Black South African English' (BSAE), which is by far the most widely spoken form of English in South Africa today, is increasingly becoming a high status variety—at least in the self-assessment of black speakers (Smit & Verhoef, 2003). Indeed, in their matched guise studies, Van Rooy, Van Rooyen, and Van Wyk (2000) and Coetzee-Van Rooy and Van Rooy (2005) found that the majority of their black participants evaluated BSAE more positively even than varieties of 'white South African English.' In this respect, Parmegiani's (2008, 2010) work on the extent to which non-native speakers of English claim *ownership* of the language is significant. These studies demonstrated that a significant number of black speakers perceive English as their own language and no longer as a colonial or imperial language imposed from the outside. This shift is both psychologically and politically significant: 'Given the extent to which English functions as a gate-keeper to symbolic and material resources, seeing the legitimate ownership of English as the exclusive prerogative of a certain group is a way to maintain the linguistic effect of this language' (Parmegiani, 2010, p. 360). In other words, the 'decolonization' of colonial language relations can also be achieved through the active *appropriation* of English.

From Attitudes to Discursive and Ideological Practices: Language Evaluation in Action

The concept of language attitudes has undeniably contributed to the study of language in society. However, even though the study of language attitudes by now reaches far beyond the confines of any one discipline, it arguably retains a number of problematic assumptions associated with mainstream social psychology. Attitudes are generally theorized in social psychology as mental structures located 'in the heads' of individuals. As such, language attitudes reflect individual evaluations of independently existing sociolinguistic facts (e.g., languages, dialects, and accents). Mainstream social psychology considers neither individual language attitudes nor the sociolinguistic phenomena these attitudes index as historically and discursively mediated. It is this deeply engrained combination of 'mentalism' and 'naïve realism' that has led Blackledge and Pavlenko (2004) to argue that social psychology tends to oversimplify real-life sociolinguistic contexts: 'As a result, they reduced diverse contexts to a few ad hoc dimensions and ignored power relations and complex sociopolitical, socioeconomic, and sociocultural factors which shaped interactions between various groups in multilingual societies' (p. 6).

According to these authors, the language attitudes tradition can thus be criticized for reifying what are in fact variable, situational and dialogical processes of evaluation into abstract, static, and above all individualistically conceived psychological structures. It treats that which is in fact a *dimension* of discursive action (e.g., expressing an evaluative judgment) as if it is an underlying *cause* of such action. Furthermore, by treating historically mediated sociolinguistic realities as unproblematically given, the social psychology of language risks obscuring vital dimensions of the political constitution of (especially colonial) language orders and practices. In order to fully acknowledge the contextual dynamics and historical specificities of sociolinguistic phenomena and processes in southern Africa, we therefore need to move the study of language attitudes beyond individualism and mere descriptivism. More specifically, we need to conceptualize language attitudes as social and ideological to the core; that is, as action-oriented rhetorical performances that are ideologically effective within historically mediated social interactions (for a reformulation of attitudes in terms of discursive action, see Durrheim & Dixon, 2006).

Some emerging work conducted in South Africa should be mentioned in this regard. In a study located in the tradition of discursive psychology, for instance, Painter and Baldwin (2004), treated language attitudes as rhetorical performances mediated by as well as reproductive of language ideologies in post-apartheid South Africa (on language ideologies, see Kroskity, 2004; also Dragojevic, Giles, & Watson, this volume). They showed how evaluations of language in a multiracial and multilingual school in South Africa were designed to defend and reproduce white privilege and public space. Importantly, even *positive* attitudes towards African languages were rhetorically mobilized against challenges to the linguistic status quo.

Similarly, Rudwick (2008) studied situated evaluations of English and Zulu in a South African township. In her study, such evaluations were articulated by participants within discursive and ideological process of manufacturing and contesting social categories and doing complex identity work. Finally, Makubalo (2007) and McKinney (2007), in their studies of identity construction among young black people in South African schools, explored the variable construction of English in relation to race. They demonstrated that English and other languages are not stable 'attitudinal objects', but are instead discursively constructed, often in contradictory ways, in relation to construction of self and others and the perceived normative requirements of a social context.

Conclusion

We began this chapter by echoing St. Clair's injunction that researchers need to reach deep into their local histories, cultures and politics if they want to understand current language attitudes. The history of southern Africa provides a stark reminder of why this is so. It is a history that reveals the complexities, contradictions and ironies of the wider contextual dynamics that now shape local 'prejudices' both for and against particular speech styles. It also demonstrates the importance of moving beyond standard methods and concepts in the study of language attitudes in order to investigate the *ideological practices* through which, over time, particular languages, dialects and accents become imbued with political significance or institutionalized as the normative ideal against which variations are judged.

In conclusion, we wish to outline three possible directions for future research. To begin with, researchers need to study more directly the social and institutional practices through which particular speech variations are accorded meaning and significance, and in turn, become incorporated within wider ideological struggles. On one level, this requires a shift in the object of research: that is, a new focus on *evaluative practices* within everyday settings (as opposed to contextually abstracted attitudes located 'in the heads' of listeners). On another level, it requires a critical awareness of the broader socio-political functions and implications of such practices. As demonstrated in the previous section, the work of Painter and Baldwin (2004), Makubalo (2007), Mckinney (2007), and Rudwick (2008), illustrates the possibilities of this kind of approach. We also note here that wider developments in discursive psychology, discourse studies, and critical discourse analysis offer an array of concepts and tools that have yet to be applied fully in the area of language attitudes.

As a second recommendation, we suggest that researchers might revisit the role of language ideologies within processes of dehumanization. As we have elaborated in this chapter, historical records of early transactions between white settlers and indigenous southern Africans revealed that language was often used to signify the animalistic nature of the latter. Although crude analogies of the kind deployed by white missionaries no longer remain in widespread use, we believe that dehumanizing attributions continue to pervade representations of linguistic variation, operating in a variety of more subtle and insidious ways. Recent social psychological work provides some clues about the potential nature of such representations (for reviews see Haslam, 2006; Leyens et al., 2007). Research on the process of *infra-humanization*, for example, indicates how dehumanization may occur not only through overt comparisons between people and animals, but also through covert denials of the so-called 'uniquely human' attributes of others, including their capacity to experience complex secondary emotions such as nostalgia, remorse, hope and pity (see, for example, Leyens et al., 2001). Similarly, dehumanization may occur through implicit practices of objectification, whereby others are portrayed in subtly mechanistic terms and thus, again, deprived of full human status (Haslam, 2006). To our knowledge, the role of language attitudes and ideologies in perpetuating such associations remains largely unexplored both in southern Africa and elsewhere.

Finally, we suggest that southern African researchers may productively engage with the emerging interest in 'linguistic landscapes' in social psychology and other fields of language study (e.g., Cenoz & Gorter, 2006; Gorter, 2006). As Jones and Merriman (2009, p. 164) argue, the 'spatialization' of language may directly contribute to the organization of 'an everyday landscape of oppression'; that is, to the often invisible spatio-linguistic boundaries that render people out of place and voiceless. This is certainly very pertinent to southern Africa, where spatial segregation and the construction of ethnolinguistic difference have historically intersected. A number of recent studies on linguistic landscapes in South Africa, which focus on the restructuring of multilingual spaces, attest to the productivity of this approach (Du Plessis, 2011; Stroud & Mpeduka, 2009, 2010).

References

Alexander, N. (1989). *Language policy and national unity in South Africa/Azania*. Cape Town, South Africa: Buchu Books.
Alexander, N. (2002). *An ordinary country: Issues in the transformation from apartheid to democracy in South Africa*. Pietermaritzburg, South Africa: University of Natal Press.
Alexander, N., & Heugh, K. (2001). Language policy in South Africa. In R. Kriger & A. Zegeye (Eds.), *Culture in the New South Africa: After Apartheid—Volume 2* (pp. 15–39). Cape Town, South Africa: Kwela Books.
Aziakpono, P., & Bekker, I. (2010). The attitudes of isiXhosa-speaking students toward language of learning and teaching issues at Rhodes University, South Africa: General trends. *Southern African Linguistics and Applied Language Studies*, 28, 39–60.
Bangeni, B., & Kapp, R. (2007). Shifting language attitudes in a linguistically diverse learning environment in South Africa. *Journal of Multilingual and Multicultural Development*, 28, 253–269
Banks, S.P. (1987). Achieving unmarkedness in organizational discourse: A praxis perspective on ethnolinguistic identity. *Journal of Language and Social Psychology*, 6, 171–189.

Bayard, D., Weatherall, A, Gallois, C., & Pittam, J. (2001). Pax-Americana? Accent attitudinal evaluations in New Zealand, Australia and America. *Journal of Sociolinguistics*, 5, 22–49.

Beukes, A.-M. (2007). On language heroes and the modernizing movement of Afrikaner nationalism. *Southern African Linguistics and Applied Language Studies*, 25, 245–258.

Bishop, H., Coupland, N., & Garrett, P. (2005). Conceptual accent evaluation: Thirty years of accent prejudice in the U.K. *Acta Linguistica Havniensa*, 37, 131–154.

Blackledge, A., & Pavlenko, A. (2004). Introduction: New theoretical approaches to the study of negotiation of identities in multilingual contexts. In A. Pavlenko & A. Blackledge (Eds.), *Negotiation of identities in multilingual contexts* (pp. 1–33). Clevedon, UK: Multilingual Matters.

Bradac, J.J., Cargile, A.C., & Hallett, J.S. (2001). Language attitudes: Retrospect, conspect, and prospect. In W.P. Robinson & H. Giles (Eds.), *The new handbook of social psychology* (pp. 137–155). New York: John Wiley & Sons.

Bradac, J.J., & Giles, H. (2005). Language and social psychology: Conceptual niceties, complexities, curiosities, monstrosities, and how it all works. In K. Fitch & R. Sanders (Eds.), *Handbook of language and social interaction* (pp. 201–230). Mahwah, NJ: Erlbaum.

Cenoz, J., & Gorter, D. (2006). Linguistic landscape and minority languages. *International Journal of Multilingualism*, 3, 67–80.

Coetzee-Van Rooy, S., & Van Rooy, B. (2005). South African English: Labels, comprehensibility and status. *World Englishes*, 24, 1–19.

Cohn, B. (1996). *Colonialism and its forms of knowledge: The British in India*. Princeton, NJ: Princeton University Press.

Coupland, N., & Bishop, H. (2007). Ideologized values for British accents. *Journal of Sociolinguistics*, 11, 74–93.

Dalvit, L., & De Klerk, V. (2005). Attitudes of Xhosa-speaking students at the University of Fort Hare towards the use of Xhosa as a language of learning and teaching (LOLT). *Southern African Linguistics and Applied Language Studies*, 23, 1–18.

De Kadt, E. (2005). English, language shift and identities: a comparison between 'Zulu-dominant' and 'multicultural' students on a South African university campus. *Southern African Linguistics and Applied Language Studies*, 23, 19–37.

De Klerk, G. (2002). Mother-tongue education in South Africa: The weight of history. *International Journal of the Sociology of Language*, 154, 29–46.

De Klerk, V. (1999). Black South African English: Where to from here? *World Englishes*, 18, 311–324.

De Klerk, V. (2000). Language shift in Grahamstown: A case study of selected Xhosa-speakers. *International Journal for the Sociology of Language*, 146, 87–110.

De Klerk, V., & Bosch, B. (1993). English in South Africa: The Eastern Cape perspective. *English World-Wide*, 14, 209–229.

De Klerk, V., & Bosch, B. (1994). Language in the Eastern Cape: A trilingual study. *South African Journal of Linguistics*, 12, 50–59.

Dixon, J.A., & Mahoney, B. (2004). The effect of accent evaluation and evidence on a suspect's perceived guilt and criminality. *The Journal of Social Psychology*, 144, 63–73.

Dixon, J.A., Tredoux, C.G., Durrheim, K., & Foster, D. (1994). The role of speech accommodation and crime type in attribution of guilt. *The Journal of Social Psychology*, 134, 465–473.

Djité, P.G. (2008). *The sociolinguistics of development in Africa.* Clevedon, UK: Multilingual Matters.

Du Plessis, T. (2011). Language visibility and language removal: A South African case study in linguistic landscape change. *Communicatio: South African Journal for Communication Theory and Research, 37,* 194–224.

Durrheim, K., & Dixon, J. (2004). Attitudes in the fiber of everyday life: The discourse of evaluation and the lived experience of desegregation. *American Psychologist, 59,* 626–636.

Dyers, C. (2004). Ten years of democracy: Attitudes and identity among some South African school children. *Per Linguam, 20,* 22–35.

Dyers, C. (2008). Language shift or maintenance? Factors determining the use of Afrikaans among some township youth in South Africa. *Stellenbosch Papers in Linguistics, 38,* 49–72.

Errington, J. (2008). *Linguistics in a colonial world: A story of language, meaning, and power.* Oxford, UK: Blackwell.

Esterhuyse, J. (1986). *Taalapartheid en skoolafrikaans.* Johannesburg, South Africa: Taurus.

Fanon, F. (2008). *Black skin, white masks.* New York: Grove Press.

Finchilescu, G., & Nyawose, G. (1998). Talking about language: Zulu students' views on language in the new South Africa. *South African Journal of Psychology, 28,* 53–61.

Giles, H., & Johnson, P. (1981). The role of language in ethnic group relations. In J. C. Turner & H. Giles (Eds.), *Intergroup behavior* (pp. 199–243). Oxford, UK: Blackwell.

Giliomee, H. (2004). *The rise and possible demise of Afrikaans as public language.* Nationalism and Ethnic Politics, 10, 25–58.

Gilmour, R. (2006). *Grammars of colonialism: Representing language in colonial South Africa.* London, UK: Palgrave Macmillan.

Gorter, D. (2006). Introduction: The study of linguistic landscape as a new approach to multilingualism. *International Journal of Multilingualism, 3,* 1–6.

Harries, P. (1995). Discovering languages: the historical origins of standard Tsonga in Southern Africa. In R. Mesthrie (Ed.), *Language and social history: Studies in South African sociolinguistics* (pp. 154–175). Cape Town, South Africa: David Phillip.

Haslam, N. (2006). Dehumanization: An integrative review. *Personality and Social Psychology Review, 10,* 252–264.

Hook, D. (2004). Fanon and the psychoanalysis of racism. In D. Hook (Ed.), *Critical psychology* (pp. 115–138). Cape Town, South Africa: UCT Press.

Hudson, N. (2004). 'Hottentots' and the evolution of European racism. *Journal of European Studies, 34,* 308–332.

Jones, R., & Merriman, P. (2009). Hot, banal and everyday nationalism: Bilingual road signs in Wales. *Political Geography, 28,* 164–173.

Joseph, J.E. (2004). *Language and identity: National, ethnic, religious.* London: Palgrave Macmillan.

Kamwangamalu, N.M. (2001). The language planning situation in South Africa. *Current Issues in Language Planning, 2,* 361–445.

Kamwangamalu, N.M. (2002). The social history of English in South Africa. *World Englishes, 21,* 1–8.

Kriel, M. (2006). Fools, philologists and philosophers: Afrikaans and the politics of cultural nationalism. *Politikon: South African Journal of Political Studies, 33,* 45–70.

Kroskity, P.V. (2004). Language ideologies. In A. Duranti (Ed.), *A companion to linguistic anthropology* (pp. 496–517). Oxford, UK: Blackwell.

Leyens, J.P., Demoulin, S., Vaes, J., Gaunt, R., & Paladino, M.P. (2007). Infra-humanization: The wall of group differences. *Social Issues and Policy Review*, 1, 139–172.

Leyens, J. P., Rodriguez, A.P., Rodriguez, R.T., Gaunt, R., Paladino, P.M., Vaes, J., & Demoulin, S. (2001). Psychological essentialism and the attribution of uniquely human emotions to ingroups and outgroups. *European Journal of Social Psychology*, 31, 395–411.

Louw, P. E. (2004). Anglicizing post-Apartheid South Africa. *Journal of Multilingual and Multicultural Development*, 25, 318–332.

Louw-Potgieter, J. (1991). Language and identity. In D. Foster & J. Louw-Potgieter (Eds.), *Social psychology in South Africa* (pp. 317–341). Johannesburg, South Africa: Lexicon Publishers.

Makalela, L. (2004). Making sense of BSAE for linguistic democracy in South Africa. *World Englishes*, 23, 355–366.

Makoni, S. (1994). African languages as European scripts: The shaping of communal memory. In S. Nuttal & C. Coetzee (Eds.), *Negotiating the past: The making of memory in South Africa* (pp. 242–248). Cape Town: Oxford University Press.

Makoni, S., & Pennycook, A. (2004). Disinventing and (re)constituting language. *Critical Inquiry in Language Studies*, 2, 137–156.

Makubalo, G. (2007). 'I don't know...it contradicts': identity construction and the use of English by high school learners in a desegregated school space. *English Academy Review: Southern African Journal of English Studies*, 24, 25–41.

Marks, S., & Trapido, S. (1987). The politics of race, class and nationalism. In S. Marks & S. Trapido (Eds.), *The politics of race, class and nationalism in twentieth-century South Africa* (pp. 1–70). London, UK: Longman.

Mazrui, A. (1997). The World Bank, the language question and the future of African education. *Race and Class*, 38, 35–48.

Mazrui, A.A., & Mazrui, A.M. (1998). *The power of Babel: Language and governance in the African experience*. Oxford, UK: James Currey.

McKinney, C. (2007). 'If I speak English, does it make me less black anyway?' 'Race' and English in South African desegregated schools. *English Academy Review: Southern African Journal of English Studies*, 24, 6–24.

Moodley, D. (2010). Language accessibility and language preference gridlocked at the University of KwaZulu-Natal. *Language Matters*, 41, 214–237.

Mostert, N. (1992). *Frontiers: The epic of South Africa's creation and the tragedy of the Xhosa people*. New York: Alfred A. Knopf.

Ndlangamandla, S.C. (2010). (Unofficial) multilingualism in desegregated schools: Learners' use of and views towards African languages. *Southern African Linguistics and Applied Language Studies*, 28, 61–73.

Ngidi, S.A. (2007). *The attitudes of learners, educators and parents towards English as a language of learning and teaching (LOLT) in Mthunzini circuit*. Unpublished Master of Arts thesis, University of Zululand, South Africa.

Painter, D. (2006). Towards a social psychology of language. In K. Ratele (Ed.), *Inter-group relations: South African perspectives* (pp. 255–273). Cape Town, South Africa: Juta.

Painter, D., & Baldwin, R. (2004). 'They all speak your language anyway...': Language and racism in a South African school. *South African Journal of Psychology*, 34, 1–24.

Parmegiani, A. (2008). Language ownership in multilingual settings: Exploring attitudes among students entering the University of KwaZulu-Natal through the Access Program. *Stellenbosch Papers in Linguistics, 38*, 107–124.

Parmegiani, A. (2010). Reconceptualizing language ownership. A case study of language practices and attitudes among students at the University of KwaZulu-Natal. *The Language Learning Journal, 38*, 359–378.

Reagan, T.G. (2002). Language planning and language policy: Past, present and future. In R. Mesthrie (Ed.), *Language in South Africa* (pp. 419–433). Cambridge, UK: Cambridge University Press.

Ridge, S. (2000). Mixed motives: Ideological elements in the support for English in South Africa. In T. Ricento (Ed.), *Ideology, politics, and language policies: Focus on English* (pp. 151–172). Amsterdam: John Benjamins.

Roberge, P.T. (1990). The ideological profile of Afrikaans historical linguistics. In J.E. Joseph & T.J. Taylor (Eds.), *Ideologies of language* (pp. 131–149). London, UK: Routledge.

Rudwick, S. (2008). 'Coconuts' and 'oreos': English-speaking Zulu people in a South African township. *World Englishes, 27*, 101–116.

Sanders, R.E. (2005). Preface to section III: Language and social psychology. In K. Fitch & R. Sanders (Eds.), *Handbook of language and social interaction* (pp. 175–178). Mahwah, NJ: Erlbaum.

Smit, U. (1996). *A new English for a new South Africa? Language attitudes, language planning and education*. Vienna: Braumuller.

Smit, U., & Verhoef, M. (2003). Language attitudes and language assessment in the classroom—an applied language attitude study on Black South African English (BSAE). *Views, 12*, 61–84.

St. Clair, R.N. (1982). From social history to language attitudes. In E.B. Ryan & H. Giles (Eds.), *Attitudes towards language variation* (pp. 164–174). London: Edward Arnold.

Stroud, C., & Mpendukana, S. (2009). Towards a material ethnography of linguistic landscape: Multilingualism, mobility and space in a South African township. *Journal of Sociolinguistics, 13*, 363–386.

Stroud, C., & Mpendukana, S. (2010). Multilingual signage: A multimodal approach to discourses of consumption in a South African township. *Social Semiotics, 20*, 469–493.

Thiong'o, N.W. (1986). *Decolonizing the mind: The politics of language in African literature*. London: J. Currey.

Van der Walt, C. (2006). University students' attitudes towards and experiences of bilingual classrooms. *Current Issues in Language Planning, 7*, 359–376.

Van Rensburg, C. (1999). Afrikaans and apartheid. *International Journal for the Sociology of Language, 136*, 77–96.

Van Rooy, B., Van Rooyen, S., & Van Wyk, H. (2000). An assessment of high school pupils' attitudes towards the pronunciation of Black South African English. *South African Journal of Linguistics, Supplement 38*, 187–213.

Verhoef, M., & Venter, T.(2008). Functional multilingualism at the North-West University as part of the institution's transformation agenda. *Southern African Linguistics and Applied Language Studies, 26*, 379–392.

Vorster, J., & Proctor, L. (1976). Black attitudes to 'white' languages in South Africa: A pilot study. *The Journal of Social Psychology, 92*, 103–108.

Webb, V. (2010). Constructing an inclusive speech community from two mutually excluding ones: The third Afrikaans language movement. *Tydskrif vir Letterkunde, 47,* 106–120.

Wiebesiek, L., Rudwick, S., & Zeller, J. (2011). South African Indian English: A qualitative study of attitudes. *World Englishes, 30,* 251–268.

Worden, N. (1994). *The making of modern South Africa: Conquest, segregation and apartheid.* Oxford, UK: Blackwell.

CHAPTER SEVEN

Language Attitudes in China Toward English

ANPING HE & SIK HUNG NG

Since the arrival of English-speaking traders to southern China in the 17th century, the English language has been in China for centuries, although much of its history has been forgotten (Bolton, 2003). In more recent times, it replaced Japanese as the chief foreign language from around 1919 when Japan invaded China. Some thirty years later, it was in turn displaced by Russian following the establishment of the Chinese communist government, and partially banished from schools and public usage during the Cold War period in the midst of antipathy to the Western world, led by English-speaking America. When China reopened to the (Western) world in the 1980s, it re-embraced English and actively promoted its teaching at schools and universities. Currently, there are more than 2 billion learners of English as a foreign language (EFL) in China. Learning English at such a huge scale in modern China consumes countless hours of learner and teacher time inside and outside the classroom, and offers a case study of the educational and cultural impact of English, public response to it, and the possible development of a Chinese variety of English, all of which are still unfolding.

Consistent with the general theme of this volume on language attitudes (Dragojevic, Giles, & Watson, this volume), we review the literature on language attitudes in China toward English. In the first section below, we outline major changes in the *government's* EFL education policies to provide an historical account of official language attitudes. This account will serve as a context for grounding later discussion on the attitudes of *teachers* and *learners* as reflected in teachers' professional identity on the one hand, and learners' language motivations and self-identity on the other. This will be followed by a discussion of the attitudes of the *general public* toward English. We shall conclude with a discussion of the debate on the nativisation of English and the emergence of a China English. As far as possible, we shall cite from indigenous studies, many of which were published in Chinese, and relate them to the international literature.

The fourfold discussion, from government to teachers and students and then the general public, will provide a fairly comprehensive account of attitudes to the extent that it covers four social categories who have a stake in English, not just any one particular category. Other social categories such as the media are beyond the scope of this chapter (see L. Gao, 2005; Liu, Murphy, Li, & Liu, 2007; Wang & Gao, 2008). Conceptually, the discussion will reflect the influence of the "language and social psychology" perspective on language attitudes as represented by the works of Lambert, Giles, and Gallois, among others (Gallois & Callan,1989; Gallois, Watson, & Brabant, 2007; Lambert, Hodgson, Gardener, & Fillenhaum, 1960; Robinson & Giles, 2001).

Government

In the current official EFL policy Chinese leaders have elevated English to the status of a national prescribed course of study no later than grade three in elementary school (about 9 years of age) right up to graduate school (about 24 years of age). This language requirement is in addition to that of Putonghua (standard Chinese) and, for some but not all ethnic minorities, also additional to their native language. The unprecedented national emphasis on English language education is the result of progressive changes in EFL policy over the past thirty years. Before 1980 the policy emphasized only a basic knowledge of English, such as grammar, pronunciation and vocabulary, regarding EFL education as a *subject knowledge* (Xu, 1964). From 1980 to 2000 the national policy continued to highlight basic language skills and language knowledge, but also broadened EFL education to include the development of communicative ability (Ministry of Education, 1993). One of the reasons for including communicative proficiency was to rectify the spread of "dumb English" shown by students who, despite their academic success in scoring high marks in English examinations, were often dumbfounded and unable to interact with English speakers.

Importantly, since 2001 humanistic goals have been added to traditional instrumental/utilitarian goals to jointly define the dual goals of the English course prescribed for students receiving free education. The purpose was to enhance students' comprehensive humanistic qualities by using English learning as a means to widen their outlook, enrich life experience, develop cross-cultural awareness, promote creative thinking and form a fine personality and correct value perception, which would lay the foundation for life long learning (Ministry of Education, 2011).

The dual instrumental/utilitarian and humanistic goals of the English course also apply to university students. Owing to the particular importance of university students in China's national development and internationalization, the policy also emphasizes the role of university English proficiency in these two strategic areas (Ministry of Education, 2007). The standard for measuring English proficiency is no longer an English vocabulary of 6,000 words or the ability to serve as an English interpreter, but rather, English proficiency entails the linguistic competence and cultural capacity to be an international ambassador for China.

It appears from the historical account above that China's current official EFL policy has been an important part of its drive for economic development and social reform, its opening to the (Western) world and entry to the World Trade Organization, as well as a response to external pressures arising from the globalization of education (see also Dai, 2008: Zhou & Sun, 2004). To China's leadership the importance of English is not restricted to its indispensable role as a link to the outside world, or its status as the international language for trade, finance, technology and diplomacy, but also as a vital tool for modernizing the country (Cortazzi & Jin, 1996; see also Rappa & Wee, 2006; Sharifian, 2009). The present positive language policy on English, which is unprecedented in the long history of English in China, constitutes an authoritative expression of the country's favorable attitude toward English.

Teachers

Whilst the positive official attitude will affect the language attitude of teachers, students and the general public, there is considerable scope for their attitudes to develop in their own ways. These attitudes will be discussed in the next three sections. In the case of EFL teachers, the literature shows that not all of them are able to endorse the official idealized goals of English teaching set by the central government. In a survey of 3,000 junior middle school (approximately grades 7 to 9) EFL teachers, based on a stratified sample of over 10,000 in Guangdong province (south China), Huang (2005) found that about 60% of the informants regarded English as just a tool, and only about 30% would go beyond this instrumental/utilitarian attitude to also endorse the humanistic goal of teaching English. Teachers accepted in principle that attention should be paid to developing students' emotional well-being, learning strategies and cultural awareness through English teaching, but most of them (80%) found it difficult to achieve such non-language outcomes in their work. These attitudes were reinforced by a perception among teachers that, after all, their (junior middle school) students were mostly driven by instrumental/utilitarian motivations of getting good grades and admission to better schools on graduation.

The reality is consistent with Beijaard, Verloop, and Vermunt's (2000) observation that most secondary teachers regarded themselves as experts in subject matter only, not in pedagogy or other extra-language teaching activities. That is, their professional identity has yet to embody fully the official EFL policy on the dual instrumental/utilitarian and humanistic goals of English teaching. As pointed out by Gao (2010) in an interview study of teachers of English who had left the teaching profession, many teachers were not confident of their English competence, much less of their ability to achieve other humanistic goals.

The picture is, however, positive with respect to university EFL teachers, especially the more senior among them. In one part of a National Education Ministry granted project, Zhu and He (2010) analyzed an 86,400-word transcription of interviewing nine retired EFL experts in south China and found that their professional identity included not only instrumental/utilitarian and humanistic values with respect to the goals of teaching university students English, but also a deep concern with students' civic development and sense of social responsibility through learning English. The professional identity of this group of retired EFL experts can be traced back to traditional Chinese culture that requires intellectuals to bear social responsibility, make contributions to the country and be a good model for younger professionals. For non-experts or younger EFL university teachers, it is doubtful that their professional identities are as full-fledged as those of these retired senior experts, because of the large classes they have to teach and lower level of self-efficacy (especially) in oral English (Chen & Goh, 2011).

Learners

Most of the Chinese research on language attitude toward English is concerned with EFL learners. Scholars have explored how learners' EFL attitudes are linked to their EFL learning motivation that jointly influence their English proficiency and self-identity. Among them are Yihong Gao and her research team (2003, 2005, 2008, 2011), whose research has covered types of EFL learning motivation and their relationship with learning behavior and learners' self-identify. In her research she developed a Chinese EFL motivation questionnaire that incorporated several motivation typologies, including Gardner and Lambert's (1959) distinction between integrative and instrumental/utilitarian motives, Dornyei's (1998) static and dynamic categorization, and Ryan and Deci's (2000) intrinsic and extrinsic classification. Using this questionnaire, Gao, Cheng, Zhao, and Zhou (2005) surveyed 2,278 learners of EFL from 30 universities in China and uncovered seven types of motivation. In descending order of self-rated importance by students, the seven types were

1) intrinsic interest, 2) immediate achievement, 3) learning situation, 4) going abroad, 5) social responsibility, 6) individual development, and 7) information medium.

Students with motivations 1, 4, 6, or 7 were found to study harder than their counterparts with other motivations. In a follow-up study, Gao, Liu, Xiu, and Ding (2008) tracked the motivation development of a thousand learners in the overall sample after they had studied English for two years at university. The results showed stable levels in motivations 1, 6, and 7 but declines in motivations 2, 3, and 5. After another two years at university, these students had increased their motivations 1, 3, and 4, maintained motivations 2 and 5, and reduced motivations 6 and 7 (Gao, Zhou, & Zhan, 2011). The pattern of motivational change indicated that by the end of their university study, learners of EFL had developed more interest and confidence in English, with less concern for academic scores but stronger expectations of furthering their training at English-speaking universities abroad.

The above research on language attitudes, and on learner motivation in particular, has opened up the interesting question of learners' "productive bilingualism" (e.g., Zhou & Gao, 2009). In its narrow sense, productive bilingualism is defined as an ideal type of bilingualism in which an increased command of English and that of Chinese positively reinforce each other, in contrast to additive bilingualism in which the increased command of English merely adds to but does not enhance the command of Chinese. Zhou and Gao (2005)used the symbols "1+1>2" to refer to productive bilingualism and "1+1=2" to refer to additive bilingualism. They found that around 40% of students in the full sample reported productive bilingualism in this narrow sense. In a broader sense, productive bilingualism includes increased awareness of the outside world, deeper appreciation of English and Chinese cultures, as well as better interpersonal understanding and communication that are associated with increased English proficiency. Between 34% and 55% of students reported these types of productive changes, which were collectively referred to as self-identity changes. Self-identity changes are interesting in showing that becoming bilingual was more than adding English to Chinese.

Zhou and Gao (2005) tracked the motivations and self-identity development of a subsample of English majors and found that after three years of university study, these learners had increased their motivations 1 and 5, and undergone self-identity changes that were characterized by a more critical attitude toward traditional Chinese culture and greater cross-cultural awareness. A similar transformational change was found in a study of non-English majors' English learning identity, which the author (Lo, 2009) interpreted as a positive restructuring of self. With reference to Giddens' (1984, 1991) social psychological structuration theory, Y. H. Gao (2005) tried to explain descriptive findings in previous research, specially the relation between learners' motivation and self-identity changes. By conducting an in-depth case study of three university English majors through "free-talk" interviews, she collected their reflections on their three year English learning and summed up key features that influenced the learners' identity during different periods of schooling. She concluded that "learning motivation and learners' self-identity construct each other."

Self-identity changes are influenced by learning motivation, but can be implicit in 'practical consciousness,' constitute 'unintended consequences of action,' and thus conditions of further action. The learning of a foreign language and culture is a process of agents turning their 'practical consciousness' into 'discursive consciousness' and increase their reflexivity, which is a necessary condition for 'productive bilingualism.' The relation between foreign language learners' self-identity and social contexts is also that of mutual construction. Learners' self-identity change is a part of China's modernization process—its outcome and constitutive force at the same time (Y. H. Gao, 2005).

The studies above, though systematic and drawn from a large sample of universities, were limited in at least two ways. First, only university students were studied. Missing from the studies are secondary school students, whose exposure to English is more limited, and correspondingly the extent of their productive bilingualism would be less evident, especially those who are from the less developed regions of the country (Hu, 2002, 2003). Second, the studies were concerned with university students of Han ancestry, the majority ethnic group in China. There are 55 ethnic minority groups in China, representing around 120 mother tongues and 110 million people, most of whom are living in the under-developed hinterland away from the coastal regions where the teaching of English has so far been concentrated. English has not yet found its way into most of these minority communities (Wang & Phillion, 2009; Yang, 2005). In a survey of 506 students representing Yi, Zhuang, Miao, and Hani minorities in Yunnan Province, Yuan (2007) found that students' minority identity in conjunction with their attitude toward and motivation of learning English, as well as expectations from parents and teachers, positively predicted their English proficiency. These and other findings were generally consistent with Gardner and Lambert's (1972) work and provided a rare glimpse of the country's minority students learning EFL as their third language, along with their first minority language and Chinese. It would be most interesting for future research to explore the extent of *productive trilingualism* among minority students for comparison with productive bilingualism among Han EFL students. For example, in what sense is becoming trilingual productive for minority members? Would it embrace all three language-based cultures and identities, including their minority culture and identity? (See also Finifrock, 2010.)

Finally, a note of caution is in order. As schools embrace English and students are expected to be successful as English learners, what financial costs do schools, parents and students have to pay in order to be successful, and what psychological costs do students have to bear for being unsuccessful? As Yu (2010) has pointed out, university students are realistic in their expectations that they are unlikely to use English frequently in their future jobs, and many of them do not believe that it should be necessary to pass the national standardized college English test in order to obtain a bachelor's degree.

General public

Given the vast Chinese population, it would be difficult to mount a representative survey of the attitudes of the general public toward English. No such research has been found in our literature search. Instead, small-scale studies have been conducted, some on the public's evaluation of different English varieties, others on their attitude toward English-Chinese code-switching, and still others on the language impact due to the hosting of major international events such as the Beijing Olympic Games. These studies will be reviewed in turn, including those that were based on student samples which shed light on the topics in question.

Two major varieties of English in China are American and British English, of which the national favorite is American English (Hu, 2005). Public attitudes toward these two accented Englishes can be described as mixed, preferring one over the other on some dimensions but showing the reverse preference on other dimensions of evaluation. This situation is evident in earlier (e.g., Ng & He, 2004) and more recent (e.g., Li, 2011; Tian & Jiang, 2011) studies. Both questionnaire and matched-guise technique (MGT: Lambert et al., 1960; see also Giles & Bourhis, 1976) results have shown a stronger preference for American to British English in terms of power, solidarity and expressiveness. Yet American English was regarded as an "informal dialect and non-standard," whereas British English was accorded "higher ranking" and considered to be "standard." Interestingly, informants who preferred American English were found to speak with a *British* English accent in tests of English pronunciation (Zhou & Chen, 2008).

English-Chinese code-switching, in which English words or sentences are inserted in a Chinese speech, has taken root among ethnic Chinese in Hong Kong (Gibbons, 1987) and English-speaking countries overseas (Li, 2009; Ng & He,

2004; Zhu, 2008). It is becoming more popular in mainland China since the economic reform and open door policy in the mid-1980s. Studies have reported positive attitudes toward code-switching among young "white-collar" workers in Guangzhou (Xu, 2008), citizens in Wu Han (L. H. Li, 2007; N. Li, 2006) and students in Nanchang (Cai, 2011). These results indicate an open-minded and tolerant attitude among the younger population toward mixing some English words in Chinese speech. The extent to which the older population would also endorse code-switching has not been studied.

Apart from EFL policy, another source of official influence on attitudes toward English is the hosting of international events in mainland China. These events have brought large numbers of foreigners to China, many of whom are native English speakers. The significance of these events for understanding changes in language attitudes toward English is twofold. First, the events have raised the profile of English through the large number of English-speaking visitors, the use of English in opening and closing ceremonies by foreign dignitaries, and occasional switching to English in an approving tone by Chinese officials. In the Beijing Olympic Games and the Shanghai World Exhibition, these English speeches and code-switching, signifying the high-status English, were widely televised in China. The international events are also significant in another way, which has to do with political pressure and social norms for Chinese people to play "host" to visitors. The host role entails, *inter alia*, accepting visitors' English and, to the extent they are capable, reciprocating with English when interacting with them. Such conversational accommodation (Gallois, Ogay, & Giles, 2005) has been an important part in the training of Chinese volunteers in the Beijing Olympic Game, numbering over a million (Li, Gui, & Shen, 2008).

Xu, Lui, and Sun (2010) conducted a survey to explore the effects of the Beijing Olympic Games and the Shanghai World Expo on the general public's language attitudes in five developed coastal cities (Shanghai, Xuzhou, Nanjing, Wuxi, and Xuzhou). The results were positive. Between 44% and 65% of the respondents in the cities believed that the two events had aroused people's passion for learning FL. A majority of them estimated that more people were learning EL after the two events. Between 47% and 64% of the respondents in the cities said they were interested in FL learning and 63% to 72% of them agreed that it was important to be competent in a foreign language. Although these figures referred to FL as a whole rather than English specifically, one could safely generalize the results to English because of its pre-eminent status among foreign languages.

An in-depth study was carried by Gao and Lin (2008, 2010) on the attitude of Chinese volunteers in the Beijing Olympics toward British, American, Black American, Indian, and Chinese Englishes. During the pre-Games period, the volunteers showed some non-correspondence between their self-reported and projected language attitudes: the former was more open-minded and non-discriminatory, whereas the latter was more conservative in giving priority to Chinese, British, and American English. During the period when the Games were held, the volunteers reported difficulties in communicating with world English speakers. Nevertheless, their language attitudes and multicultural awareness changed as well as sustained, towards both being more open (that is, with more tolerance to non-native-like accents of speakers from non- English speaking countries) and more conservative (that is, still regarding British and American accents as the "Standards" in comparison with other varieties of English). The researchers thus suggest that "receptive world English skills and multicultural awareness should be included as pedagogical components in long-term language education as well as short-term English training programs" (Gao & Lin, 2010, p. 105).

Conclusion

Given the influential role of English as an international language and its increasing penetration into Chinese society, it is unlikely that English will meet the same fate of decline as Japanese or Russian did in 20th century China. The positive language attitudes reviewed in the present chapter pertaining to the central government, EFL teachers and students, as well as the general public, all point to this prospect. Under China's official and popular embrace, the power of English to stay and prosper in this populous country is formidable, and will be strengthened further by the increasing presence of English-speaking expatriates coming to China to work and former students returning from overseas English-speaking universities.

Yet there are controversies beneath the surface of generally positive language attitude toward English. There is doubt over the feasibility of "the whole nation learning English" movement, and the burden that this movement has placed on students, parents and schools (Li, Long, & Li, 2007; Long, Li, & Li, 2007). Rural areas, in particular, have to make do with a shortage of EFL teachers, and students there are less well supported to achieve compared to their counterparts in the more affluent urban areas (Wang, 2011). The English language disparity will widen the existing rural-urban gap.

Compulsory English in elementary and secondary schools can be a burden on students, especially for students whose home language is not Putonghua and who have to make extra efforts in their trilingual education (native language + Putonghua + English). This situation applies to some though not all minority students. Unless minority parents have been able to provide Putonghua learning for their children at a young age (perhaps to better prepare them for educational and economic advancement in mainstream, Putonghua-dominated society), learning Putonghua when they enter school is already hard enough. For many minority students, the chances are that they will fall behind their Han counterparts in both Putonghua and English. Even worse, their home language may suffer decline through neglect, thus aggravating the endangerment of minority languages (Bradley, 2005). On the other hand, English as part of trilingual education is not without benefits for minority students and their home towns. In a review of the debate, Blachford and Jones (2011) point to the benefits of English in giving minority students an advantage to find better employment, and the positive role played by a critical mass of English-proficient minorities in turning their villages into prosperous tourist destinations in Yunnan and other provinces. Individual and collective successes such as these help to promote a positive, albeit utilitarian attitude toward English among minority groups.

Another concern relates to ethnolinguistic pride. In the context of World Englishes, one might argue that English now is no longer the property of only one country, or even that of the collective "inner circle" of English-speaking countries (America, Australia, Britain, Canada, and New Zealand), but one that belongs to the world. However, as long as English remains as a "foreign" language, learning it signifies that Chinese are late comers trying to imitate or approximate the idealized or "standard" English. Standard English, up until now, is British or American English, although some studies have found that the former has an edge over the latter (Hu, 2006; Zhu & Chen, 2008). Due to cross-linguistic influence (Selinker, 1992), L_1 (Chinese) will inevitably influence the acquisition and usage of L_2 (English), resulting in the development of a local variety of English known by many names. "Chinglish," which carries pejorative meanings, is not welcome in China; "Chinese English," apparently a neutral term, nonetheless implies bad English or beginner's English and is similarly resisted though to a less extent. The search for a better meaning name led some to switch to the term "China English" (e.g., Li, 1993; Yi, 2004). After a review of various definitions of China English, He and Li (2009) conclude that the term is most accurately defined as "a performance variety of English which has the standard Englishes as its core but is colored with characteristic features of Chinese phonology, lexis, syntax and discourse pragmatics, and which is particularly suited for expressing content ideas specific to Chinese culture through such means as transliteration and loan translation." As Chinese people are more likely to use English with other English speakers in Asia than in Anglo-American countries, some authors have argued that China English would be a more culturally appropriate model of English than any superimposed 'Anglo' norm (Kirkpatrick & Xu, 2002).

The search for a more acceptable name is not merely academic or simply for greater accuracy. From the language and social psychology perspective referred to earlier, more specifically the theory of ethnolinguistic identity (e.g., Giles, 1978), the name search and debate over it is an expression of assertive ethnolinguistic pride. In a paper that carries the assertive rhetorical title "Why China English should stand alongside British, American, and other 'World Englishes'," Hu (2006) questions the need for the teaching and learning of EFL in China to conform to any of the existing standard varieties, arguing that Chinese should be learning China English instead. Later surveys of Chinese teachers of English found that the majority of teachers considered that China English will eventually become a standard variety of English in its own right, pending proper codification and official recognition (He, 2007; Hu, 2005).

The emergence of China English raises serious questions for language attitudes research. From the language and social psychology perspective, speakers of China English make interesting comparison vis-à-vis speakers of "standard" English with respect to status and solidarity evaluations, perceived personality and persuasion/influence, and ingroup identification. In the Asian context, comparisons with speakers of other Asian varieties of English are especially relevant, because English has become the de facto *lingua franca* of trade, finance, technology and diplomacy in this part of the world (Lazaro & Medalla, 2004). The results of comparison would shed light on ethnolinguistic relations in this part of the world. At a more fundamental level, the emergence of China English will re-open the debate on the role of English learning in the country's quest for modernity. Skeptics may argue, for example, that China English will diminish the humanistic values of EFL learning by diverting learners' interest away from Western cultures and values that are more closely associated with Anglo-American English. Against this, advocates may claim that there is more than one (Western) path to and model of modernity, and that it is more important for the nation to be at ease with its characteristic way of speaking English rather than to hide its *Chineseness* in classrooms, boardrooms, and international fora.

References

Beijaard, D., Verloop, P., & Vermunt, J. D. (2000). Teachers' perceptions of professional identity: An exploratory study from a personal knowledge perspective. *Teaching and Teacher Education, 16,* 49–764.
Blachford, D. R., & Jones, M. (2011). Trilingual education policy ideals and realities for the Naxi in rural Yunnan. In A. Feng (Ed.), *English language education across greater China* (pp. 228–259). Clevedon, UK: Multilingual Matters.
Bolton, K. (2003). *Chinese Englishes: A sociolinguistic history.* Cambridge, UK: Cambridge University Press.

Bradley, D. (2005). Introduction: language policy and language endangerment in China. *International Journal of the Sociology of Language, 173,* 1–21.
Cai, C. (2011). Language attitude of college students under the perspective of multicultural education, *Journal of Nanchang College of Education,* Vol.26 (2). (In Chinese.) 蔡晨. 多元文化教育视野下的大学生语言态度研究, 南昌教育学院学报, 2011(2).
Chen, Z., & Goh, C. (2011). Teaching oral English in higher education: Challenges to EFL teachers, *Teaching in Higher Education,16,* 333–345.
Cortazzi, M., & Jin, L. X. (1996). English teaching and learning in China. *Language Teaching, 29,* 61–80.
Dai, W. D. (Ed.) (2008). *A report of foreign language teaching at universities of China (1978–2008).* Shanghai: Shanghai Foreign Language Education Press. (In Chinese.) 戴炜栋（主编）(2008) 高校外语专业教育发展报告 (1978–2008) 上海：上海外语教育出版社.
Dornyei, Z. (1998). Motivation in second and foreign language learning. *Language Learning,31,* 117–135.
Finifrock, J. E. (2010). English as a third language in rural China: Lessons from the Zaidang Kam-Mandarin Bilingual Education Project. *Diaspora, Indigenous, and Minority Education, 4,* 33–46.
Gallois, C., & Callan, V. J. (1989). Attitudes to spoken Australian English: judgments of ingroup and ethnic outgroup speakers. In D. Bradley, R. D. Sussex, & G. K. Scott (Eds.), *Studies in Australian English* (pp. 149–160). Bundoora, Australia: Department of Linguistics, La Trobe University for the Australian Linguistic Society.
Gallois, C., Ogay, T., & Giles, H. (2005). Communication accommodation theory: A look back and a look ahead." In W. B. Gudykunst (Eds.), *Theorizing about intercultural communication* (pp. 121–148). Thousand Oaks, CA: Sage.
Gallois, C., Watson, B., & Brabant, M. (2007). Attitudes to language and communication. In M. Hellinger & A. Pauwels (Eds.), *Handbook of language and communication: Diversity and change* (pp. 597–620). Berlin: Mouton de Gruyter.
Gao, L. (2005). Bilinguals' creativity in the use of English in China's advertising. In J. Cohen, K. T. McAlister, K. Rolstad, & J. MacSwan (Eds.), *Proceedings of the 4th international symposium on bilingualism* (pp. 827–837). Somerville, MA: Cascadilla Press.
Gao, X. (2010). To be or not to be: Shifting motivations in Chinese secondary school English teachers' career narratives. *Teacher Development: An International Journal of Teachers' Professional Development, 14,* 321–334.
Gao, Y. H. (2005). A structuation theory perspective of the social psychology of foreign language learning. *Research in Foreign Language and Literature,5*(2), 25–34. (In Chinese.) 高一虹. 外语学习社会心理的结构化理论视角. 外国语言文学，2005(2).
Gao, Y. H., & Cheng, Y. (2003). The relationship between types of English learning motivation and motivation intensity. *Foreign Language Research, 1,* 60-64. (In Chinese.)高一虹，程英. 英语学习动机类型与动机强度的关系—对大学本科生的定量考察，外语研究, 2003(1).
Gao, Y. H., Cheng, Y., Zhao, Y., & Zhou, Y. (2005). Self-identity changes and English learning among Chinese undergraduates. *World Englishes, 24,* 39–51.
Gao, Y. H., Liu, L., Xiu, L. M., & Ding, L. P. (2008). A tracked report on English learning motivation development of Chinese college undergraduates. *Journal of Tianjin Foreign Studies*

University, 6, 67–73. (In Chinese.)高一虹，刘璐，修立梅，丁林棚. 大学生基础阶段英语学习动机跟踪——综合大学英语专业样本报告，天津外国语学院学报, 2008(6).

Gao. Y. H., & Lin, M. Q. (2008). The attitude towards World Englishes among volunteers of Olympic Games. *Journal of Xinjiang Normal University (Edition of Philosophy and Social Sciences), 4,* 86–92. (In Chinese.) 高一虹，林梦茜. 大学生奥运志愿者对世界英语的态度——奥运会前的一项主观投射测试研究, 新疆师范大学学报：哲学社会科学版, 2008(4).

Gao, Y. H., & Lin, M. Q. (2010). Olympic Games volunteers' attitudes towards World Englishes and multicultural awareness: An investigation before and during Beijing Olympic Games. *Foreign Languages in China, 2,* 99–105. (In Chinese.) 高一虹，林梦茜. 奥运志愿者对世界英语的态度与多元文化意识—北京奥运会前、奥运会中的考察. 中国外语, 2010(2).

Gao, Y. H., Zhou, Y., & Zhan, F. M. (2011). English study and development of learners' self-identity. *Foreign Languages Research, 2,* 56–62.(In Chinese.) 高一虹，周燕，战凤梅. 英语学习与学习者的认同发展——五所高校高年级阶段跟踪研究. 外语研究, 2011(2).

Gardner, R. C., & Lambert, W. E. (1959). Motivational variables in second language acquisition. *Canadian Journal of Psychology, 13,* 266–272.

Gardner, R. C., & Lambert, W. E. (1972). *Attitudes and motivation in second language learning.* Rowley, MA: Newbury House.

Gibbons, J. (1987). *Code-mixing and code choice—A Hong Kong case study.* Clevedon, UK: Multilingual Matters.

Giddens, A. (1984). *The constitution of society.* Berkeley, CA: University of California Press.

Giddens, A. (1991). *Modernity and self-identity.* Stanford, CA: Stanford University Press.

Giles, H. (1978). Linguistic differentiation in ethnic groups. In H. Tajfel (Ed.), *Differentiation between social groups: Studies in the social psychology of intergroup relations* (pp. 361–393). London: Academic Press.

Giles, H., & Bourhis, Y. (1976). Methodological issues in dialect perception: Some social perspectives. *Anthropological Linguistics, 18,* 294–304.

He, D. (2007). *'China English' or native speaker based standard? : A study of college teachers' and students' perceptions of the ideal pedagogic model of college English in mainland China.* Unpublished MPhil thesis, City University of Hong Kong. http://lib.cityu.edu.hk/record=b2218141. (Accessed 18 February, 2012.)

He, D., & Li, D. C. S. (2009). Language attitudes and linguistic features in the 'China English' debate. *World Englishes,28,* 70–89.

Hildebrandt, N., & Giles, H. (1983). The Japanese as subordinate group: Ethnolinguistic identity theory in a foreign language context. *Anthropological Linguistics, 25,* 436–466.

Hu, G. W. (2002). Potential cultural resistance to pedagogical imports: The case of communicative language teaching in China. *Language, Culture and Curriculum,15,* 93–105.

Hu, G. W. (2003). English language teaching in China: Regional differences and contributing factors. *Journal of Multilingual and Multicultural Development, 24,* 290–318.

Hu, X.Q. (2005). China English, at home and in the world. *English Today, 21,* 27–38.

Hu, X. Q. (2006). Why China English should stand alongside British, American, and the other "World Englishes." *Journal of Basic English Education, 12,* 34–39. 基础教育外语教学研究, 2006(12).

Huang, Z. H. (2005). *Program report on mid & long-term plan of EFL education development in Guangdong* (2007–2016). (Personal communication.)

Kirkpatrick, A., & Xu, Z. (2002). Chinese pragmatic norms and 'China English'. *World Englishes,21,* 269–79.
Lambert, W. E., Hodgson, R. C., Gardner, R. C., & Fillenbaum, S. (1960). Evaluational reactions to spoken language. *Journal of Abnormal and Social Psychology,60,* 44–51.
Lazaro, D. C., & Medalla, E. M. (2004). English as the language of trade, finance and technology in APEC: An East Asia perspective. *Philippine Journal of Development, number 58, second semester 2004, xxxi,* 2, 277–300.
Li, L. H. (2007). On Wuhan young students' attitudes to Wuhan dialect, Mandarin and English. *Journal of Technology College Education,6,* 122–125. (In Chinese.) 李腊花．论武汉青年学生对武汉方言、普通话和英语的态度，理工高教研究, 2007(6).
Li, N. (2006). Chinese citizens' attitude towards English—an investigation of some people in Wuhan city. *Journal of Xianning University,5,* 127–129. (In Chinese.) 黎娜．中国人对英语的语言态度—对武汉市部分城市人口的一个调查，咸宁学院学报, 2006(5).
Li, S.Q. (2009). *A study on the post-'80 generation's attitude towards Chinese-English code-mixing.* Unpublished MA thesis, Xiangtan University, Hu Nan, China.
Li, W. Z. (1993). China English and Chinglish. *Foreign Language Teaching and Research, 4,* 18–24. (In Chinese.) 李文忠．中国英语与中国式英语，外语教学与研究, 1993(4).
Li, X. Y., Long, Y. & Li, J. (2007). Brand strategy on education of foreign language in China. *Research in Teaching,30(2),* 111–115. (In Chinese.) 李雪岩，龙耀，李娟．中国外语教育品牌战略思考，教学研究, 2007(2).
Li, Z., Gui, T., &Shen, Y. (2008). *Opportunity of Olympic Games' promotes volunteerism in China towards systematization.*(In Chinese.) http://news.xinhuanet.com/newscenter/2008-08/25/content_9708602.htm.
Li, Z. R. (2011). On university students' preference towards British and American English. *Examination Weekly, No.47,* 88–90. (In Chinese.) 李子容．本科生对英国英语和美国英语的喜好态度，考试周刊, 2011(4).
Liu, F., Murphy, J., Li, J., & Liu, X. (2007). English and Chinese? The role of consumer ethnocentrism and country of origin in Chinese attitudes store signs. *Australasian Marketing Journal, 14,* 5–16.
Lo, B. J. (2009). The more I learned, the less I found my self. In J. B. Lo, J. Orton, & Y. Gao (Eds.), *China and English: Globalization and the dilemmas of identity* (pp. 155–168). Clevedon, UK: Multilingual Matters.
Long, Y., Li, X. Y., & Li, J. (2007). The education system of foreign language in China: Problems and reform. *Research in Teaching, 30,* 18–23. (In Chinese.) 龙耀，李雪岩，李娟．中国外语教育制度：问题与改革．教学研究, 2007(1).
Ministry of Education of People's Republic of China. (1993). *English Syllabus for Junior Middle Schools.* Beijing: People's Education Press. (In Chinese.) 教育部（1993).初中英语教学大纲．北京：人民教育出版社．
Ministry of Education of People's Republic of China. (2007). *University English teaching requirements.* (In Chinese.) 教育部（2007). 大学英语课程教学要求． http://www.moe.gov.cn/publicfiles/business/htmlfiles/moe/s3857/ 201011/xxgk_110825.html.
Ministry of Education of People's Republic of China. (2011). *The National English Curriculum Standard for Compulsory Education* (2011 Version). Beijing: Beijing Normal University Publishing Group. (In Chinese.) 教育部（2011）义务教育英语课程标准（2011）版），北京：北京师范大学出版社．

Ng, S. H., & He, A. P. (2004). Code-Switching in trigenerational family conversations among Chinese immigrants in New Zealand, *Journal of Language and Social Psychology, 23,* 28–48.

Rappa, A. L., & Wee, L. (2006). *Language policy and modernity in Southeast Asia: Malaysia, the Philippines, Singapore and Thailand.* New York: Springer.

Robinson, W. P., & Giles, H. (Eds.). (2001). *The new handbook of language and social psychology.* Chichester, UK: John Wiley.

Ryan, R., & Deci, E. (2000). Intrinsic and extrinsic motivations: Classic definitions and new directions. *Contemporary Educational Psychology, 25,* 54–67.

Selinker, L. (1992). *Rediscovering interlanguage.* London, UK: Longman.

Sharifian, F. (Ed.). (2009). *English as an international language: Perspectives and pedagogical issues.* Clevedon, UK: Multilingual Matters.

Tian, L., & Jiang, Q. (2011). A study on middle school students' attitude towards English teachers' code-switching, *Anhui Literature, No.1.* (In Chinese.)田莉, 蒋琴. 中学生对英语教师语码转换的语言态度研究, 安徽文学（下半月）, 2011(1).

Yu, Y. (2010). *Attitudes of learners toward English: A case of Chinese college students.* Unpublished Ph.D. dissertation, The Ohio State University. http://etd.ohiolink.edu/send-pdf.cgi/Yu%20Yang.pdf?osu1283303545

Wang, W., & Gao, X. (2008). English language education in China: A review of selected research. *Journal of Multilingual and Multicultural Development, 29,* 380–399.

Wang, W. J. (2011). Current situation of English teaching in primary schools of west China rural areas. *New Curriculum Study, Teacher Education, No.7.* (In Chinese.) 王文君. 西部农村地区小学英语教学现状，新课程研究. 教师教育，2011(7).

Wang, Y., & Phillion, J. (2009). Minority language policy and practice in China: The need for multicultural education. *International Journal of Multicultural Education, 11,* 1–14.

Xu, G. Z. (Ed.). (1964). *English* (Book 1). Shanghai: Commercial Press.许国璋（主编）（1964）英语（第一册），上海：商务印书馆.

Xu, Y. H., Liu, N., & Sun, H. (2010). Investigating influence of Beijing Olympics and World Exhibition on Chinese citizens' attitudes towards foreign language learning. *Science & Technology Information, Vol.36.*

Xu, Z. H. (2008). On interaction between language and society from the language attitudes of young people in Guangzhou. *Foreign Language Teaching and Research, 4*(4), 310–313. (In Chinese.) 徐真华. 从广州年轻人的语言态度看语言与社会的互动关系，外语教学与研究, 2008(4).

Yang, J. (2005). English as a third language among China's ethnic minorities. *International Journal of Bilingual Education and Bilingualism, 8,* 552–567.

Yi, Z. (2004). A study of standard English, China English and Chinese English. *Journal of Jimei University, 5,* 72–77.

Yuan, Y. C. (2007). Differences in attitude and motivation and English learning of ethnic minority students in Yunnan. In X.M. Yu (Ed.), *Hani culture and Yunnan endangered ethnic minority languages.* Melbourne, Australia: La Trobe University Press.

Zhou, M., & Sun, H. (2004). *Language policy in the People's Republic of China: Theory and practice since 1949.* New York: Springer.

Zhou, R., & Chen, G. H. (2008). Study of Chinese university students' attitude to American and British English. *Modern Foreign Languages, 31,* 49–57. (In Chinese.) 周榕，陈国华. 英语专业大学生英美英语态度偏好与实际口音特点研究，现代外语, 2008(1).

Zhou, Y., & Gao, Y. H. (2009). The development of English learning motivation types. *Foreign Language Teaching and Research, 41,*113–118. (In Chinese.) 周燕，高一虹．大学基础阶段英语学习动机的发展—对五所高校的跟踪研究，外语教学与研究, 2009(2).

Zhu, H. (2008). Dueling languages, dueling values: Code-switching in bilingual intergenerational conflict talk in diasporic families. *Journal of Pragmatics, 40,*1799–1816.

Zhu, X. Y., & He, A. P. (2010). *The professional identity of teachers of English as a Foreign Language (EFL) in Mainland China.* Paper presented at the 12th International Conference on Language and Social Psychology, Brisbane, Australia.

CHAPTER EIGHT

Language Attitudes in South Asia

ITESH SACHDEV & TEJ BHATIA

This chapter focuses on South Asia (SA)—India, Pakistan, Nepal, Bangladesh, Sri Lanka, Bhutan, and the Maldives. SA represents an astonishing array of linguistic diversity that challenges those who are accustomed to monolingual situations and models. This diversity is not reflected in official ideologies in SA, which range from the monolithic one-language-one religion-one nation type to pluralistic official multilingualism and multiculturalism.

We first outline this diversity, and then consider ideology and language attitudes in a broad historical perspective in SA. The next section considers the case of India today, considered by many to be the best example of pluralistic ideology enacted in SA. Speakers of several SA languages were divided by national boundaries following partition in 1947. How speakers of one SA language—Punjabi—have fared under different ideological regimes post-independence in SA and elsewhere in the world is considered next. The impact of English on the SA linguistic landscape precedes the penultimate section, which considers that most prevalent behavioral manifestation of multilingualism—code-switching. The chapter closes with some brief conclusions.

Linguistic Diversity in SA

Linguistic diversity is a hallmark of SA. More has been written about charting the linguistic diversity of India relative to other SA countries. In India, Abbi (2008,

2009) argues that there are six language families (Indo-European, Dravidian, Austroasiatic, and Tibeto-Burman, Angan, Great Andamese) and more than 650 languages as well as numerous geographical, social, ethnic, religious and rural varieties or dialects (more than 3000). In Pakistan, Coleman (2010, British Council) estimates there to be 72 living languages (not including English), with 14 having speakers greater than a million. Even in the smaller SA countries, where relatively little research has been conducted, there is evidence of great linguistic diversity. Thus, Nepal had 104 languages at the last count (Giri, 2010), Bangladesh over 30 (Rahman, 2010), Sri Lanka 7 (Lewis, 2009), and even the multi-island Maldives is listed as having several 'dialects' (Lewis, 2009). Note that definitions of languages, dialects and other varieties of linguistic variation are socio-politically charged (cf. "a language is a dialect with an army and a navy," oft-attributed to Max Weinriech, 1945; see Kachru & Bhatia, 1978 for more on dialect conflict in the Hindi-speaking area).

The wide linguistic diversity on the ground in SA has not resulted in nations systematically engaging in multilingual policies. As in the rest of the world (see Edwards, 1994), SA countries tend to promote fairly restrictive language ideologies, policies and laws (Giri, 2011; Mohanty, 2010; Rahman, 1996). Thus Bangladesh and the Maldives have one official language (Bengali and Dhivehi, respectively); Nepal (Nepali and English) and Sri Lanka (Sinhala and Tamil) have two; and Pakistan, which has one national language (Urdu) and two official languages (Urdu and English). Even India, considered by many as a paragon of national multilingualism, has "only" 22 constitutionally so-called "scheduled" (national) languages that map onto state boundaries within the country (the consequence of a political process begun in 1956 that is still ongoing) out of hundreds or even thousands (depending on definitions).

Today, speakers of Indo-European languages are dominant in all SA countries. In India, where there are six language families, speakers of Indo-European languages are greater in numerical strength (over 60% of the population) as well as social influence and significance; for example, in the media, political and economic institutions and literary traditions (Bhatia & Ritchie, 2006). In Pakistan, the majority language (Punjabi, approximately 60% of population speak it as a mother tongue), and the national language (Urdu, 8%) are Indo-European. With the exception of Brahui (1%), a Dravidian language, the remaining 39% of the population speak languages of either Indo-Aryan or Indo-Iranian stock. The official languages of other SA countries are also Indo-European: Sinhala (Sri Lanka; spoken by 75% of the population); Nepali (Nepal; 90%); Bengali (Bangladesh; 90%), and Dhivehi (the Maldives).

A History of Language Contact

Three millennia of contact between ethnolinguistic groups led to the convergence of four major language families in SA: Indo-European, Dravidian, Austroasiatic, and Tibeto-Burman. Bhatia and Ritchie (2006) provide a historical overview of how three languages, in particular, played a significant role in SA history: Sanskrit, Persian, and English. Each has had a significant impact on multilingualism right up to today, promoted and justified by ideologies based on religious, commercial and colonial interests.

Sanskrit education, promoted by Brahmins (under royal patronage) from the 6th century B.C., promoted Sanskrit as the language of Hindu scriptures, philosophical and technical literature throughout much of SA. Bhatia and Ritchie (2006) outline how Sanskrit significantly altered the form, function and use not only of north Indian languages, but also of Dravidian and other languages in south India such that "Sanskrit became the single most important marker of Indian culture—both in the north and in the south" (p. 788).

The advent of the Mogul empire from the 12th century heralded the influence of Islam and Persian in SA that probably reached its zenith in the mid-late 18th up to the early part of the 19th century. During this time, Persian became the official language of the court of the Mogul empire, and was dominant in administrative, social and educational domains over other SA languages. For instance, Kachru (1997, p. 563) observes that:

> The hegemony of Persian lasted over four centuries, resulting in the Persianization of Kashmiri literary and intellectual culture. The ancestral Sanskrit language was reduced to essentially ritualistic roles. The Pandits of Kashmir gradually turned to Persian and used it as a language of access, even to the study of their own Hindu religious and cultural texts such as the Mahabharata, Ramayana, Shivapurana, and the Bhagavad-Gita.

In contrast to Sanskrit, Persian was viewed as an imposed language in much of SA and, under the Moghuls, it became identified with Islam. Post-independence (1947–), extensive Persianization and Arabicization of Urdu has led to greater differentiation of the Urdu of Pakistan from the Urdu of India. Conversely, in India, there appears to have been an increase in the Sanskritization of Urdu (Abidi & Gargesh, 2008; Bhatia & Ritchie, 2006).

The British colonial era introduced English education in the 19th century to India, succinctly articulated in Lord Macaulay's stated mission for the British Raj in his oft-quoted Minute (Feb. 2, 1835) of creating "a class of persons, Indian in blood and color, but English in taste, in opinions, in morals and intellect." Macaulay's own attitudes to SA languages were negative (Bhatia & Ritchie, 2013: 854),

> I have no knowledge of either Sanskrit or Arabic. But I have done what I could to form a correct estimate of their value....I am quite ready to take

the oriental learning at the valuation of the orientalists themselves. I have never found one amongst them who could deny that a single shelf of a good European library was worth the whole native literature of India and Arabia.

The high prestige language, English, introduced a new phase of multilingualism in SA and continues to have a powerful impact across SA (see below).

Indian Multilingualism Today

India, considered by many as a paragon of national multilingualism, has 22 constitutionally "scheduled" (national) languages that map onto state boundaries within the country, the consequence of a political process begun in 1956 that is still ongoing. Official Government of India figures from the last (2001) Census, report a total of 122 languages being spoken across India—'rationalized' and reduced from 6661 in the original raw data—and 234 mother tongues, and not counting languages which have fewer than 10,000 speakers (see on interpreting Census data, Bhatia & Ritchie, 2006; Ladousa, 2010; Pattanayak, 1981).

Factors responsible for classification as 'scheduled' languages in the country's constitution vary on various dimensions of group vitality (see Giles, Bourhis, & Taylor, 1977; Sachdev & Bourhis, 1993), and include the numeric strength, literary tradition, regional representation and power of the speakers of the major languages, as well as the success of political and ideological pressure groups (Kachru, 1997; for the criteria used, see Annamalai, 2001; Krishnamurti, 1998). The notion of a national 'scheduled' language in India is a dynamic one, with new ones expecting to be elevated as processes of ideological conflict and differentiation (Sachdev & Giles, 2004) interplay with migration, advances in technology and trade globalization (Bhatia & Ritchie, 2013).

Hindi (including its varieties) is not only the most widely spoken regional language (across several states, approx 40% according to 2001 Indian Census figures), but it is also the 'official' language of the nation. Contrary to expectations pre-independence, English has continued to enjoy 'associate official language' status. In India, although English and Hindi are high vitality languages, Hindi (and its varieties) is associated with greater economic and cultural power as it has wider communicative access within India, while English is associated with greater social mobility, and has no competitor at the elite and global levels (Bhatia & Ritchie, 2006).

Interestingly, high vitality languages may also feel threatened by other high vitality languages in multilingual settings. For instance, Bhatia and Ritchie (2006) discuss how abolishing English was the aim of protests in one Hindi-speaking state in north India (Uttar Pradesh) in the 1990s, while those in a neighboring one

(Bihar) favored making English compulsorily in the school curriculum. Overall in India, English and Hindi occupy the top of a four-tiered language pyramid outlined by Bhatia and Ritchie (2006); the second tier is represented by the 22 'scheduled' languages, followed by several hundred languages of widespread currency (over 100, third tier), and an even greater number of local vernaculars (over 200 and possibly into the thousands, fourth tier) at the lowest level.

According to the 2001 Indian census, 77–78% of the total population of India lives in more than half a million (638,365) villages and speaks in numerous vernaculars. Communication with rural India is either in Hindi (and varieties) or the regional languages and their local vernaculars as English proficiency is very low there. The influence between rural vernaculars and Hindi is bidirectional and boundaries have become very fluid given the strong literary past in regional languages (e.g., with devotional poetry) combined with popular media today. Bollywood is perhaps the most celebrated force for bridging the gap between the urban/rural (and regional), and mutual intelligibility between spoken Hindi and rural language varieties continues to grow.

Due to a number of factors associated with globalization, the technology revolution and economic liberalization, Bhatia and Ritchie (2006) suggest that not only are there new patterns of migration (e.g., Hindi speaking out-of-state Indians going to work in rural Punjab), but that middle-class rural India appears to have more disposable income than urban India. Thus, media and marketers tailor their messages (and products) in dozens of major and minor languages, providing for a multilingualism planted/developed in local vernaculars (see Bhatia, 2007; Bhatia & Ritchie, 2013). Rural markets, fairs, festivals and pilgrim sites are extremely fertile contexts for the promotion of multilingual communication on the ground (see Bhatia, 2000, 2007; Masica, 1991).

Indian educational policies are also favorable to the promotion of multilingualism and multiculturalism (Kachru, 1997; Krishnamurti, 1998; Schiffman, 1999; Sridhar, 1996). For instance, not only does the National Academy of Letters (The Sahitya Akademi and its regional counterparts) promote literary activities in at least eighteen of the "scheduled" languages, but 47 languages are used in primary education, and the national 'Three Language Formula' aims for trilingualism (or quadrilingualism) in education. However despite these, only some are privileged amongst the huge array of languages in India, and many minority and tribal groups face language endangerment due to their extremely low vitality in terms of demography, institutional support and status (Abbi, 2008; Bhatia & Ritchie, 2006; Giles et al., 1977; Sachdev & Bourhis, 1993).

The Constitution of India provides various measures to safeguard the rights of linguistic, religious and ethnic minorities, including the right to mother tongue instruction during primary years for linguistic minority group children. However, despite such constitutional measures, linguistic minorities of Tibeto-Burman and Munda origin are unable to withstand the linguistic and cultural attraction of the high vitality languages around them. Bhatia and Ritchie (2006) argue that, in some cases, some members of the urban tribal population even take "special pride in confessing a lack of knowledge of their mother tongue and take pride in associating with the dominant language of the region (i.e., Hindi) while interacting with members of their linguistic group" (p. 803). The newly formed state of Jharkhand aims, in part, to reverse this trend (Bhatia & Ritchie, 2013).

Punjabi: One SA Language across Borders

Speakers of Punjabi (and its varieties, estimated to be greater than 100 million worldwide, Sachdev, 1995)—and Punjabi is considered to be among the top twenty languages in the world by sheer numbers of speakers (Lewis, 2009)—span across the border between India and Pakistan in northwest SA. The majority are to be found in Pakistan (over 70%), with a large number of the remainder in India, where they form less than 4% of the national population, but are in the majority (over 70%) in the state of Punjab.

A number of researchers, including Bhatia (2008), argue that Punjabi speakers "form a single (socio) linguistic area" (p. 127) in spite of the multiple, criss-crossing categorizations along lines of nationality (Pakistani-Indian), religion (Sikh-Muslim-Hindu), writing (4 scripts for Punjabi), language (and dialectal) variation, literary tradition, and socio-cultural ethnicity. The suggestion is that that Punjabi speakers are united by a common heritage (stretching hundreds of years) and culture, referred to as 'Punjabiyat' (Punjabiness), consisting of distinctive songs, art, literature (poetry, story, tradition) and belief systems (Khubchandani, 1997). Speaking Punjabi is associated with qualities of rurality, openness, liveliness, and fun-loving nature, and its use mainly as a marker of intimacy, humor and informality (Bhatia, 2000, 2007).

The fate of Punjabi has varied across national borders as a consequence of the partition of the sub-continent in 1947. It provides, therefore, a useful illustration of comparative ideologies and attitudes at the national level. India, following a pluralistic ideology (Sachdev & Bourhis, 2001), has re-drawn state boundaries to create a state, Punjab, where Punjabi is the official language. As a consequence, Punjabi has flourished in India, where Punjabi speakers have access to government services and education. Additionally, even though Punjabi is a mother-tongue of many Muslims, Hindus, and Sikhs in India, it is Sikhs who claim it as their language (see below).

In contrast, after partition Pakistan followed a one nation-one religion-one language ideology. Punjabi became a majority language (approx 60% of population) with no official status in Pakistan, where Urdu was declared the only national language, despite only being spoken by a minority (approx 8% of population). There are no official policies in Pakistan to promote Punjabi, in spite of its speakers being in the majority.

Bhatia (2008) reports on how Punjabi Pakistanis have responded to the perceived threats to their linguistic identity by reducing the amount of Urdu vocabulary in Punjabi, "even at the cost of intelligibility and risk of being labelled anti-Islamic" (p. 128; for the Punjabi language movement, see Rahman, 1996). Given the dynamic nature of ethnolinguistic relations and the diversity of the Punjabi sociolinguistic area (and typical of SA), it is noteworthy that there are also movements aiming for separate language status for varieties previously been labelled as Punjabi dialects/varieties in Pakistan, such as Siraiki, Hindko, and Pothohari (see Bhatia, 2008).

Brass (1994) discussed how linguistic identities in north-western India were shaped by conflict along political and religious dimensions in the 19th and 20th centuries. Vis-à-vis Punjabi, Sachdev (1995) argued that:

> ...the polarization of religious differences in the Punjab, the bi-national 1947 partition of the region of Punjab and the further 1966 partition of the Indian state of Punjab into three separate entities divided along linguistic lines, left Sikhs as the prime 'owners' and promoters of the Punjabi language. (p 176)

The Sikhs, who consider Punjabi as being the language of their religion, are in a majority in the state of Punjab (59%, India Census 2001), and are also highly visible in the larger urban centres of North India, such as Delhi, outside of the Punjab (the current Prime Minister of India, Dr Manmohan Singh, is a Sikh). There are also significant and vital Punjabi-speaking Sikh communities outside of India, such as in the UK, USA and Canada (Sachdev, 1995).

India is perhaps the most favorable country for Sikhism and Punjabi vitality as a consequence of its plural ideology and multilingual policies. It has its own official version of geo-linguistic language planning, where most of the national languages are generally majorities in their home state—in this case, the state of Punjab. The school education system also aims to promote the teaching and learning of three languages, which includes Punjabi (but see critique by Mohanty, 2010).

Canada also has a pluralistic approach, encapsulated by an official policy of federal multiculturalism. However, this is designed to operate through the official languages, that is, English and/or French and, as such, it does not provide much support for 'non-official' language maintenance. Education in Canada is under provincial jurisdiction, conducted through the medium of one (or more infrequently both) of the official languages. Recently (in the last decade or so), with the help of the provincial government, schools in places like Vancouver with significant Sikh populations have begun to provide support for 'non-official' languages like Punjabi, though not without opposition from significant sections of the dominant group (Sachdev, 1995).

In the UK, Punjabi language teaching has largely been in the hands of the family and the community. Government support for community languages, in a country where English is the official language (also Welsh in Wales), has generally been sparse and unsystematic in spite of repeated community demands (McPake & Sachdev, 2010). There has been some success, in that a handful of schools in London and other parts of the UK now offer Punjabi as a subject on the curriculum. However, given the low status ascribed to 'community languages' (McPake & Sachdev, 2010), Punjabi language teaching has an uncertain future in the UK. Unlike India and Canada, the UK has no national policy supporting cultural pluralism, in spite of the fact that all major urban centers and many UK citizens are multilingual and multicultural.

Sachdev (1995) explored the maintenance of Punjabi linguistic identities amongst Sikh adolescents in India, Canada and the UK. His participants came from four urban centres: in Amritsar (capital of the state of Punjab, India, a Punjabi-dominant majority setting); in Delhi (the national capital, a Hindi-dominant, Punjabi minority setting in India); and also in the two of largest populations of Sikhs outside of India—in London, UK (English dominant, a Punjabi minority outside of India) and in Vancouver, Canada (English dominant, Punjabi minority setting outside of India).

Sachdev's (1995) main findings were unambiguous in that identification as Punjabi Sikh was high and resilient and able, in large part, to resist the stretching of regional and national boundaries due to migration and mobility. Importantly, in all national contexts, Punjabi linguistic identities were consistently and positively related to 'Punjabiness' (i.e., Punjabi cultural identity), reinforcing Bhatia's (2008) arguments above as well as supporting the widely recognized view that language and culture are intricately intertwined. There was also good evidence that identification with Sikhism positively predicted Punjabi linguistic identity in northern India, but not outside of India. Interestingly, and as might be expected from a macro-level analysis of national ideologies and their impact, national identities subtracted from linguistic identity outside of India, in Canada and UK, but not in India. Supportive national and regional ideologies and policies (and their implementation) are important for the maintenance of minority linguistic identities. This is likely to enhance social cohesion between members of majorities and minorities, as well as acceptance and participation as full citizens of modern democratic societies.

English in SA: Glocal and Global

"People who know English are more exposed, more knowledgeable and therefore, more successful in life than those who don't. Without English, there is no academic or occupational future." (Nepali interviewee, Giri, 2011, p. 213)

More than one and a half centuries after its introduction to SA, English is no longer associated with just the colonial power, and is a critical part of the SA linguistic landscape. Bhatia and Ritchie (2006, 2013) even discuss how Englishization of Indian languages has not only paralleled Sanskritization and Persianization, but also that English has undergone significant changes itself as a consequence of being in India (referred to as 'nativization' of Indian English: Bhatia, 1982; Kachru, 1983). Multilingualism in English is increasing, but it still at fairly low levels overall in SA, and is confined largely to the elite. It enjoys high vitality in all national and international spheres and domains including education, law, government, media, science and technology. Domains of language use that once belonged to Sanskrit or Persian are now dominated by English.

In most SA countries, as a consequence of globalization, English language education is booming, especially for the elite and middle classes (Coleman, 2010; Giri, 2011; Imam, 2005; Ladousa, 2010). By all accounts, in India, private English language education has also mushroomed since 1991, when the nation altered its economic path from a socialist to a market-based one in the globalized world. As Hornberger and Vaish (2009) suggest, this change has also resulted in huge demand for English-medium instruction at younger ages (in primary school). Indeed, given the population, age distribution, demand and increasing economic clout of India, there may be some validity to Graddol's (2006) claim that India is an important player in maintaining the status of English as a global language.

However, as a number have cautioned, there are severe challenges ahead in terms of teacher education, pedagogy and curriculum (Graddol, 2006; Hornberger & Vaish, 2009). Some have also questioned the potential negative and subtractive impact of the rise of English on regional and minority languages in SA, especially given that English-medium schools are usually better equipped and staffed than non-English medium schools (e.g., Giri, 2011; Imam, 2005; Skutnabb-Kangas & Phillipson, 2010;). English opens major doors to social mobility in India and across SA generally; alas, it is one whose key most members of the general population are unable to obtain. Inequalities between elites and the general population appear to be increasing since the economic reforms in the 1990s (e.g., Ansari & Akhtar, 2012), and the future does not augur well for the have-nots.

Code-switching

Thus far, the discussion has focussed on ideologies, policies, attitudes in broad societal and historical perspective, but not on actual language behavior in SA.

> The maternal tongue of a Bombay spice merchant is a Kathiawari dialect of Gujerati; he usually speaks Kacchi at work, however. In the market place he speaks Marathi and, at the railway station, Hindustani. English is the medium when he flies with Air India to New Delhi, and he sometimes watches English-language films at the cinema. He reads a Gujerati newspaper written in a dialect more standard than his own. (Edwards, 1994, p. 2)

This illustrates not only the multilinguality that is characteristic of SA, but also exemplifies how 'normal' interactions in India involve switching between many different languages, revealing the dynamics of language usage and constant negotiation of identities. Code-switching can be broadly defined as "the alternate use of two or more languages" (Grosjean, 1982, p. 145; also termed translanguaging) is a normal defining feature of interactions in India, as in other bilingual and multilingual societies around the world (Garcia, 2009; Gardner-Chloros, 2009; Hamers & Blanc, 2000; Lawson & Sachdev, 2000; Milroy & Muysken, 1995; Myers-Scotton, 1993; Romaine, 1995; Sachdev & Bourhis, 2001). Bhatia and Ritchie (2006) suggest that in addition to the constant shifting between the various languages, "intra- and inter-sentential code-mixing within a single discourse unit is a way of life" in India (p. 797). They quote a trilingually switched English-PERSIAN-*Hindi* rebuke of a husband by his wife:

> vil yuu shat ap! baRaa *MARDAANAA RUAAB* jhaaR rahe ho...samajh kayaa rakhaa hai mujhe! gaav-gavaii kii chuii-muii, baikvard, *JAAHIL AURAT*, ghar kii *BAANDII* yaa apne *HUKAM KII GULAAM*? ghar aur bachion kii jitnii *ZIMMEDAARII AURAT* kii hai, utnii *MARD* kii bhii, bhuul se bhii apne ko *TIISMAARKHAAN* samajhne kii *ZURRAT* na karnaa.

> (translation: 'Will you shut up! Why are you shedding off your male egoistic dominant behaviour/act. What do you think of me? I am not a submissive, backward, rustic, slave, village woman—slave to (your) order. The responsibility of children is as much of men as of women. Don't you ever dare to consider yourself a brave hero. (pp. 797–798)

Relatedly, there is also evidence of SA societies in diaspora (Punjabi speakers in UK) code-mixing at rates many times higher than other groups (Cheshire &

Gardner-Chloros, 1998). Thus, it may appear that perhaps the most common form of multilingual communication amongst Indians is code-switching, given its frequency, fluency and all pervasive nature (Bhatia, 2011; Bhatia & Ritchie, 1996; Kachru, 1978; Pandharipande, 1990; Singh, 1981).

Not only is code-switching prevalent in everyday interactions, a historical perspective would suggest that it may have led to profound changes to the syntax of languages in contact in India. For instance, Bhatia and Ritchie (2006) write that:

> Centuries-old coexistence and an ongoing process of convergence has led to an unmarked pattern of wide-spread naturalistic linguistic coalescence rather than separation, dominance and disintegration. Large-scale diffusion of linguistic features across genetic and areal boundaries has resulted in mutually-feeding relationships and reciprocity. (p. 795)

Bhatia and Ritchie (2013) discuss the large variety of linguistic and sociolinguistic factors underlying code-switching/mixing in India, including identities, attitudes, social mobility, degree of economic and socio-political power associated with languages (e.g., Ritchie & Bhatia, 2006). In examining everyday conversations, they refer to determinants of code-switching in terms of social psychological affiliations and also various discourse features such as code-switching to emphasize, to interject, to quote, to reiterate, to qualify, to elaborate, to change addressee and to provide extra comments on topic (Bhatia and Ritchie, in press).

Sachdev and Bourhis (2001) modelled these and other factors in terms of the interaction between macro-level variables (e.g., state ideologies, language policies, power, and status of groups), micro-level variables (e.g., discourse markers, sociolinguistic domain norms and rules) as mediated by social psychological variables (e.g., attitudes, perceptions and identities). The determinants of code-switching are multifactorial and interact dynamically throughout the course of communication to affect various proximal outcomes in the immediacy of the interaction, including multilingual accommodation, discoursal attuning, and non-verbal accommodation, and more distal patterns of additive/subtractive bilingualism (Lambert, 1975) and multiculturalism. This, in turn, contributes to the longer-term maintenance and loss, shift and revival of languages and cultures (Bourhis, 2000; Fishman, 1991; Giles, Leets, & Coupland, 1990; Sachdev & Giles, 2004).

Conclusion

SA presents rich, natural and complex multilinguality on the ground that challenges conceptions and understandings based on monolingual ideological models.

An ideology of multilingualism as a resource differentiates and enriches. Language mixing/code-switching by multilinguals aims to attain the optimal result by the accommodation and augmentation of the linguistic and socio-psychological meaning of the message, identities and ideologies (Bhatia, 2011; Lawson & Sachdev, 2000). While there is no question that such creative and communication needs cannot be filled either by English or by Hindi and/or any other language alone, it is also important to realize that language mixing is undergoing rapid and significant changes in both qualitative and quantitative terms as communicative needs of SA speakers change. For instance, future research may focus on the question of language(s) used by media and advertising in the age of hyper-globalization, where advances in communication technology are enabling in multiple modes and means at an exponential rate.

Much of the analysis presented in this chapter is drawn from previous research on language in SA that uses historical and sociolinguistic methodologies. Studies employing social psychological evaluative methodologies, such as the matched-guise technique (Lambert, 1975), are very rare in SA, though some do exist. For example, Booth (2009) in multilingual Darjeeling (in northeastern India with Nepali, Bengali, Hindi, & English), Dorjee, Giles, and Barker (2011) amongst Tibetan refugees in India (with Tibetan and Tibetan-Hindi code-switching), and Senaratne (2009) amongst urban Sinhala-English bilinguals in Sri Lanka (with Sinhala, English and code-switching), employed the matched-guise technique. Although the aims and foci of these studies varied, their findings are supportive of some of the analyses in this chapter. For instance, the high status of English in SA was reflected amongst evaluations by urban Sinhalas in Sri Lanka and amongst Indians of Nepali origin in north-eastern India. The multilingual code-switching character of communication in India (referred to above) appears to be found amongst long-term Tibetan refugees in India so that their use of Tibetan-with-some-Hindi is considered 'normative'. Interestingly, perhaps in an echo of the analysis concerning the Punjabi Sikhs above, Dorjee et al. (2011) also discuss whether there were lessons to be learnt from the high levels of language, culture and identity maintenance amongst Tibetans in India relative to those in the West (who appear to be assimilating).

The socio-historical analyses presented in this chapter may serve as a useful springboard for future attitudinal work in SA employing social psychological methodologies. For instance, programmes of research may focus on some of the distinctive characteristics of linguistic diversity in SA that are different from those in other regions of the world identified in this chapter such as (i) multilingualism and code-switching (especially as they appear to be normative and so widespread); (ii) Variation of evaluations of the same and different languages and varieties at local, regional and national levels; by groups and segments in society (such as the urban elite, rural majority, males, females, ethnicities). The potential range of studies in this genre, and in the field, is huge given the paucity of social psychological research on linguistic diversity in SA.

Processes of iconicity, fractal recursivity, and erasure referred to in the introductory chapter (Dragojevic, Giles, & Watson, this volume) in the pursuance of narrow nationalist ideologies (e.g., one language-one nation-one religion) post-independence have operated together to rationalize, justify and officially promote considerably reduced linguistic diversity across SA. The wide linguistic diversity on the ground has not led SA nations to engage in multilingual policies systematically, and, in several cases, has led to language endangerment and death.

In taking a long term historical perspective, Bhatia and Ritchie (2006) discussed the ideologies of prescriptivism dating back from the Sanskritization (6th century BC), through Persianization (12-18/19th centuries) and Englishization (from 19th century onwards). They also reported on instances of linguistic conflict in SA, including the anti-Hindi movements in the Tamil and Dravidian south in India in the 20th century (Das Gupta, 1970), the resistance to Urdu imposition for independence in Bangladesh (Rahman, 1996), and the creation of new 'scheduled' languages in the last decade. Using historical, social and linguistic analyses, they suggested that India represents a good example of long-term stable multilingualism where, despite prescriptivist ideologies and ongoing linguistic conflict, language diversity has flourished and the languages from outside the subcontinent have become a natural and integrated part of the landscape inside.

References

Abbi, A. (2008). Tribal languages. In B. Kachru, Y. Kachru, & S. N. Sridhar (Eds.), *Language in South Asia* (pp. 153–74). Cambridge, UK: Cambridge University Press.
Abbi, A. (2009). Is Great Andamanese genealogically and typologically distinct from Onge and Jarawa? *Language Sciences, 31*, 791–812.
Abidi, S. A. H., & Gargesh, R. (2008). Persian in South Asia. In B. Kachru, Y. Kachru, & S. N. Sridhar (Eds.), *Language in South Asia* (pp. 103–120). Cambridge, UK: Cambridge University Press.
Annamalai, E. (2001). *Managing multilingualism in India: Political and linguistic manifestations.* New Delhi: Sage.
Ansari, I., & Akhtar, S. (2012). Incidence of poverty in India: Issues and challenges. *International Journal of Multidisciplinary Research, 2*, 443–449.
Bhatia, T. (1982). English and vernaculars of India: Contact and change. *Applied Linguistics, 3*, 235–245.
Bhatia, T. (2000). *Advertising in rural India.* Tokyo: Tokyo Press.
Bhatia, T. (2007). *Advertising and marketing in rural India.* Delhi: Macmillan.

Bhatia, T. (2008). Major regional languages [of South Asia]. In B. Kachru, Y. Kachru, & S. N. Sridhar (Eds.), *Language in South Asia* (pp. 121–131). Cambridge, UK: Cambridge University Press.

Bhatia, T. (2011). The multilingual mind, optimization theory, and Hinglish. In R. Kothari & R. Snell (Eds.), *Chutneying English: The phenomenon of Hinglish* (pp. 37–52). New Delhi: Penguin Books.

Bhatia, T. & Ritchie, W. (1996). Bilingual language mixing, universal grammar, and second language acquisition. In W. C. Ritchie & T. K. Bhatia (Eds.), *Handbook of second language acquisition* (pp. 627–682). San Diego, CA: Academic Press.

Bhatia, T., & Ritchie, W. (2006). Bilingualism in South Asia. In T. Bhatia and W. Ritchie (Eds.) *Handbook of bilingualism* (pp. 780–807). Oxford, UK: Blackwell.

Bhatia, T., & Ritchie, W. (2013). Bilingualism and Multiculturalism in South Asia. In T. Bhatia & W. Ritchie (Eds.), *Handbook of bilingualism and multilingualism* (pp. 843–870). Oxford, UK: Wiley-Blackwell.

Booth, C. (2009). "An ocean of culture": Language ideologies and the social life of language in multilingual Darjeeling, India. *Texas Linguistic Forum, 53*, 8–17.

Bourhis, R. Y. (2000). Reversing language shift in Quebec. In J. Fishman (Ed.), *Reversing language shift: Can threatened languages be saved?* (pp. 5–38). Oxford, UK: Blackwell.

Brass, P. (1994). *Language, religion and politics in north India*. Cambridge, UK: Cambridge University Press.

Cheshire, J., & Gardner-Chloros, P. (1998). Code-switching and the sociolinguistic gender pattern. *International Journal of the Sociology of Language, 129*, 5–34.

Coleman, H. (2010). *Teaching and learning in Pakistan: The role of language in education*. Islamabad, Pakistan: The British Council.

Das Gupta, J. (1970). *Language conflict and national development. Group politics and national language policy in India*. Berkeley: University of California Press.

Dorjee, T., Giles, H., & Barker, V. (2011). Diasporic communication: Cultural deviance and accommodation among Tibetan exiles in India. *Journal of Multilingual and Multicultural Development, 32*, 343–350.

Edwards, J. (1994). *Multilingualism*. London, UK: Routledge.

Fishman, J. (1991). *Language and ethnicity*. Amsterdam: John Benjamins.

García, O. (2009). *Bilingual education in the 21st century: A global perspective*. Oxford: Wiley/Blackwell.

Gardner-Chloros, P. (2009). *Code-switching*. Cambridge, UK: Cambridge University Press.

Giles, H., Bourhis, R., & Taylor, D. (1977). Towards a theory of language in ethnic group relations. In H. Giles (Ed.), *Language, ethnicity, and intergroup relations* (pp. 307–334). New York: Academic Press.

Giles, H., Leets., L., & Coupland, N. (1990). Minority language group status: A theoretical conspexus. *Journal of Multilingual and Multicultural Development, 11*, 37–55.

Giri, R. A. (2010). Cultural anarchism: The consequences of privileging languages in Nepal. *Journal of Multilingualism and Multilingualism Development, 31*, 87–100.

Giri, R. A. (2011). Languages and language politics: How invisible language politics produces visible results in Nepal. *Language Problems and Language Planning, 35*, 197–221.

Graddol, D. (2006). *English next: Why global English may mean the end of 'English as a Foreign Language'*. London: British Council.

Grosjean, F. (1982). *Life with two languages*. Cambridge, MA: Harvard University Press.
Hamers, J., & M. Blanc, M. (2000). *Bilinguality and bilingualism*. Cambridge, UK: Cambridge University Press.
Hornberger, N., & Vaish, V. (2009). Multilingual language policy and school linguistic practice: Globalization and English language teaching in India, Singapore and South Africa. *Compare, 4/5*, 305–320.
Imam, S. R. (2005). English as a global language and the question of nation-building education in Bangladesh. *Comparative Education, 41*, 471–486.
Kachru, B. (1978). Toward structuring code-mixing: An Indian perspective. *International Journal of the Sociology of Language, 16*, 28–46.
Kachru, B. (1983). *The Indianization of English: The English language in India*. Delhi: Oxford University Press.
Kachru, B. (1997). Language in Indian society. In S. N. Sridhar & N. K. Mattoo (Eds.), *Ananya: A portrait of India* (pp. 555–585). New York: The Association of Indians in America.
Kachru, B., & Bhatia, T. (1978). The emerging 'dialect' conflict in Hindi: A case of glottopolitics. *International Journal of the Sociology of Language, 16*, 47–56.
Khubchandani, L. (1997). *Revisualizing boundaries: A pluralism ethos*. New Delhi: Sage.
Krishnamurti, Bh. (1998) *Language, education and Society*. New Delhi: Sage.
Ladousa, C. (2010). On mother and other tongues: Sociolinguistics, schools, and language ideology in Northern India. *Language Sciences, 32*, 602–14.
Lambert, W. E. (1975). Culture and language as factors in learning and education. In A. Wolfgang (Ed.), *Education of immigrant children* (pp. 55–83). Toronto: Ontario Institute for Studies in Education.
Lawson, S., & Sachdev, I. (2000). Codeswitching in Tunisia: Attitudinal and behavioral dimensions. *Journal of Pragmatics 32*, 1343–61.
Lewis, P. (2009) *Ethnologue: Languages of the world*. http://www.ethnologue.com/
Masica, C. P. (1991). *The Indo-Aryan languages*. Cambridge, UK: Cambridge University Press.
McPake, J., & Sachdev, I. (2010). Community languages: Mapping provision and matching needs in higher education in England. *Sociolinguistic Studies, 4*, 509–534.
Milroy, L., & Muysken, P. (1995). *One speaker, two languages*. Cambridge, UK: Cambridge University Press.
Mohanty, A. (2010). Multilingualism and predicaments of education in India. In O. García, T. Skutnabb-Kangas & M. E. Torres-Guzmán (Eds.), *Imagining multilingual schools: Languages in education and glocalization* (pp. 262–283). Bristol, UK: Multilingual Matters.
Myers-Scotton, C. (1993). *Social motivations for codeswitching: Evidence from Africa*. Oxford, UK: Clarendon Press.
Pandharipande, R. (1990). Formal and functional constraints on code-mixing. In R. Jacobson (Ed.), *Code-switching as a worldwide phenomenon* (pp. 33–39). New York: Peter Lang.
Pattanayak, D. P. (1981). *Multilingualism and mother tongue education*. New Delhi: Oxford University Press.
Rahman, T. (1996). *Language and politics in Pakistan*. Karachi, Pakistan: Oxford University Press.
Rahman, T. (2010). A multilingual language-in-education policy for indigenous minorities in Bangladesh: challenges and possibilities. *Current Issues in Language Planning, 4*, 341–359.

Ritchie, W. C., & Bhatia, T. K.. (2006). Social and Psychological factors in language mixing, In T. K. Bhatia & W. C. Ritchie (Eds.), *Handbook of bilingualism* (pp. 336–352). Oxford, UK: Blackwell.

Romaine, S. (1995*). Bilingualism*. Oxford, UK: Blackwell.

Sachdev, I. (1995). Predicting Punjabi linguistic identity: From high to low in-group vitality contexts, *International Journal of Punjab Studies, 2*, 175–194.

Sachdev, I., & Bourhis, R. Y. (1993). Ethnolinguistic vitality and social identity. In D. Abrams & M. A. Hogg (Eds.), *Group motivation: social psychological perspectives* (pp. 33–51). Hemel Hempstead, UK: Harvester Wheatsheaf.

Sachdev, I., & Bourhis, R. Y. (2001). Multilingual communication. In W. P. Robinson & H. Giles (Eds.), *The new handbook of language and social psychology* (pp. 407–428). Chichester, UK: Wiley & Sons.

Sachdev, I., & Giles, H. (2004). Bilingual accommodation. In T. Bhatia & W. Ritchie (Eds.), *The handbook of bilingualism* (pp. 353–378). Oxford, UK: Blackwell.

Schiffman, H. (1999). South and Southeast Asia. In J. A. Fishman (Ed.), *Language and ethnic identity* (pp. 431–443). Oxford, UK: Oxford University Press.

Senaratne, C. D. (2009). *Sinhala-English code-mixing in Sri Lanka: A sociolinguistic study*. Utrecht, the Netherlands: LOT.

Singh, R. (1981). Grammatical constraints on code-switching. *Recherches linguistics Montreal, 17*, 155–163.

Skutnabb-Kangas, T., & Phillipson, R. (2010). The politics of language in globalisation: maintenance, marginalization, or murder. In. N. Coupland (Ed.), *The handbook of language and globalization* (pp. 77–100). Malden, MA: Wiley-Blackwell.

Sridhar, K. (1996). Language in education: Minorities and multilingualism in India. *International Review of Education, 42*, 327–347.

Weinriech, Max. (1945). The YIVO faces the postwar world. *YIVO Bletter, 25*, 3–18.

CHAPTER NINE

Language Attitudes in Australia and New Zealand

ANN WEATHERALL

This chapter discusses language variation in New Zealand and Australia and its social meanings. It considers the languages spoken in each country, with a focus on indigenous languages and distinctive varieties of English. Institutional support in terms of governmental policies on indigenous and minority languages will be discussed in terms of societal language attitudes. English is the dominant language in both countries, and distinctive varieties and subvarieties of Australian English (AusE) and New Zealand English (NZE) have emerged. Speaker evaluation studies that have investigated Australasian attitudes towards their accents will be reviewed. Future challenges to the study of language attitudes in New Zealand and Australia will be considered at the conclusion of this chapter.

Australia and New Zealand have distinctive language environments, but there are important points of confluence for language attitude matters. Both countries were colonised by Britain. The racist attitudes of the settlers towards indigenous peoples and their languages characterized early language contact and, arguably, continue to haunt language revitalization efforts today. With respect to the emergence of AusE and NZE, the linguistic heritage of the settlers importantly shaped the development of the distinctive varieties of English that currently exist in each country (for New Zealand English, see Hay, Maclagan, & Gordon, 2008; for Australian English, see Blair, 1989; Cochrane, 1989). Immigrants to New Zealand were typically working class and came to the country to better their lives. In contrast, Australia was used initially as a penal colony. Furthermore, current patterns of immigration continue to exert a powerful influence on language in the two societies, with visible immigrant language communities particularly within Australia's much larger population (Clyne, 1991).

Work in language and social psychology, here as well as elsewhere, has long recognised that attitudes towards language and communication are inseparable from social identity and intergroup relations (e.g., Giles, 2012; Giles & Coupland, 1991). Thus, evaluations of a language, dialect, accent or register can be taken as indicating some judgement of the social group or groups to which the speaker belongs, which may or may not translate into discriminatory practices (Gallois, Watson, & Brabant, 2007). The close relationships between language variation, social identities and patterns of advantage and disadvantage in society mean that language attitudes are deeply political matters. The current endangerment of Aboriginal languages in Australia and Te Reo Māori in New Zealand are a continuing legacy of the racist world-views that were part and parcel of European colonisation (Benton, 1991; McKay, 2011; Tatz, 1999).

Social identity is an important aspect of language and communication attitudes. A positive and distinctive sense of self arises in part from the social groups of which one is a member. One manifestation of social identity (or social identities) is the languages, dialects and/or registers one speaks. The existence of dictionaries of New Zealand English (Orsman, 1997) and Australian English (Butler, 1981) is one illustration of the importance of linguistic distinctiveness as a marker of national identity. Furthermore, ethnolinguistic vitality has long been recognised as crucial for the psychological health and well-being of its community of speakers (Giles, Bourhis, & Taylor, 1977). Linguistic distinctiveness and innovation are interesting to document in their own right, but they are also closely linked to matters central to social psychology.

Attitudes towards language and communication are incredibly complex, given multiple dimensions of linguistic diversity and the roles of cognition, affect and interactional dynamics which shape them and/or their expression (Gallois et al., 2007). Classification frameworks usefully describe the important aspects of language attitudes research (Garrett, Coupland, & Williams, 1993; Ryan, Giles, & Hewstone, 1988). One aspect identified in those frameworks, already alluded to, is the treatment of language at a societal level. This chapter has as one focus the status of indigenous languages and governmental policy and practices around their use and survival. Two other important areas of language attitude research are studies that have solicited people's opinions about language matters explicitly, and studies using indirect measures such as the speaker evaluation paradigm.

In what follows, some research using direct and indirect measures of language attitudes in New Zealand and Australia will be reviewed. An important concern being addressed in language attitude surveys in New Zealand is to document non-

Māori compared to Māori attitudes towards Te Reo Māori (the indigenous language of New Zealand). Promoting positive attitudes towards Te Reo Māori is part of a government strategy to support the language, and surveys have been conducted to evaluate the success of those strategies. A rather different focus is evident from a research program that examined New Zealand and Australian attitudes towards their accents where matters of intergroup identity were brought to the fore.

Language Attitudes in New Zealand and Australian Societies

An aspect of language attitudes is the ways in which language is treated in society. Historically, in both New Zealand and Australia racist world views of colonialists included negative attitudes towards indigenous languages. Contemporary ethnic relationships continue to be evidenced by governmental support for indigenous and other minority languages. The dominance of English in New Zealand and Australia can be viewed neutrally as merely a response to its increasing status as an international language, or more critically, as a new kind of linguistic imperialism. New Zealand policy regarding what languages can be used for government business illustrates the important symbolism of language status at a societal level.

In New Zealand there are two official languages—Te Reo Māori and New Zealand sign language—which are formally accorded special status in law (by comparison, no Australian languages have this). English is a third de facto 'official' language in New Zealand by virtue of its pervasiveness across all areas of social life, which is also the case in Australia. After English, Samoan is the most widely spoken language in daily contexts in New Zealand. Pacific Islanders are one of New Zealand's largest ethnic groups, and Samoans constitute a Pacific majority. Advocates of the community are calling for a specific language policy, so that Pacific languages can also be accorded formal official status (Donoghue, 2012). These calls show language recognition by statute symbolises formally, at least an acknowledgement and appreciation for minority and marginalised social groups' status within society.

The official status of minority languages in law is symbolic. English has no special legal status in either New Zealand or Australia. because its dominance means no such recognition is required. Nevertheless, language recognition in law is an important political strategy to promote and support members of linguistic minorities. For example, New Zealand now has, for the first time, a profoundly hearing impaired Member of Parliament (MP). As a hearing impaired MP, Mojo Matthew's presence resulted in maiden speeches being translated into sign language, for the first time in the history of New Zealand. Furthermore, the official status of New Zealand sign language was used to argue for a controversial increase in resources to pay for note-takers to enable the honourable Matthew to follow parliamentary debate (O'Brien, 2012). The case of Mojo Matthew is a compelling illustration of the complex and ambivalent interplay between policy, politics and practice in relation to minority languages. Indigenous languages are a special case of minority languages because of their distinctiveness to New Zealand and Australian societies, respectively.

Indigenous languages

New Zealand and Australia are very different with respect to their Indigenous languages. Precolonisation, New Zealand had only one indigenous language—Te Reo Māori, with some regional variation (Benton, 1991). In contrast, it is thought that around 250 distinct languages were spoken in Australia before significant European contact, with most languages also having considerable dialectal variation (Dixon, 1980). An unfortunate similarity between the two countries is that patterns of language contact, of colonisation and rather shameful histories of racist attitudes and institutional practices, have resulted in significant undermining of the linguistic vitality of indigenous language/s. In the case of Australia, the extent of language endangerment or death (around 98%) has been understood as part of a history of race-relations that effectively constitutes cultural genocide (Tatz, 1999).

The extent of language loss in New Zealand and Australia are unfortunate cases that powerfully illustrate Giles et al.'s (1977) model of ethnolinguistic vitality. An important factor in that model is attitudes towards a language, with positive ones linked to language maintenance. In the case of Australia, there was an often-held assumption from the earliest days of European colonization that Aboriginal languages were of lesser value than English (Walsh, 1993). The burden of language learning for communication was thus on the Aboriginal people, not the settlers. A striking example of a lack of will to accommodate linguistically was the colonisation of the Sydney area, where capture and force were used to ensure English language learning and use (Troy, 1993).

In contrast in New Zealand, and perhaps less typical of general patterns of cololonisation, the European settlers did accommodate, at least initially, by learning Te Reo Māori and by using it, for example, in the missionary schools as the medium for education (Spools, 1993). In the early days, and more similar to Australia, was the New Zealand government's assimilationist attitudes, whereby the ultimate goal was towards English monolingualism. For example, the 1867 Native Schools Act discouraged the use of and teaching in Te Reo Māori. In both New Zealand and Australia colonisation, and the more or less racist attitudes that were brought with it, resulted in significant, albeit variable, language loss within 100 years of early European settlement. During this time indigenous peoples also became over-represented as socially and economically disadvantaged groups. The loss of their own languages has been widely linked to negative indicators of well-being, which in the case of Te Reo Māori at least resulted in a negative feedback loop that led to further degeneration of the indigenous language (Benton, 1991).

Around the middle of the 20th century intense concern for ethnic identities was noted, which resulted in grassroots movements and governmental language policy for language revival, not only in Australasia but world-wide (Kirkpatrick, 2007). The link between language and well-being was again being recognised, albeit in a more positive way—native language preservation was acknowledged as crucial for the psychological health of indigenous speakers and for the safe-guarding of cultures. Evidence to support the close relationship between language and well-being is easy to find. For example, young Aboriginal and Torres Strait Islander people who speak an Indigenous language are less likely to abuse illicit drugs and alcohol (McKay, 2011).

In Australia, this period of recognition and support for indigenous languages was evidenced by a national policy on languages, published in 1987 (McKay, 2011). The policy was quite comprehensive considering the status of languages, teaching and learning of languages and language services in three language groupings—Aboriginal and Torres Strait Islander languages (including creoles), English, and other languages such as Australian sign language. A concrete and celebrated outcome of the policy was the nationwide establishment of Aboriginal language centres that attracted considerable local, grassroots involvement.

Despite improved institutional support for Indigenous Aboriginal Languages, McKay (2011) noted that national government attitudes towards them are inconsistent. On the one hand, a national indigenous languages policy was established in 2009 that aims to promote, maintain and develop critically endangered Indigenous languages and their speakers. On the other hand, Australia's support for the United Nations Declaration of Rights of Indigenous Peoples, that includes support for languages, was declared by relevant government officials as aspirational, rather than binding.

In Australia, as in the USA, state level policies powerfully influence key institutional practices that can affect social change. Few Australian States have an Aboriginal languages policy, and those that do are primarily focused on language awareness and language learning rather than language maintenance and revitalisation (McKay, 2011). As a consequence, much state-based policy is in the field of school-based education, which even if implemented effectively is unlikely to be sufficient to change attitudes and instigate practices that will support language revival. Furthermore, there is no evidence that indigenous languages will be given precedence, particularly in the Northern territories where the indigenous community languages are still surviving. In sum, if policies and their implementation are taken as a proxy for societal attitudes towards indigenous languages, then at best they seem equivocal in Australia.

In two important respects the situation regarding indigenous language differs between New Zealand and Australia. In New Zealand there is only one main language other than English, and there is no second-tier state-level government. Those differences aside, compared to Australia, government structures in New Zealand point to a more positive and committed approach to the promotion of Te Reo Māori (De Bres, 2011). As previously mentioned, Te Reo Māori has been established in statute—the Māori Language Act, 1987—as an official language. Further, there is a government agency—Māori Language Commission—whose responsibilities include promoting Te Reo Māori as a living language and as an ordinary means of communication. Positive attitudes—in both Institutional policies and at an individual level—are viewed as key to its missions. Initiatives include television advertising, a Māori language week and the development of targeted resources for more and less advanced speakers.

Government commissioned language attitude surveys (see below) are being used in an attempt to systematically evaluate the Commission's effectiveness at promoting Te Reo Māori. However, there is considerable anecdotal evidence of a generally positive attitude. For example, the New Zealand National anthem is now routinely sung in both English and Te Reo Māori at, for example, important cultural and sporting events. Also, Radio New Zealand (New Zealand's national public radio) announcers routinely use Māori greetings and introductions. National television has Māori language programmes, and there is a television channel that broadcasts exclusively in Te Reo Māori.

In New Zealand there is also a strong and well-known grassroots movement, which begun in the 1980s, that involved the establishment of language nests or Kōhanga Reo for pre-school children. The establishment of a Kura Kaupapa Māori independent school movement followed, to provide primary and then secondary immersion schools for the children coming out of Kōhanga Reo. There is some evidence that the loss of vitality of Te Reo Māori has been stemmed, with the 2006 New Zealand census reporting a small increase in the number of speakers who have conversational fluency. However, language scholars remain ambivalent about the future of Te Reo Māori as a living language, not because of negative attitudes towards it, but due to a lack of evidence of intergenerational transmission (Spolsky, 1995).

The large majority of Māori in New Zealand and Aboriginal people in Australia do not speak their native language. The existence of a distinctive Māori English in New Zealand (Holmes, 1997) and Aboriginal English in Australia (Malcolm

& Grote, 2007) is another way of marking ethnic group identification. The emergence of distinctive varieties of English is not restricted to indigenous communities. For example, in New Zealand Hay et al. (2008) point to the newly developing Pacific Islands New Zealand English or Pasifika English, which they predict will become more distinctive as Pasifika youth seek to create a unique identity for themselves. Perhaps a notable feature shared by these varieties is that they are marked—they are not 'just' English but a non-standard variety. What counts as standard and non-standard varieties is a social judgement that can be understood as part of an attitude towards that variety.

Attitudes towards Varieties of English

A naturalistic example of language attitudes relevant to the New Zealand and Australian context was a recent article by a New Zealand reporter that was published in the *Dominion Post*, a major daily newspaper. It reported that a British air traffic control training company planned to set up a school in New Zealand. The reason attributed to the decision to set-up in New Zealand over Australia was that the Kiwi accent was less harsh than the Australian one. Learning good English in the right environment was reported as important for the air traffic control students, where clear and fluent speech was fundamental to the job (Van Den Bergh, 2012).

People have been expressing opinions about varieties of spoken English in New Zealand and Australian for a long time. Typically, Australasian accents are derided in comparison to standard forms of British English. Gordon and Abell (1990) documented evidence of negative attitudes towards New Zealand English from the very early 20th century. What was glossed as a colonial twang was attributed to a variety of ills, including weak mindedness, laziness and poor-upbringing—effectively *bad* English, rather than a legitimate variety of English in its own right. Of course, it is a linguistic given that no language variety is inherently superior, so evaluations of them, like those on different Australasian accents, point to issues of identity and intergroup dynamics. Furthermore, evidence suggests that non-Australasians are poor at accurately differentiating between New Zealand and Australian form of English (Bayard, 1995), an ability that may only be developed after repeated exposure to the different accents.

The existence of attitudes towards particular language varieties, even in the absence of skill at identifying them, is explained theoretically in important social psychological theories of communication including accommodation and ethnolinguistic vitality theories (Gallois, Ogay, & Giles, 2005; Giles & Coupland, 1991). Empirically, research has typically used questionnaire methods, as the next section that focuses on New Zealand language attitude research illustrates.

Language Attitude Surveys

In New Zealand, attitudes towards Te Reo Māori and varieties of Māori English have been relatively well surveyed more or less systematically. Purely academic as well as government commissioned research has documented attitudes towards Te Reo Māori as well as Māori English. The academic studies have revealed some interesting patterns (Boyce, 2005). For example, there is some evidence that when attitudes towards language and language varieties are couched in very general terms, responses tend to be more positive than when items are more specific. This pattern of response is actually consistent with what has been described as new forms of racism, where positive attitudes are espoused but practices that would affect social change in support of disadvantaged groups are disavowed (Wetherell & Potter, 1992).

Government commissioned language attitude research has been focused on evaluating the effectiveness of the New Zealand government's Māori Language Strategy. So there have been a series of surveys asking Māori and non-Māori New Zealanders about their knowledge of, and attitudes towards, the Māori language (Te Puni Kokiri, 2010). Responses to the survey indicate that people generally have positive attitudes towards the Te Reo Māori, with Māori attitudes being even more positive than non-Māori. Encouragingly, non-Māori attitudes have become increasingly more favorable, and this may be due in part to Government-led initiatives. Indeed, there are strongly held beliefs that the Government has an important role in language vitalization. However, a worrying gap exists between positive attitudes towards the language and participation in Māori language. Thus, the positive attitudes are not translating into patterns of language use that will actually result in language vitalization.

Gallois et al. (2007) noted that the lack of correspondence between measured attitudes and actual language behaviours is the Achilles heel of language attitude surveys. Measured attitudes provide an indication of respondents' thoughts and feelings about a particular language variety, which gives a useful snapshot of judgements at a particular point in time and a way of documenting what people believe. Speaker evaluation studies developed as a more subtle way of documenting the source of language attitudes.

Speaker Evaluation Studies

"I explained the whole story (.) I get some person up in India somewhere (0.2) struggling to understand what I'm saying (0.2)"

The above quote is taken from a transcript of an actual telephone call to a dispute resolution service for complaints about utilities. The caller is recounting his experience of ringing the company's call-centre, which happens to be off-shore. Part of his dissatisfaction is that the "person up in India somewhere" cannot easily understand him. An implication is that the person, as a non-native New Zealander, cannot function satisfactorily in their role because they cannot comprehend the speech of the callers they are employed to serve. Accents may indeed produce trouble in understanding, but conversational repair practices exist to address them. Nevertheless, the negative attitude expressed above seems as much about cultural intolerance as misunderstanding.

A desire to tease out and quantify what underpins opinions or attitudes about others based on their speech, like that expressed in the above quote, motivates speaker evaluation studies, where an assessment of the way a person sounds (or in the particular case above, the recipients' ability to understand a local accent) is taken as a proxy for attitudes towards a class of person. Already mentioned is that theoretically, attitudes towards a class of person are understood as being related psychologically to social identity issues and matters of intergroup dynamics (Giles, 2012). There has been a large range of studies conducted on attitudes towards languages, as this volume attests.

One broad and well-known pattern that emerged from early empirical language attitude work was that generally speakers of a standard language variety are associated more with social status traits (e.g., intelligence, confidence and power) than non-standard speakers. In contrast, speakers of non-standard varieties tend to be associated more with traits relating to solidarity (e.g., social attractiveness, integrity and benevolence) than standard varieties (Giles & Coupland, 1991). It is widely accepted that people continue to use lower prestige or non-standard varieties of language because they are part and parcel of a language community's distinctive social identity.

One of the most extensive research programmes of New Zealanders' attitudes towards accents, informed by social identity theory, was a series of studies conducted by Bayard (1995). He systematically investigated the ways New Zealanders rated their own and other English accents, including AusE. Following the 'Lambert-Gilesian' research tradition (Giles & Coupland, 1991) the evaluations were understood as being manifestations of intergroup dynamics. New Zealanders' evaluations of differently accented English speakers were interpreted as reflecting their sense of themselves in terms of their national identity.

One of the more controversial of Bayard's (1995) claims was that New Zealanders demonstrated a kind of cultural cringe towards their own accent. Bayard's assertion of a cultural cringe was based on his interpretation of a pattern of results, counter to those found in previous evaluation studies, whereby his New Zealand research participants rated New Zealand accented speakers lower than Australians, British or Canadian accented speakers, on scales designed to measure solidarity traits, More consistent with prior research was that the non-New Zealand accents were also rated lower on items designed to measure high social status (e.g., intelligence and leadership).

A limitation of Bayard's (1995) work was that it was based on only one Australian middle-class male speaker. Weatherall, Gallois, and Pittam (1998) sought to further refine Bayard's findings by increasing the range of New Zealand English (NZE) and Australian English (AusE) accents evaluated. They found that both New Zealanders and Australians were able to identity their own accents accurately, with correct identification being slightly lower for accents from the other country. Evaluations of the accents on standard measures of social status and solidarity measures showed no clear pattern. Gender, nationality of accent and accent type (broad, general or cultivated) interacted in ways that showed that all three factors can shape the way an accent is evaluated (Bayard, Weatherall, Gallois, & Pittam, 2001).

Accent evaluations are interpreted as indirect indicators of beliefs about social groups such as gender and class, as well as ethnicity. The above-mentioned studies, for example, both noted that speaker evaluations could function as covert measures of prejudice. In Weatherall et al.'s (1998) study the broad male NZE accent was more likely to be identified as Maori, which was taken to point to negative beliefs about the social status of Maori. Also, the cultivated female NZE accent was down-graded on social status measures relative to the same male accent—a possible indication of sexism.

Empirical accent evaluation investigations are a powerful research tool for measuring social beliefs associated with different language varieties. The experimental design of such work is both a strength and a weakness. As has been documented elsewhere (e.g., Weatherall, 2007), important confounds such as speaker idiosyncrasies and speech content are controlled for. In addition, a standard set of measures permit systematic comparisons across accents and also across different studies. However, like all experiments the contrived nature of speaker evaluations studies is also a weakness. Perhaps more important is the challenge of identifying exactly which linguistic variant (or variants) of what is glossed as an accent is triggering the variation in the evaluative responses.

Linguistic variation research documents sound shifts, which are linked with broader patterns of social interaction. Social identity, stereotypes and inter-group dynamics are psychological forces that come into play as people go about their everyday business. The inextricability of language variation and psycho-social dynamics provides fertile ground for on-going research collaborations between social psychologists and linguists.

Conclusion

The topic of attitudes towards language and communication has a long history. The contemporary examples of language attitudes used to illustrate this chapter show its continuing relevance. Language use is a pervasive aspect of being human, and the psychological investment in the languages and language varieties one speaks is indisputable. That investment can provoke strong feelings and responses—the widespread outrage that New Zealand's first severely hearing impaired MP, Mojo Matthews, wasn't getting sufficient translation resources to do her job is a case in point.

In view of the long history of language attitude research and its continuing relevance in today's world, it is perhaps timely to consider what work remains to be done and where new insights may come from. An assumption underpinning the earliest research, that language variation has social significance, holds strong. Thus, it continues to be important to track societal attitudes towards indigenous and minority languages, not least because it can function as an alert to policies and practices that condone patterns of advantage and disadvantage on the basis of social group membership alone.

The intractability of identity and intergroup dynamics in language attitudes and communication has been comprehensively mapped out in theory. Carefully conducted experimental and survey research has confirmed the complex interplay between speech perception, communication behaviours and social dynamics. A remaining challenge for a traditional language attitude research approach is to pin down exactly what linguistic or communicative variants are causing differential responses. It is work that will require a unique combination of linguistic and social psychological expertise.

A potentially fruitful new direction for research in the area may be a systematic study of the actual expression of language attitudes. The illustrative quote used in this chapter, which was taken from a complaint call to a dispute resolution agency, is the kind of phenomenon that could collected. From this single case, it can be noted that interactional dissatisfaction can be achieved by making a negative assessment of how someone speaks. Of course, getting such data is difficult, because it is not amenable to targeted data collection methods.

Although potentially difficult to collect, examining actual instances of language attitude articulation in everyday or institutional talk is likely to provide new and innovative insights into their use in everyday life. A newly emergent social context of interest might be call-centres for organisations such as telecommunication companies or computer help desks, which can be located off-shore. In off-shore call-centres callers and call-takers will be likely to speak different varieties of the same language. In that environment, what occasions an explicit noticing or reference to accent? To my knowledge, no work of this kind has been done, and it would make a welcome, innovative and valuable contribution to the field.

References

Bayard, D. (1995). *Kiwitalk. Sociolinguistics and New Zealand society.* Palmerston North, New Zealand: Dunbar Press.

Bayard, D., Weatherall, A., Gallois, C., & Pittam, J. (2001). Pax Americana? Accent attitudinal evaluations in New Zealand, Australia, and America. *Journal of Sociolinguistics, 5,* 22–49.

Benton, R. (1991). The history and development of the Māori language. In G. McGregor & M. Williams (Ed.), *Dirty silence* (pp. 1–18). Auckland, New Zealand: Oxford University Press.

Blair, B. (1989). The development and current state of Australian English. In P. Collins & D. Blair (Eds.), *Australian English. The language of new society* (pp. 171–176). St Lucia, New Zealand: University of Queensland Press.

Boyce, M. (2005). Attitudes towards Māori. In A. Bell, R. Harlow, & D. Starks (Eds.), *Languages of New Zealand* (pp. 86–110). Wellington, New Zealand: Victoria University Press.

Butler, S. (Ed.). (1981). *Macquarie dictionary of Australian English.* Sydney, Australia: Macquarie Dictionary Publishers.

Clyne, M. (1991). *Community languages: The Australian experience.* Cambridge, UK: Press Syndicate.

Cochrane, G.R. (1989). Origins and development of the Australian accent. In P. Collins & D. Blair (Eds.), *Australian English: The language of a new society* (pp. 176–187). St Lucia, Australia: University of Queensland Press.

De Bres, J. (2011). Promoting the Māori language to non-Māori: Evaluating the New Zealand government's approach. *Language Policy, 10,* 361–376.

Dixon, R.M.W. (1980). *The languages of Australia.* Cambridge, UK: Cambridge University Press.

Donoghue, T. (2012, January 31) Labin seeks status for island languages. *Stuff.co.nz.* Retrieved February 1, 2012, from http://www.stuff.co.nz/national/6337988/Laban-seeks-status-for-island-languages

Gallois, C., Ogay, T., & Giles, H. (2005). Communication accommodation theory: A look back and a look ahead. In W.B. Gudykunst (Ed.), *Theorizing about intercultural communication* (pp.121–148). Thousand Oaks, CA: Sage.

Gallois, C., Watson, B., & Brabant, M. (2007). Attitudes to language and communication. In M. Hellinger & A. Pauwels (Eds.), *Handbook of language and communication: Diversity and change* (pp. 597–620). Berlin: Mouton de Gruyter

Garrett, P., Coupland, N., & Williams, A. (2003). *Social meanings of dialect, ethnicity and performance.* Cardiff, UK: University of Wales Press.

Giles, H. (Ed.). (2012). *The handbook of intergroup communication.* New York: Routledge.

Giles, H., Bourhis, R. Y.,& Taylor, D.M. (1977). Towards a theory of language in ethnic group relations. In H. Giles (Ed.), *Language, ethnicity and intergroup relations* (pp. 307–348). London: Academic Press.

Giles, H., & Coupland, N. (1991). *Language: Contexts and consequences.* Milton Keynes, UK: Open University Press.

Gordon, E., & Abell, M. (1990). "This objectionable colonial dialect": Historical and contemporary attitudes towards New Zealand speech. In A. Bell & J. Holmes (Eds.), *New Zealand ways of speaking English* (pp. 21–48). Clevedon, UK: Multilingual Matters.
Hay, J., Maclagan, M., & Gordon, E.(2008). *Dialects of English: New Zealand English*. Edinburgh, UK: Edinburgh University Press.
Holmes, J. (1997). Māori and Pakeha English: Some New Zealand social dialect data. *Language in Society, 26,* 65–101.
Kirkpatrick, A. (2007). Linguistic imperialism? English as a global language. In M. Hellinger & A. Pauwels (Eds.), *Handbook of language and communication: Diversity and change* (Vol. 9, pp. 333–364). Berlin: Mouton de Gruyter.
Malcolm, I.G., & Grote, E. (2007). Aboriginal English: Restructured variety for cultural maintenance. In G. Leitner & I.G. Malcolm (Eds.), *The habitat of Australia's Aboriginal Languages* (pp. 153–180). Berlin: Mouton de Gruyter.
McKay, G. (2011). Policy and Indigenous languages in Australia. *Australian Review of Applied Linguistics, 34*(3), 297–319.
O'Brien, T (2012, February, 15) Speaker staunch on MP's technology funding. TV3 News. Retrieved February 15 2012, from http://www.3news.co.nz/Speaker-staunch-on-deaf-MPs-technology-funding
Orsman, H.W. (Ed.). (1997). *The dictionary of New Zealand English*. Auckland, New Zealand: Auckland University Press.
Ryan, E. B., Giles, H., & Hewstone, M. (1988). The measurement of language attitudes. In U. Ammon, N. Dittmar, & K. J. Mattheier (Eds.), *Sociolinguistics: An international handbook of the science of language* (Vol. II, pp. 1068–1081). Berlin: Mouton de Gruyter.
Spolsky. B. (2005). Māori lost and gained. In A. Bell, R. Harlow, & D. Starks (Eds.), *Languages of New Zealand* (pp. 67–85). Wellington, New Zealand: Victoria University Press.
Tatz, C. (1999). Genocide in Australia. *Journal of Genocide Research, 1,* 315–352.
TePuniKokiri (2010). *Attitudes towards the Maori language*. TePuniKokiri, Wellington, New Zealand: Hongongoi.
Troy, J. (1993). Language contact in early colonial New South Wales 1788–1791. In M. Walsh & C. Yallop (Eds.), *Language and culture in Aboriginal Australia* (pp. 33–50). Canberra, Australia: Aboriginal Studies Press.
Van den Burgh, R. (2012, January 31). Air traffic control academy planned for Wellington. *The Dominion Post,* p. C1.
Walsh, M. (1993). Language and their status in Aboriginal Australia. In M. Walsh & C. Yallop (Eds.), *Language and culture in Aboriginal Australia* (pp.1–15). Canberra, Australia: Aboriginal Studies Press.
Weatherall, A. (2007). Language. In A. Weatherall, D. Harper, M. Wilson, & J. McDowall (Eds.), *An introduction to psychology in Aotearoa New Zealand*. Auckland: Pearson Education New Zealand.
Weatherall, A., Gallois, C., & Pittam, J. (1998). Australasian attitudes towards Australasian accents. *Te Reo, 41,* 153–162.
Wetherell, M., & Potter, J. (1992) *Mapping the language of racism. Discourse and the legitimation of exploitation*. New York: Harvester Wheatsheaf.

EPILOGUE

Language Attitudes in Context

CINDY GALLOIS [1]

It is a real pleasure to write this Epilogue. I have never seen a book like this one, with such a comprehensive—yet focused—coverage of language attitudes around the world. There are chapters on too little-studied parts of the world (e.g., Davies & Bentahila, chapter 5; Sachdev & Bhatia, chapter 8), which I hope will provide strong encouragement to researchers to develop these areas further. There are very new angles on parts of the world that have been studied previously (e.g., Gluszek & Hansen, chapter 2; Kristiansen, chapter 4). Almost every chapter at some point applies an original lens to the well- (one might even say over-) studied area of attitudes to English (e.g., Painter & Dixon, chapter 6; He & Ng, chapter 7). There is important work here on language-based discrimination and on group vitality, which develop long-established themes. Overall, this book is a refreshing and innovative compendium of language attitudes around the world, with many implications for language policy, language education, and theory.

The introductory chapter (Dragojevic, Giles, & Watson, chapter 1) lays out the book and draws out the similarities among the chapters. In this Epilogue, however, I would also like to highlight some of the *differences* across the chapters, and explore briefly what this may mean for research into language attitudes in the future. In reading the book, I was surprised again and again by these differences, most of which can be attributed to the linguistic and historical context of their research. To me, this is a—if not the—major theme in the book. I found myself questioning many of my assumptions about language attitudes, and about how they should best be studied. In particular, I will take up the following questions, all of which implicate the sociohistorical context in major ways to

- What are language attitudes—language or attitudes?
- What is a language?
- What counts as group vitality?
- What do attitudes to English tell us about language attitudes?
- And finally, how should we study language attitudes?

I will not be able to answer all (perhaps any) of these questions comprehensively, but I hope they will point to some directions that future research in this vibrant field could go. Inevitably, my impressions are colored by my own context: Australia is arguably the most English-dominant country in the world, in spite of there being about 200 languages here (with 80-100 viable ones), and this situation has important consequences; for example, there is no official language here, and encouraging foreign-language learning is a continuing struggle. This is a very different context from the ones discussed in this book (I take this issue up again below).

Researchers in the field of language attitudes (and I include myself) have always acknowledged the important differences across cultures and groups. Yet we have still tended to act as if a small and controllable set of variables, mainly centred around group identity, prejudice and discrimination, and intergroup relations, can predict the most important aspects of language attitudes. Perhaps at a very high level of abstraction this is true, but these chapters show the extent to which context can change things. Thus, it is worth revisiting the very concept of language attitudes.

What Are Language Attitudes—Language or Attitudes?

The first question that these chapters raised for me is this: What are language attitudes really about, language or attitudes? Of course, most researchers would answer (resoundingly) BOTH. Nevertheless, each of these chapters puts a strong emphasis *either* on the details of productive language (a more linguistic approach), *or* on the impact of language on impressions, attitudes, and intergroup relations (a more socio-psychological approach).

In fact, these chapters reflect the field of language attitudes from its earliest days. Social psychologists usually count the start of language attitudes research from the late 1950s, with the work in Canada of Lambert and his colleagues (e.g., Lambert, Gardner, Hodgson, & Fillenbaum's classic paper in 1960), followed closely by the theoretical work of Giles and his colleagues (e.g., Giles, 1973) in the UK. Lambert (1967) argued that language is a key marker of ethnic or social group, which is the first judgement that people make about others. The approach these scholars took was experimental. A key contribution was the development of the matched-guise technique (MGT), in which the same speakers would present content-neutral passages in more than one language, dialect, or accent, to be judged by listeners who were not aware that they were listening to the same people. Much subtle and interesting work was done in this tradition over many years—indeed, MGT and other experimental research is returning, as some of the chapters in this book indicate (e.g., chapters 6, 7, and to some extent 2). Even so, criticism came early and often, from linguists who questioned the experimental controls and the authenticity of the language (e.g., Nolan, 1983), and from critical psychologists who argued that attitudes were being inappropriately reified (e.g., Potter & Wetherell, 1995).

On the other hand, linguists count the development of language attitudes research from the same period, but from different sources—like the seminal work of Hall (e.g., 1959), the ethnography of communication (Gumperz & Hymes, 1964), or the sociolinguistic work on style conducted by Labov (e.g., 1972). This work took the opposite approach to that in social psychology, emphasizing small and subtle changes in productive language as markers of identity. For example, Labov theorized the phenomenon of hypercorrection—the production of overstandardized language—as a marker of a desire for upward social mobility. Indeed, there are some resonances to the latter process in this volume, for example in the attitudes to modern standard Arabic explored by Davies and Bentahila (chapter 5) and those toward Norwegian explored by Kristiansen (chapter 4). The approach of linguists (and linguistic anthropologists) has been observational, with small details of language in either naturally occurring or elicited language providing the corpus of data. Once again, much invaluable work has been done, and is reflected in some of the chapters in this book (e.g., chapters 4 in particular, 8, and to some extent 2 and 3). This work, however, has attracted criticism for inferring people's thoughts and feelings from their language, rather than asking people for them.

In reality, of course, there is merit in both approaches, and even more merit in combining them. Unfortunately, we tend to be the prisoners of our favorite methodologies, which are tied to the training, understanding, and editorial gatekeeping of our disciplines. Thus, it is hard to design a research agenda that assesses both language production and attitudes, and does this in a global way—yet there is a great need for such an agenda (see Gallois, Cretchley, & Watson, 2012, for a discussion of this issue).

What Is a Language Anyway?

What counts as a language (as against a dialect, variety, or something else) has long been a vexed question in linguistics, yet I thought I had a good rule of thumb: Two languages are different if they are not mutually intelligible and if they both have (formal or informal) status or (institutional or other) support. But my assumptions about what a language is, and thence what group vitality is, are also challenged by these chapters. For example, Sachdev and Bhatia (chapter 8) point to the thousands of languages spoken on the Indian sub-continent, where multilingualism is a way of life and where code-switching is a given. They do not draw strong distinctions between languages and dialects, although others would do so—but to what end in this context, where only 22 of the more than 5000 languages have any official status and institutional support in India? How could one measure the vitality of these many languages, each one of which may have more speakers than many European (and Australian) languages that guard their vitality zealously (see Rakić & Steffens, chapter 4)? Likewise, our efforts to elucidate the sociolinguistic meanings of code-switching may not mean very much in this kind of context; Sachdev and Bhatia argue that code-switching is a necessity of daily life.

On the other hand, Davies and Bentahila (chapter 5) describe the status of written classical Arabic (Fusha), a language with arguably no speakers but with very high vitality and prestige, to which speakers look to symbolize their identity. Thus, speakers (whose own languages, or varieties of Arabic, may not be mutually intelligible) identify as Arabic speakers and turn to Fusha for support and validation. Add to this the highly delineated concepts of what constitutes a language in the Nordic countries (Kristiansen, chapter 4) and more generally in Western Europe (Rakić & Steffens, chapter 3), and it is clear that we often compare apples with oranges (to put it mildly) when we generalize about linguistic standardization, prestige, or vitality. Kristiansen makes a persuasive case for the role of specific historical events in determining the versions of Norwegian and other languages that are preferred in the Nordic countries—in this case, with a *smaller* total number of speakers than there are in Australia, much less in big countries.

I am not sure that we can ever determine what a language is in a global context. Perhaps this is less important than explicating attitudes about languages (or dialects or varieties) as they are defined by *speakers in their contexts*. Linguists do this currently in describing languages, but language attitudes research has not yet really come to grips with this issue. In the future, we should do so. For example, there is an opportunity for very interesting systematic research that extends group vitality (Giles, Bourhis, & Taylor, 1977) and ethnolinguistic identity (Giles & Johnson, 1987) theories by taking more account of languages in their overall contexts, and especially the extent of multilingualism. Such research, however, requires a global perspective. Furthermore, it requires multi-site comparative approach, something that almost never happens at present.

What Counts as Group Vitality?

As Dragojevic et al. (chapter 1) point out, group vitality (and ethnolinguistic identity more broadly) is inextricably tied up with language-based status, prejudice, and discrimination—overall, with the impact of intergroup relations. Most of their propositions, indeed, concern the ways in which the prestige and ideology around a language are expressed and received, and thus how intergroup relations are subtly signalled by sociolinguistic moves. These interesting propositions are consonant with communication accommodation theory (Giles, Mulac, Bradac, & Johnson, 1987), perhaps the most useful theory for describing such moves. The chapters in this book characterize the ways in which dominant groups create versions of a standard or prestige language to suit their own purposes; that is, they increase the vitality if their preferred languages, at the expense of other languages or varieties. For example, Gluszek and Hansen (chapter 2) explore the standard Mexican accent created in the media to neutralize the impact of other variants of Spanish. Chapters 3, 4, and 5 all include close analyses of the languages in their areas (Western Europe, the Nordic countries, and North Africa) and the ways in which prestige and ideology are expressed through language forms, differential use of the host language by immigrant groups, and code-switching. If there is a general theme in language attitudes research, this is it: language is used to express prestige and discrimination.

Nevertheless, group vitality and indeed ethnolinguistic identity more generally, as Giles and his colleagues have always argued (e.g., Giles & Johnson, 1987; Giles et al., 1977), is a very subjective thing. The indicators they propose to measure the vitality of a language—status, institutional support, and the like—turn out to be largely in the eye of the beholder (or the eyes of the speakers and listeners). All the chapters in this book illustrate this point, and Dragojevic et al. highlight it in chapter 1. Researchers need to take this seriously, and to find context-specific measures of vitality that nonetheless have analogues across contexts. Allard and Landry (1986) aimed to do this systematically for French versus English in Canada, and their approach is useful at least in that context. Other researchers could follow this lead, and could also go further than Allard and Landry to look for analogous measures of vitality across contexts. I know that this is not an easy or straightforward task, but it is well worth undertaking.

One theme through many of the chapters—attitudes to English—captures the interaction of prestige, vitality, and context very clearly; it is addressed in the next section. It is interesting that attitudes to English figure so large in a book where pains have been taken to foreground lesser-known languages and contexts. Perhaps in the world today, English is the great comparison language.

What Do Attitudes to English Tell Us?

I had always assumed—but now that I have read these chapters, I think perhaps simplistically—that attitudes to English constitute a good index of threat to the vitality of a local language in the contemporary world. English is so dominant in certain spheres—the internet, business, science, and so forth—that speakers of other languages have accommodated to the point that many countries (e.g., Singapore) have English as an official language, along with several generations of native speakers. This situation goes beyond the post-colonial use of the colonial language that we see with English in the Indian sub-continent (Sachdev & Bhatia, chapter 8), French in North Africa (Davies & Bentahila, chapter 5), and Afrikaans in South Africa (Painter & Dixon, chapter 6)—and of course English in Australia and New Zealand (Weatherall, chapter 9). Of course, there is good evidence that people in many places do think of English as the modern colonial language (e.g., see the discussion by Gluszek & Hansen, chapter 2), and react accordingly.

The context of the People's Republic of China (He & Ng, chapter 7) is especially striking. Chinese, Mandarin in particular, is an extraordinarily high-vitality language, with billions of speakers located throughout the world, and majority populations in many East Asian countries. Perhaps because of this high vitality, there is no reason for Chinese to be threatened by any language, including English. Yet across their history, as He and Ng point out, attitudes to English have varied from condemnation and taboo to educational requirement. Today, not only is English viewed as important to success in the world (at a group as well as—perhaps more than—at an individual level), but as a way of encouraging humanist and culture-aware ideas and behavior.

Even so, He and Ng present the argument that China English (as they label it) should be established as a world variant of English, alongside Indian English, Singaporean English (not to mention the older variants of Scottish, Welsh, American, Australian, and New Zealand English), which have developed organically over time and through generations of speakers. This is an interesting argument, given that there are not yet any native speakers of China English; once again it raises the issue of what a language is. It is worth asking—and studying systematically—what this says about Chinese perceptions of the vitality of Mandarin and English. It is also worth asking how Chinese people would react to, say, America Chinese (should this unlikely situation ever arise).

The chapters in this book do not mention (although Dragojevic et al. allude to them in chapter 1) the English-only movement in the USA and the French-only movement in Québec. The difference between the reactions of people in these movements to a perceived threat (and it can only be a perceived threat) to their extremely high-vitality languages, and the reactions of the Chinese to English in their country, is astonishing. I was once involved in a study of subjective group vitality here in Australia (Pittam, Gallois, & Willemyns, 1991), where some Anglo-Australian residents of a suburb with a high concentration of Vietnamese refugees believed that in the future, English would have lower vitality than Vietnamese in Australia. I am confident that this result, like the perceptions of advocates of English-only (e.g., Barker et al., 2001) and French-only (e.g., Bourhis, Moïse, Perreault, & Sénécal, 1997), can be explained (as they traditionally have been) through prejudice. Many chapters in this book tell a similar story, and Dragojevic et al.'s propositions theorize it. Why are things in these countries so different from China?

At the other end of the spectrum is Australia—different even from New Zealand (see Weatherall, chapter 9) in having no official language and no competitors to English (Pittam et al., 1991, notwithstanding). In this country (and this is also true in a number of other Anglo-Saxon majority countries), it is very difficult to get people to learn any other language, even when it is the language of their own immigrant community. In Australia, they simply have too little reason to do so, and the intrinsic motivation to learn a language, theorized by Gardner and his many colleagues (see Gardner, 2010, for a recent discussion), does not seem to be a sufficient push. Indeed, even some urban indigenous people (and some immigrant groups) in Australia have concluded that they can preserve only enough of their heritage languages to use in ceremonies like welcomes to country. Thus, as Australia broadens to a greater appreciation of indigenous culture, the use of heritage languages can only be symbolic (Austin, 2010). An important part of the future of group vitality theory, to me, lies in exploring the sociohistorical context to explain this type of situation compared to that in China, Western Europe (chapter 3), South America (chapter 2), or elsewhere. Harwood, Giles, and Bourhis (1994) theorized the sociohistorical status of a language as a predictor of its vitality long ago; in future, we need to develop better measures to explore this key aspect of context much more deeply.

Conclusion: How Should We Study Language Attitudes?

As I noted earlier, for me the message of this book is that context—and sociohistorical context in particular—trumps everything else in influencing language attitudes. In taking language attitudes research forward for another fifty years, we must, therefore, give much more attention to context, global and regional as well as local, than we have in the past. Our most basic assumptions are challenged if we take context seriously, yet this is our best chance of developing truly global theories of language attitudes and methods of studying them.

At the applied level, the chapters in this book have interesting implications for language policy and planning. It is clear that policy is also a function of context, and our hopes for a global approach to language policy are probably vain. Nevertheless, it would be very interesting to compare different contexts—for instance, places with more than one official language (Canada, Belgium, New Zealand) with other countries that have no, one, or many official languages. How do non-official languages fare (in the case of Canada, this includes indigenous languages) in these different environments? We have tantalizing hints in this book, but there is much more work to be done here.

In terms of research, this book shows clearly the need for good theory. Fortunately, there is good theory in abundance. The early research in Canada, along with the ethnography of communication (Gumperz & Hymes, 1964) and sociolinguistic theory developed by Labov (1972) and Milroy (1980) is seminal, of course. Much current research tests or is framed by social identity theory (Tajfel & Turner, 1979). More specific theories include those already mentioned, ethnolinguistic identity theory (Giles & Johnson, 1987) and especially communication accommodation theory (Giles et al., 1987; Gallois, Ogay, & Giles, 2005), which originally looked at convergence in language or accent—how far it has come since then.

The chapters in this book do not make great mention of theory, but rather concentrate on drawing the literature together. This exercise is very valuable, but if anything it highlights the need to explore these many contexts theoretically. For example, what counts as accommodation in India, as against Sweden or South Africa, and why does it? What underpins high vitality in these contexts? How does a language function to enhance positive social identity when it has no speakers? In exploring questions like these and many others, the theories will naturally be extended and better grounded in the reality of everyday language use.

Finally, the language attitudes approach has proved to be a very useful way of understanding other intergroup communication, for example in health, across genders or generations, intergroup communication at work, institutional-individual relations, and so forth. One example is explored here—the small extension of language attitudes to deaf sign language (Weatherall, chapter 9). If one broadens the concept of language attitudes to include mode, style, register, accent, and so forth, then it is only another step to broaden it to contexts associated with other types of intergroup relations. The major theories in the area have already been extended in this way (indeed, my own work these days is mainly in intergroup health communication; see Giles, 2012, for many examples of this kind of extension to new contexts). To get the full benefit of this approach, however, it will be important to ground research in linguistic and communicative reality. This probably means, at the very least, complementing an experimental approach with observation of what people actually say and how they react to others. Researchers in these newer domains of intergroup communication can learn much from the work on language presented in this book.

Overall, then, this collection is exciting and challenging—it tells us much about the ways in which language attitudes play out around the world. At the same time, this work raises many questions about whether there are commonalities in language attitudes, and if so, what they are and how they work. These chapters point the way to a mixed-methods, context-aware, global approach to language attitudes, and to a long and productive future for research in this area.

Note

1. I would like to thank Howie Giles and Bernadette Watson very deeply for undertaking this enterprise. It is an amazing honor to me personally, and I am indeed most honoured (and completely surprised). It is also an excellent contribution to the field of language attitudes, and more generally to the social psychology of language and communication. Having had the shoe on the other foot from time to time, I know how much effort—recruiting good contributors, persuading them to meet deadlines and stick to the content guidelines, editing and copy editing—goes into a collection like this. Howie and Bernadette have risen to the occasion admirably, and produced a great collection of chapters. I would also like to thank the individual authors very much—they have shown great confidence in the field to put so much intellectual work into producing this unified and comprehensive collection.

References

Allard, R., & Landry, R. (1986). Subjective ethnolinguistic vitality viewed as a belief system. *Journal of Multilingual and Multicultural Development, 7*, 1-12.

Austin, P. (2010, June). Going, going, gone? Australian indigenous languages: Endangerment and revitalization. Paper presented at 12th International Conference on Language and Social Psychology, Brisbane.

Barker, V., Giles, H., Noels, K., Duck, J., Hecht, M. L., & Clément, R. (2001). The English-only movement: A communication analysis of changing perceptions of language vitality. *Journal of Communication, 51*, 3-37.

Bourhis, R. Y., Moïse, L. C., Perreault, S., & Sénécal, S. (1997). Towards an interactive acculturation model: A social psychological approach. *International Journal of Psychology, 32*, 369-386.

Gallois, C., Cretchley, J., & Watson, B. (2012). Methodology in intergroup communication: Eclectic approaches to communicating identity. In H. Giles (Ed.), *The handbook of intergroup communication* (pp. 31-43). New York: Routledge.

Gallois, C., Ogay, T., & Giles, H. (2005). Communication accommodation theory: A look back and a look ahead. In W. B. Gudykunst (Ed.), *Theorizing about intercultural communication* (pp. 121-148). Thousand Oaks, CA: Sage.

Gardner, R. C. (2010). *Motivation and second language acquisition: The socio-educational model.* New York: Peter Lang.

Giles, H. (1973). Accent mobility: A model and some data. *Anthropological Linguistics, 15,* 87-109.

Giles, H. (Ed.). (2012). *The handbook of intergroup communication.* New York: Routledge.

Giles, H., Bourhis, R. Y., & Taylor, D. M. (1977). Towards a theory of language in ethnic group relations. In H. Giles (Ed.), *Language, ethnicity, and intergroup relations* (pp. 307-348). London: Academic Press.

Giles, H., & Johnson, P. (1987). Ethnolinguistic identity theory: A social psychological approach to language maintenance. *International Journal of the Sociology of Language, 68,* 69-99.

Giles, H., Mulac, A., Bradac, J. J., & Johnson, P. (1987). Speech accommodation theory: The first decade and beyond. In M. McLaughlin (Ed.), *Communication yearbook, 10,* 13-48.

Gumperz, J. J., & Hymes, D. (Eds.). (1964). The ethnography of communication. *American Anthropologist, 66,* part 2 (special issue).

Hall, E. T. (1959). *The silent language.* New York: Doubleday.

Harwood, J., Giles, H., & Bourhis, R. Y. (1994). The genesis of vitality theory: Historical patterns and discoursal dimensions. *International Journal of the Sociology of Language, 108,* 167-206.

Labov, W. (1972). *Sociolinguistic patterns.* Philadelphia: University of Pennsylvania Press.

Lambert, W. E. (1967). A social psychology of bilingualism. *Journal of Social Issues, 23,* 91-109.

Lambert, W. E., Gardner, R. C., Hodgson, R. C., & Fillenbaum, S. (1960). Evaluational reactions to spoken languages. *The Journal of Abnormal and Social Psychology, 60,* 44-51.

Milroy, L. (1980). *Language and social networks.* Oxford, UK: Blackwell.

Nolan, F. (1983). *The phonetic basis of speaker recognition.* Cambridge, UK: Cambridge University Press.

Pittam, J., Gallois, C., & Willemyns, M. (1991). Perceived changes in ethnolinguistic vitality in dominant and minority subgroups. *Journal of Multilingual and Multicultural Development, 12,* 449-458.

Potter, J., & Wetherell, M. (1995). Natural order: Why social psychologists should study (a constructed version of) natural language, and why they have not done so. *Journal of Language and Social Psychology, 14,* 216-222.

Tajfel, H., & Turner, J. C. (1979). An integrative theory of intergroup conflict. In W. G. Austin & S. Worchel (Eds.), *The social psychology of intergroup relations* (pp. 33-47). Monterey, CA: Brooks-Cole.

Contributors

ABDELALI BENTAHILA holds a PhD in sociolinguistics from the University of Wales. He has taught at universities in a number of Moroccan cities, including Tangier, Tetouan, and Fez where he was head of the English Department. He has published widely on the multilingual situation in Morocco, exploring issues including code-switching, language choice, language planning and education, and intercultural communication. His current research interests include the use of code-switching in song lyrics and in medieval poetry.

TEJ K. BHATIA is Professor of Linguistics and Director of South Asian Languages at Syracuse University. He was also a Fellow at the Center for the Study of Popular Television at the S. I. Newhouse School of Public Communication. He has published a number of books, articles, and book chapters in the areas of bilingualism, multiculturalism, media (advertising) discourse, socio- and psycho-linguistics, and the structure and typology of English and South Asian languages (particularly Hindi, Urdu, and Punjabi).

EIRLYS DAVIES is Lecturer at King Fahd School of Translation in Tangier, Morocco where she teaches translation, translation theory and research methodology. She obtained a PhD in syntax and semantics from the University of Wales, after which she became a lecturer at the Faculty of Arts of Fez, Morocco. Her publications cover a wide range of areas including translation, multilingualism, intercultural communication, language teaching and learning, stylistics, and pragmatics.

JOHN DIXON is Professor of Social Psychology at the Open University (UK). He has published extensively around themes of prejudice, inequality, and social change. His research has appeared in *American Psychologist, Behavioral and Brain Sciences, Psychological Science, Current Directions in Psychological Science, Journal of Social Issues, Political Psychology*, and the *European Journal of Social Psychology*. He is currently co-editor (with Jolanda Jetten) of the *British Journal of Social Psychology* and is co-author (with Kevin Durrheim) of *Racial Encounter: The Social Psychology of Contact and Desegregation*. London: Routledge.

MARKO DRAGOJEVIC is a doctoral student in the Department of Communication at the University of California, Santa Barbara, USA, and obtained his MA from the Davis campus. He studies intergroup communication and persuasion. In particular, his research focuses on understanding the effects of linguistic variation, such as accents and politeness, on speaker evaluations and other communication outcomes. His most recent publications have appeared in *Communication Research* and the *Journal of Health Communication*.

CINDY GALLOIS is Emeritus Professor of Psychology and Communication at The University of Queensland, Australia. She is a Fellow of the Academy of the Social Sciences in Australia and the International Communication Association, and is a past President of the International Communication Association and the International Association of Language and Social Psychology. Her research interests encompass intergroup communication in health, intercultural, and organizational contexts.

HOWARD GILES is Professor of Communication at the University of California, Santa Barbara, USA. He is founding Editor and Co-Editor of the *Journal of Language and Social Psychology* and the *Journal of Asian Pacific Communication*. Giles was past President of International Communication Association and the International Association of Language and Social Psychology. His research interests encompass language attitudes and intergroup communication in intergenerational, police-civilian, and other settings, and he is the editor of the recent *Handbook of Intergroup Communication*.

AGATA GLUSZEK received her PhD in social/personality psychology from Yale University, USA. Her research interests focus on the stigma of nonnative accents. She consults in education and industry on the impact of accents in organizations.

KAROLINA HANSEN is a doctoral candidate at the Friedrich Schiller University in Jena, Germany. Her research interests are in the fields of social psychology, sociolinguistics, and cross-cultural psychology.

ANPING HE is Professor of English at the School of Foreign Studies, South China Normal University, Guangzhou, China. She obtained her PhD in Applied Linguistics from the Victoria University of Wellington.

TORE KRISTIANSEN is Professor of Sociolinguistics at the Nordic Research Department, Copenhagen University, Denmark, and member of the leader team of the Danish National Research Foundation's LANCHART Centre (Language Change in Real Time) at Copenhagen University. The central theme of his research is 'linguistic norm and variation', with a main theoretical focus on the role of social psychological processes (representations, attitudes, ideology) in language variation and change, but also with a strong interest in the more 'applied' (pedagogical, political) aspects of the norm vs. variation issue.

SIK HUNG NG is a professor at the School of Psychology, South China Normal University, Guangzhou, China. He is a Fellow of the Royal Society of New Zealand and a past President of the International Association of Language and Social Psychology and the Asian Association of Social Psychology.

DESMOND PAINTER is Senior Lecturer in the Department of Psychology at Stellenbosch University. He has edited two books, *Interiors: A History of Psychology in South Africa* (with Clifford van Ommen) and *Research in Practice: Applied Methods for the Social Sciences* (with Martin Terre Blanche and Kevin Durrheim). He is currently interested in the intersections of discourses on language, ethnicity and race in postcolonial contexts, with specific emphasis on the politics of Afrikaans in South Africa.

TAMARA RAKIC is Research Associate at the Person Perception Research Unit at the Department of Psychology at Friedrich Schiller University Jena (since 2009), Germany. She studied psychology at University of Padova and did her doctorate at International Graduate College at Friedrich Schiller University Jena (2009). In 2011/12 she was a Visiting Scholar at University of California, Santa Barbara. Her research interests include the influence of accents on person perception and categorization, and different language and cross-cultural aspects of social psychology.

ITESH SACHDEV is Professor of Language and Communication at the School of Oriental & African Studies (SOAS), University of London, England. He was born and brought up in Kenya, completed secondary and undergraduate education in the UK (Psychology, University of Bristol), received doctoral training in Social Psychology in Canada (McMaster University, Ontario), and then taught in Applied Linguistics at Birkbeck College, University of London. He has also been Director of the SOAS-UCL Centre for Excellence in Teaching and Learning 'Languages of the Wider World', served as President of the British Association for Canadian Studies, and is the current (20010-2012) President of the International Association for Language and Social Psychology.

MELANIE STEFFENS is Professor for Social Cognition and Cognitive Psychology at the Department of Psychology at the Friedrich Schiller University Jena (since 2004). She did her doctorate at the University of Trier (1998). In 2001, she was a Visiting Fellow at Yale University. Her research interests comprise implicit and explicit attitudes and stereotypes of social groups, social categorization and impression formation, in addition to memory phenomena. She is a faculty member of the Max Planck research school "Adapting behavior in a fundamentally uncertain world."

BERNADETTE WATSON is Senior Lecturer in psychology at The University of Queensland and completed her PhD under the supervision of Professor Cindy Gallois. She is a health psychologist who studies communication. Her research focuses on effective communication between health professionals and patients. She researches on the influence of identity and intergroup processes both on patient-health professional communication and on communication in multi-disciplinary health teams.

ANN WEATHERALL is Reader in the School of Psychology at Victoria University of Wellington, New Zealand. Her interests include conversation analysis, discursive psychology, feminist psychology and language and social psychology. She has been mentored by Cindy Gallois and collaborated with her on a number of projects including studies of Australasian language attitudes and on work that considers the theoretical and methodological confluences and conflicts within various approaches to language and social interaction.

Index

A

AAVE *See* Language, African American Vernacular English
Aboriginal language centres, 161
Académie Française, 5
Accent
   Australasian, 163
   Bavarian, 53
   Black, 109
   Canadian, 166
   Cockney, 9
   Dublin, 52,57
   Evaluation, 113, 166
   Fez, 98
   Foreign, 7, 10, 39, 46, 50–51
   Københavnsk, 70
   Mexican,10, 31, 174
   Non-native, 28, 31, 80
   Non-standard, 28, 34–37
   Oxbridge, 10
   Received pronunciation, 48, 51–52, 57
   Regional, 10, 28, 33, 46, 51–53
   Standard, 28,31,34-37,48-49,53,57
   Type, 57, 166

Accommodation, 48–50, 54, 109, 132, 151–152, 163, 174, 177
Afrikaner nationalism, 110–111
Alphabets and scripts
   Arabic, 92–93, 95
   Roman, 92–93, 95, 101
   Tifinagh, 95
Americas
   Central America, 27, 34
   Latin America, 10, 29–33, 35–36
   North America, 15
   South America, 15, 27, 176
Anbehetelse, 74
Anglification, 72
Anglophone, 91
Apartheid state,106, 109
Approaches to language, geo-political and historical, 46
Arabic diglossia, 84
Arabicization, 143
Arabic-speaking world, 84
Arabization, 85, 89–90, 94, 97–98, 100
Arab nationalism, 88
Arabophones, 95
Arrogance, 56

Ascription, 12, 45, 97
Assimilationist, policies and attitudes, 13, 160
Attitudinal surveys, 89
AusE *See* Languages, Australian English

B

Beijing Olympic Games, 131–132
Bilingual, 15, 20, 29–32, 38, 47–48, 55, 73, 75, 80, 90, 94, 98, 100, 111, 129–131, 150–152
Bilingual education, 30, 32, 90
Bilingualism, 30, 38, 48, 75, 129–131, 151
Billboards, 92–93
Black varieties of English, 116
Bollywood, 17, 145
Brahmins, 143
British colonial era   *See* British Raj
British Raj, 143
BSAE *See* Languages, Black South African English

C

CAT *See* Communication accommodation theory
Cities
  Amritsar, 148
  Delhi, 147–148, 150
  Guangzhou, 132
  London, 148
  Nanchang, 132
  Soweto, 111
  Vancouver, 148
  Wu Han, 132
  Code-switching, 12, 17, 49, 53, 85, 97–100, 131–132, 141, 150–152, 173–174
Colonialism, 18, 105–108, 112
Communication accommodation theory, 48–49, 174, 177
Communication behavior, 14
Communication norms, 51
Communication technology, 101, 152
Comparative philologists, 107
Competence, 9, 11, 17, 28, 50, 52–57, 78–80, 127–128
Comunidades Autónomas, 48

Constitution of India, 145
Convergence, 35, 151, 177
Conversational repair practices, 165
Countries and regions
  Åland, 64–65, 73
  Algeria, 16, 84–85, 88–90, 94–97
  Argentina, 26, 31, 33
  Australia, 9, 18, 134, 157–163, 166, 171, 173, 175–176
  Austria, 46
  Bangladesh, 17, 141–142, 153
  Bejaia, 89
  Belgium, 15, 46–48, 51, 55, 177
  Bhutan, 141
  Bihar, 145
  Bolivia, 26, 29–31, 34, 36, 39
  Brazil, 15, 27, 34
  Britain, 6, 10, 15, 48, 134, 157
  Canada, 27, 29, 31–32, 134, 147–148, 171, 174, 177
  Cape Colony, 110
  Caribbean, 27, 34, 40
  Chile, 26
  China, 17, 125–135, 175–176
  Costa Rica, 31–32
  Cyprus, 51
  Denmark, 5–6, 15, 64–67, 70–73, 75–76, 78–79, 81–82
  Eastern Cape, 114
  Ecuador, 3, 26, 30
  European Union, 45–47
  Faroes, The, 67, 73–74, 78
  Finland, 5, 15–16, 64–65, 69–70, 73, 76–79
  France, 5, 9, 46–47, 50, 52–53, 55
  Friesland, 47, 54
  Germany, 5, 15, 46–47, 49–50, 53, 56, 65
  Greece, 15, 47
  Greenland, 64–65, 69, 73–74, 80
  Guatemala, 29–30, 32
  Guangdong province, 127
  Hawai'i (USA), 2, 11
  Hong Kong, 131
  Iceland, 15, 64–65, 68, 70, 73–79
  India, 6–7, 12, 16–17, 115–116, 132, 141–153, 165, 173, 175, 177
  Iraq, 88
  Ireland, 46–47, 57
  Italy, 15, 46–47, 53, 55
  Jharkhand, 146

Countries and regions, *cont.*
 Kabylia, 85
 Kashmir, 17, 143
 Luxembourg, 15, 46–47
 Maghreb, 16, 84–85, 87–89, 91–92, 96–97, 100–102
 Maldives, The, 17, 141–142
 Malta, 15, 46–47, 55
 Mexico, 7, 27, 29, 33
 Morocco, 16, 84–85, 87–89, 91–92, 94–95, 97
 Nepal, 141–142, 149, 152
 Netherlands, The, 15, 47, 50, 92
 New Zealand, 18, 134, 157–160, 162–167, 175–177
 Nordic countries, 15–16, 64–65, 74, 76, 78–80, 173–174
 North Africa, 85, 91, 95, 97, 174–175
 Northern Ireland, 57
 Norway, 15–16, 64–65, 67, 69–74, 76, 78–79, 81–82
 Orange Free State, 110
 Pacific Islands, 163
 Pakistan, 17, 141–143, 146–147
 Paraguay, 28, 31
 Peru, 10, 26, 29–30, 32–33, 36
 Punjab, 17, 141–142, 145–148, 152
 Quebec, 26, 36
 Republic of South Africa, 106, 112
 Saharan, 85
 Sápmi, 65
 Scotland, 47
 South Asia, 17, 141
 Southern Africa, 4, 105–107, 109–110, 112–113, 115, 117–119
 South Tyrol, 46–47, 56
 Spain, 33, 46, 48, 54–55, 90
 Sri Lanka, 141–142, 152
 Sweden, 15, 64–67, 69–70, 72–73, 75–79, 82, 177
 Switzerland, 12, 15, 46–48, 51, 55–56
 Transvaal, 110
 Tunisia, 16, 84–85, 87–88, 91–92, 98–101
 UK, 46–48, 147–148, 150, 172
 USA, 7, 27, 29–33, 36, 39, 147, 176
 Uruguay, 27, 35
 Uttar Pradesh, 144
 Wales, 47, 148
 Western Cape, 115
 Yunnan province, 130
Critical discourse analysis, 118
Cross cultural awareness, 127, 130
Cultural alienation, 108, 110
Cultural cringe, 165
Cultural heritage, 101

D

Dehumanization, 108, 118–119
Diachronic change, 88
Dialect
 Chicano English, 29
 Colloquial dialect, 84, 91, 99
 Ile de France dialect, 5, 9
 Non-standard dialect, 32
Dialects, 1, 5, 9–10, 14–16, 26–29, 34–37, 39, 45–47, 50–51, 53–54, 57, 67–71, 74, 81, 84–85, 91, 99, 113, 117–118, 142, 147, 158, 173
Diaspora, 91
Direct questioning, 66, 70–71, 90, 99
Discourse markers, 151
Discourse studies, 118
Discrimination
 Accent, 7, 28, 38
 Age, 58
 Employment, 31
 Ethnic and racial, 106, 109, 113
 Foreign-accent, 7
 Language based, 7, 26–28, 32, 38–39, 58, 116, 170, 174
Discriminatory practices, 109, 158
Discursive psychology, 117–118
Domination, 12, 15, 20, 66, 72, 105, 108–109
Dubbing, 58
Dumb English, 126
Dynamism, 28, 72

E

Ecological variety, 53
Economically disadvantaged groups, 161
Economic power, 37, 111
EFL *See* English as a foreign language
ELIT *See* Ethnolinguistic identity theory
Elites, 110–111, 149
Employment, 27–29, 31–32, 39, 52, 134
Endoglossic, 66–67, 74

English as a foreign language, 125
Englishization, 17, 149, 153
English-medium schools, 149
English proficiency, 127–130, 145
Ethnic group, 32, 130, 159, 163
Ethnic groups
  Han, 130–132, 134
  Miao, 130
  Yi, 130, 134
  Zhuang, 130
Ethnic identities, 115, 161
Ethnicity, 1, 6, 30, 38, 48, 91, 105, 109, 114, 146, 166
Ethnic minorities, 126, 145
Ethnic relationships, 159
Ethnist policy, 13
Ethnolinguistic
  groups, 26
  identity, 48, 58, 135, 173–174, 177
  landscapes, 106, 109
  vitality, 49, 54, 158, 160, 163
Ethnolinguistic identity theory (ELIT), 48–49, 177
European colonization, 160
EV *See* Ethnolinguistic vitality
Evaluative practices, 118
Exoglossic, 66
Expressiveness, 131
External purism, 68, 73

F

Fanon, Frantz, 107–108
Fennicisms, 73
First language, 51, 73, 80, 86
Formal purism, 66, 68
Francophone, 96
Functional purism, 66

G

Gender, 1, 101, 105, 166, 177
Gender difference, 101
Globalization, 19, 39, 72, 75, 110, 127, 144–145, 149, 152
Grammatical errors, 89
Grammatical morphemes, 91

H

Hamito-Semitic language, 85
High Commission for Amazighity, 94
High social status, 166
High status, 9, 12, 48, 53, 57, 110, 116, 152
High status variety, 116
Hindu scriptures, 143
Hispanic Americans, 32, 37
Hochdeutsch *See* High German language

I

Identities, 1–3, 16, 18, 45, 50, 54, 56, 106, 109, 112, 115, 128, 131, 147–148, 150–152, 158, 161
Identity
  Bosnia and Herzegovina, 2
  Catholic, 2
  Croatian, 2
  Ethnolinguistic, 48, 58, 135, 173–174, 177
  Maghrebi, 97
  Markers, 91
  Muslim, 2
  National, 4–5, 30, 51, 89–90, 112, 158, 165
  Orthodox Christian, 2
  Professional, 126, 128
  Serbian, 2
  Social, 2, 19, 48, 55–56, 58, 94, 158, 165–166, 177
Identity construction, 117
Ideological practices, 118
Ideology, 4–5, 7–8, 10, 28, 30–31, 39, 45, 66–69, 78–79, 84, 108, 141, 146–147, 152, 174
  Dialect, 67
  Nationalist, 4–5, 7, 66
  Nativeness, ideology of, 7, 79
  One nation–one religion–one language, 146
  Pluralistic, 141, 146
  Standard language, 8, 10, 30–31, 39, 66
Imaghizen people, 95
Immigrant communities, 50
Immigrant groups, 50, 79, 174, 176
Immigrant language communities, 158
Immigration, 37, 65, 79
Indigenous peoples, 107, 111, 157, 161
Indigenous populations, 30, 108
Indirect questioning, 66

Infra-humanization, 119
Ingroup and outgroup, 26–27, 37, 91
Institutionalized, 7, 36, 118
Institutional norms, 51
Intergenerational transmission, 162
Intergroup, 14–15, 19, 35–36, 49, 110, 112, 158–159, 163, 165, 167, 171, 174, 177–178
Intergroup attitudes, 49
Intergroup dynamics, 19, 163, 165, 167
Intergroup identity, 159
Intergroup relations, 112, 158, 171, 174, 177
Inter-language and intra-language dynamics, 45
Internet forums, 93
Interviews, 66, 82, 86, 130
Intra-language dynamics *See* Inter-language and intra-language dynamics
Islam *See* Religion, Muslim

K

Kohanga Reo, 162
Københavnsk *See* Accent, Københavnsk
Koran, 84–85, 88
Kura Kaupapa Maori independent school movement, 162

L

Label ranking method, 70–71
LANCHART project, 72
Language
  Academies, 16, 88
  Accents, 55
  Accommodation, 109
  Administrative, 73
  Ancestral, 84, 143
  Battle, 67
  Behaviour, 164
  Change, 70–72
  Colonial, 16, 106, 108, 110, 112, 116, 175
  Community, 148, 162
  Death, 153, 160
  Discrimination, 58
  Endangerment, 145, 153, 160
  Evaluation, 48

Language, *cont.*
  Foreign, 37, 50, 58, 74, 79, 99, 125, 130, 132
  Global, 149
  Governmental policies, 12, 80, 157
  High variety, 84, 90
  High vitality, 144, 146
  Ideologies, 2–3, 11–13, 18, 38, 105, 107, 117–118, 142
  Immigrant, 39, 158
  Institutional support for, 12, 16, 18–19, 49, 55, 69, 81, 145, 157, 161, 173–174
  International, 46, 55, 127, 133, 159
  Learned, 84
  Loss, 36, 160–161
  Low variety, 84
  Low vitality, 13, 17–18, 145
  Majority, 46, 80, 142, 146
  Minority, 11–13, 15, 17–18, 36–37, 46, 54–55, 58, 80, 130, 134, 149, 157, 159–160, 167
  Missionary, 4
  Motivation, 126
  National, 4–5, 16, 36, 46, 55, 58, 75–76, 80–81, 94, 101, 115, 127, 133, 142, 147, 159
  Nests *See* Kohanga Reo
  Non-standard, 31–32, 38, 113
  Official, 3, 12, 17, 45–48, 52, 55, 66, 73–75, 79, 86, 94, 125, 142–144, 146–148, 159, 162, 171, 175–177
  Outsiders, 84–85
  Planning, 16, 81, 85–86, 101, 147
  Policy, 29, 75, 79, 89, 109, 112, 115, 127, 159, 161, 170, 177
  Political status of, 88, 90
  Politics, 46, 66, 69, 73–74, 79, 109
  Prestige, 174
  Purity, 16, 79, 81, 88
  Revival, 161
  Rights, 58, 80, 106
  Scheduled, 142, 144–145, 153
  Shift, 94, 115
  Standard, 5, 8–11, 13, 28, 30–33, 38–39, 49, 51, 53–54, 57, 66–67, 72, 74, 113, 165
  Standardized, 172
  Stereotype, 46
  Variation research, 166
  Variety/varieties, 1, 10–11, 13, 16–17, 19–20, 29, 31, 33, 37, 46, 48–49, 52, 54, 57, 84, 145, 163–167
  Vernaculars, 9, 13, 28–29

Language, *cont.*
   Vitality, 12–13, 15, 17–19, 49, 52–55, 70, 144–147, 149, 158, 160, 162–163, 170–171, 173–177
Language and social psychology, 126, 134–135, 158
Language Change in Real Time LANCHART, 72
Language community, 16, 18, 29, 48, 54–55, 78, 81, 95, 158, 165
Language families, 64, 142
   Angan, 142
   Austroasiatic, 142
   Dravidian, 142–143, 153
   Eskimo-Aleutic, 64
   Finno-Ugric, 64
   Great Andamese, 142
   Indo-Aryan, 142
   Indo-European, 64, 142
   Indo-Iranian, 142
   North-Germanic, 64, 74
   Tibeto-Burman, 142–143, 146
   Uralic, 64
Languages
   Aboriginal, 18, 158, 160–162
   African, 4, 16, 112, 114–115, 117
   African American Vernacular English, 9, 15, 28
   Afrikaans, 4, 16, 110–114, 175
   Amazigh, 16, 85–86, 89–90, 93–95
   American English, 9, 28, 131, 133–135
   Arabiyya, 84, 86, 93
   Australian English, 157–158, 166
   Aymarain, 30
   Basque, 15, 54–55
   Bengali, 142, 152
   Berber *See* Amazigh
   Black American English, 132
   Brazilian Portuguese, 8, 33–35
   British English, 9, 33, 79, 131, 163
   Cape Afrikaans, 113–114
   Casablanca variety, 91
   Castilian, 9, 46, 48, 54–55
   Catalan, 15, 46, 49, 54–55
   China English, 17, 126, 132, 134–135, 175
   Chinese English *See* China English
   Chinglish *See* China English
   Classical Arabic, 84, 89, 173
   Colloquial Arabic, 16, 85–86, 89, 91–93, 97, 100
   Creole language, 111

Languages, *cont.*
   Cypriot-Greek dialect, 52
   Danish, 6, 15–16, 64–65, 67, 70, 72–82
   Dhivehi, 142
   Dutch, 4, 47, 50–51, 53–54, 91, 111
   Egyptian Arabic, 91
   English, 2, 5–7, 9, 11–13, 15–18, 26–30, 32–33, 36–40, 46–49, 51–52, 55, 57, 64, 72, 75–82, 85, 87–88, 99–100, 108, 110–111, 113–118, 125–135, 141–145, 147–150, 152–153, 157–166, 170–171, 174–176
   European, 3–4, 33, 37, 45–48, 50, 64, 67, 91, 107–110, 142, 144, 158, 160–161, 173
   Faroese, 64–65, 67–68, 74, 77
   Finnish, 64–65, 68–70, 73, 76–78
   Flemish, 54
   French, 5, 9, 15–16, 26, 36, 46–52, 55–56, 72, 85, 87–92, 94–101, 108, 147, 174–176
   Frisian, 54
   Fusha, 8, 16, 84–86, 88–90, 92, 99, 173
   Galician, 54
   German, 4–5, 12, 15, 33, 46–47, 49–51, 53, 56, 59, 64–65, 72–75
   Greek, 6, 50, 52, 107
   Greenlandic, 64–65, 69, 73–74, 80
   Guarani, 15, 31
   Gujarati (Gujerati), 150
   Haitian Creole, 26
   Hamito-Semitic, 85
   Hanseatic Low German, 73
   High German, 5, 12, 46, 73
   Hindi, 17, 142, 144–146, 148, 150, 152–153
   Hochdeutsch *See* High German
   Icelandic, 64–65, 68, 70, 74, 77
   Indian English, 115–116, 149, 175
   Indigenous, 3, 15–16, 18, 30–32, 34–39, 65, 105–112, 114, 118, 126, 157–163, 167, 176–177
   International English, 6
   Irish, 15, 47–49, 57
   isiZulu, 114
   Italian, 47–49, 53, 55–57
   Japanese, 125, 133
   Khoikhoi, 107
   Kurdish, 4
   Ladino, 47, 56
   Latin, 10, 13, 29–33, 35–36, 72, 85, 152, 164–165
   Luxembourgish, 47

INDEX | 191

Languages, *cont.*
  Maltese, 47,55
  Maori English, 18, 162, 164
  Maya, 30
  Modern Standard Arabic (MSA), 84, 88–92,
    99–100, 172
  Moselfränkisch, 46
  Moroccan Arabic, 50, 86, 88–93, 95–98
  Moroccan-flavored Dutch, 91
  Nepali, 142,149,152
  New Zealand English (NZE), 157–158, 163,
    166, 175
  New Zealand sign language, 159–160
  Non-native language, 34
  Nordic Countries (*see also* The North), 15–16,
    64–65, 74, 76, 78–80, 173–174
  Norwegian, 64–65, 67–68, 70, 74, 77–80, 172–173
  Old English, 5
  Old Norse, 64
  Pasifika English, 163
  Persian, 17, 143, 149–150, 153
  Portuguese, 8, 15, 26–27, 30, 32–35, 39, 50, 107
  Putonghua, 126,133–134
  Quechua, 20, 26, 30, 36
  Quichua, 3, 15, 20
  Russian, 33, 65, 73, 125, 133
  Sámi, 64–65, 69, 80
  Samoan, 18, 159
  Sanskrit, 143, 149, 153
  Sinhala, 142, 152
  Spanish, 3, 7, 9–10, 15, 26–35, 37–39, 85, 92, 97, 174
  Standard Chinese *See* Puonghua
  Standard French, 9, 15, 47–48, 50, 52
  Swedish, 5, 15–16, 64–65, 67–70, 73, 75–78
  Swiss German, 12,56
  Tamil, 142, 153
  Te Reo Maori, 158–162, 164
  Tunisian Arabic, 91, 99, 101
  Turkish, 6, 15, 50, 91
  Urdu, 142–143, 147, 153
  Valencian, 54
  Welsh, 15, 47, 51, 54, 148, 175
  Xhosa, 16, 113–115
  Zulu, 16, 114–115, 117
Languaging, 81, 150
Learner motivation, 129
Legitimacy, 5–6, 13, 49

Lexical diversity, 48
Lingua franca, 2, 15, 45, 47, 85, 88, 135
Linguistic
  Borders, 46,79
  Capital, 10
  Community, 3,11–12, 49
  Conflict, 153
  Difference, 2, 5, 10, 105–107, 119
  Diversity, 2–4, 11, 39, 46, 49, 106, 141–142, 152–
    153, 158
  Imperialism, 18, 30, 159
  Indices, 2
  Landscape, 4, 8, 15–18, 36–37, 49, 87, 106, 109,
    119, 141, 149
  Minorities, 12, 146, 159
  Norm, 66
  Performance, 56
  Purism, 6
  Superdiversity, 6
  Vitality, 49, 53–54, 158, 160, 163
Literacy rates. 88, 101
Literary tradition, 68, 142, 144, 146
Living language, 28, 142, 162
Local patriotism, 16, 70–71

M

Majority language, 46, 80, 142, 146
Matched guise technique, 87, 98, 113–114
Metroethnicity, 6
Middle-class, 115, 145, 166
Minorities, 12–13, 50, 126, 130, 134, 145–146, 148, 159
Minority languages, 11–13, 15, 17, 36, 46, 54–55, 58,
    80, 134, 149, 157, 159–160, 167
Min project 69, 77, 82
Missionary schools, 160
Mogul empire, 143
Monolingualism, 160
Maori Language Act, 1987
Maori Language Commission, 162
Maori language strategy, 164
Maori *See* Languages, Te Reo Maori
Mother tongue, 4, 12, 17, 80, 84, 93, 109, 130, 142,
    144–146
Motivation, 17, 20, 49, 51, 58, 79, 93, 126, 128–130,
    176

MSA *See* Languages, Modern Standard Arabic
Multicultural awareness, 133
Multiculturalism, 6, 36, 141, 145, 147, 151
Multiethnic youth groups, 91
Multilingualism. 6, 17, 58, 80, 141–145, 149, 152–153, 173–174
Multiracial, 117

N

National Academy of Letters *See* Sahitya Akademi
National identity, 4–5, 30, 51, 89–90, 112, 158, 165
Nationalist ideology, 4–5, 7, 66
Nationality, 5, 91, 105, 146, 166
National languages, 4, 16, 75, 80–81, 147
National policy on languages, 161
National purism, 73, 78–79
Native language, 4, 18, 26, 34, 40, 51, 79, 126, 133, 161–162
Native speakers, 7–8, 26, 56, 86, 89–90, 95, 175
Nativisation, 126
Negotiation of identities, 150
Neo-nationalist, 111
New Zealand national anthem, 162
Non-native speakers, 7, 8, 36, 38, 116
Non-standard language, 31–32, 38, 113
Nordic Council of Ministers, 75
Nordic countries *See* Countries and regions, Nordic countries
Normative, 19, 118, 152
North, The, 17, 53, 64–65, 68, 80, 143, 162
    See also Countries and regions, Nordic countries
Norwegian-Icelandic oral tradition, 68
Norwegian, standardization of, 67
NZE *See* Languages, New Zealand English

O

Official language *See* Language, official
Oral communication, 47
Oral English, 128
Otherness, 105
Outgroup *See* Ingroup and outgroup

P

Pacific Islanders, 159
Parisian French *See* Languages, Standard French
Partition (of India), 141, 146–147
Patterns of migration, 145
Perceived personality, 135
Performance, 20, 32, 46, 56–57, 77, 112, 117, 134
Persianization, 17, 143, 149, 153
Persuasion, 135
Phonetic orthography, 68
Phonetic variation, 68–69
Pidgin, 11
Plurilingual, 15
Postcolonial, 30, 106, 108, 110, 112
Power, 4, 8, 10, 12, 19, 37, 48–49, 79, 95, 106, 108–113, 115, 117, 131, 133, 144, 149, 151, 158, 160–161, 165–166
Prejudice, 2, 26–27, 31–32, 118, 166, 171, 174, 176
Prescriptivism, 6, 153
Prestige, 9–12, 17, 29, 31, 36, 52, 57, 84, 88, 91, 100, 165, 173–174
Productive bilingualism, 129–131
Productive trilingualism, 130
Professional identity, 126, 128
Pronunciation, 1–2, 8–9, 27–28, 31, 34–36, 38, 48, 50, 53, 68, 74, 126, 131
Propositions, 18, 174, 176
Public discourse, 39, 68, 77, 92–93
Public space, 117
Purism, 6, 65–66, 68, 72–74, 77–79, 81

Q

Quadrilingualism, 145
Questionnaires, 66, 86, 97

R

Race, 5, 7–8, 14, 19–20, 38, 55, 75, 87–88, 90, 96–97, 105, 107, 109–112, 114–115, 118, 125, 128, 131, 133, 160
Racial discrimination, 106, 109
Racially pure, 111

Racial stereotyping, 113
Racism, 7, 18, 107–108, 112–113, 164
Racist, 108, 157–160
Radio New Zealand, 162
Recall test, 57
Reformation, 66, 68
Regional accent, 10, 28, 33, 46, 51–53
Register, 109, 158, 177
Religion
  Catholic, 2, 57
  Hindu, 143, 146, 150
  and language, 5, 38, 68, 93, 98–99, 107–108, 142–143, 145–147, 153
  Muslim, 2, 146
  Protestant, 57
  Sikh, 146–148, 152
Rhetorical performances, 117
Rigsdansk, 70
Royal Institute of Amazigh Culture (IRCAM), 94
R.P. *See* Accents Received Pronunciation
Russification, 73

S

Sahitya Akademi, The, 145
Same language countries, 55
Sanskritization, 143, 149, 153
Schema, 2, 11–12, 19
Scientific racism, 107
Second language, 27, 49, 55–56, 58
SEE *See* Speaker evaluation experiment
Self-efficacy, 128
Self-identity, 37, 128–130
Semiotic processes, 3–4
  Erasure, 3–4, 6, 11, 153
  Fractal recursivity, 3–4, 153
  Iconicity, 4, 153
Sense of self, 158
Settlers, 4, 111, 118, 157, 160
Shanghai World Expo, 132
Sikhs, 146–148, 152
SIT *See* Social identity theory
Social attractiveness, 19, 28, 52, 54–55, 57, 165
Social class, 1, 9
Social groups, 7, 9, 20, 106, 158–159, 166

Social identity, 2, 19, 48, 55–56, 58, 94, 158, 165–166, 177
Social identity *See* Identity, Social
Social identity theory, 48, 165, 177
Social mobility, 10, 20, 108–112, 144, 149, 151, 172
Social norms, 38, 49, 132
Social psychological theories of communication, 163
Social psychology of language, 2, 112–113, 117, 178
Social purism, 78
Social status traits, 165
Social treatment of language, 66, 72–76, 80, 158
Socio-cultural ethnicity, 146
Sociolinguistic contexts, 117
Sociolinguistic domain norms, 151
Sociolinguistics, 2, 71, 87, 112
Socio-politically charged, 142
Socio-political power, 151
Solidarity, 11–12, 19, 28, 52–53, 56–57, 78, 91, 95, 99, 110, 131, 135, 165–166
Speaker evaluation, 66, 157–158, 164–166
Speaker evaluation experiment, 66, 71–72, 76–80
Speech perception, 167
Speech style, 14, 48, 113–115, 118
Spoken standards of Swedish, 69, 77
Standardization, 5–6, 8–10, 12–13, 45, 66, 72, 82, 173
Standard language, 5, 8–11, 13, 28, 30–33, 38–39, 49, 51, 53–54, 57, 66–67, 72, 74, 113, 165
Standard language ideology, 8, 10, 30–31, 39, 66
Status difference, 54, 56
Status traits, 98–99, 165
Stereotypes, 1, 32, 46, 53, 76, 166
Stigmatization, 16, 80, 109, 113–114
Structuration theory, 130
Studies with adults, 52
Studies with children, 50
Subjectification, 105, 110
Subjective ethnolinguistic vitality, 49, 54
Subjugation, 109
Subordination, 12, 20, 66, 72
Superiority, 72, 88

T

Te Reo Maori, 18, 158–162, 164
Text messages, 93

Three language formula, 145
Torres Strait Islander people, 161
Tribal groups, 145
Trilingual education, 133–134
Trilingualism, 17, 130, 145
TV and radio, 8, 15, 33–35, 37, 55, 68–70, 76–77, 91, 162

U

Unconscious language attitudes, 87, 98
UNESCO, 32, 88
United Nations Declaration of Rights of Indigenous Peoples, 161
Upward mobility, 106
Us/Them dichotomy, 7

V

Variationist sociolinguistics, 71
Varieties of English, 9, 29, 76, 115–116, 131, 133, 135, 157, 163
Verbal guise, 71
Verwoerd, H. F., 109
Viking age, 15, 64
Volk, 4–5

W

White nationalism, 111
World English speakers, 133
WW II, German occupation, 73